THE MORAL ECONOMY
OF ACTIVATION

Also available in the series

Welfare, populism and welfare chauvinism
By **Bent Greve**

Why, in a time of increasing inequality, has there been a recent surge of support for political parties who promote an anti-welfare message? Using a mixed methods approach and newly released data, this book aims to answer this question and to show possible ways forward for welfare states.

HB £75.00 **ISBN** 9781447350439
168 pages June 2019

Dualisation of part-time work
The development of labour market insiders and outsiders
Edited by **Heidi Nicolaisen, Hanne Cecilie Kavli** and **Ragnhild Steen Jensen**

This book brings together leading international authors from a number of fields to provide an up to date understanding of part-time work at national, sector, industry and workplace levels.

HB £75.00 **ISBN** 9781447348603
248 pages June 2019

Forthcoming titles

Local policies and the European Social Fund
Employment policies across Europe

By **Katharina Zimmermann**

Comparing data from 18 local case studies across 6 European countries, and deploying an innovative mixed-method approach, this book presents comparative evidence on everyday challenges in the context of the European Social Fund (ESF) and discusses how these findings are applicable to other funding schemes.

HB £75.00 **ISBN** 9781447346517
224 pages October 2019

For a full list of all titles in the series visit:

**bristoluniversitypress.co.uk/
research-in-comparative-and-global-social-policy**

THE MORAL ECONOMY OF ACTIVATION

Ideas, Politics and Policies

Magnus Paulsen Hansen

First published in Great Britain in 2019 by

Policy Press
University of Bristol
1-9 Old Park Hill
Bristol
BS2 8BB
UK
t: +44 (0)117 954 5940
pp-info@bristol.ac.uk
www.policypress.co.uk

North America office:
Policy Press
c/o The University of Chicago Press
1427 East 60th Street
Chicago, IL 60637, USA
t: +1 773 702 7700
f: +1 773-702-9756
sales@press.uchicago.edu
www.press.uchicago.edu

British Library Cataloguing in Publication Data
A catalogue record for this book is available from the British Library

Library of Congress Cataloging-in-Publication Data
A catalog record for this book has been requested

978-1-4473-4996-9 hardback
978-1-4473-4997-6 ePdf
978-1-4473-4998-3 ePub

Cover design by Andrew Corbett
Printed and bound in Great Britain by CPI Group (UK) Ltd, Croydon, CR0 4YY
Policy Press uses environmentally responsible print partners

Contents

List of tables and figures

Tables

Figures

List of abbreviations

AC !	Act Together Against Unemployment (*Agir ensemble contre le chômage*), French social movement
ALMP	Active labour market programme/policy
ALMPA	Active Labour Market Policy Act (*Lov om aktiv arbejdsmarkedspolitik*)
ANPE	National Employment Agency (*Agence nationale pour l'emploi*)
Apeis	Association for Employment, Information and Solidarity of Unemployed and Precarious Workers (*Association pour l'emploi, l'information et la solidarité des chômeurs et des précaires*)
Assedic	Association for Employment in Industry and Trade (*Association pour l'emploi dans l'industrie et le commerce*)
AUD	unique diminishing allowance (*allocation unique digressive*)
CARE	aid contract for return to employment (*contrat d'aide au retour à l'emploi*)
CFDT	French Democratic Confederation of Labour (*Confédération française démocratique du travail*)
CFTC	French Confederation of Christian Workers (*Confédération française des travailleurs chrétiens*)
CGC	General Confederation of Executives (*Confédération générale des cadres*)
CGPME	General Confederation of Small and Medium Companies (*Confédération générale des petites et moyennes entreprises*)
CGT	General Confederation of Labour (*Confédération générale du travail*)
CGT-chômeurs	General Confederation of Labour-unemployed (*Comité national de lutte et de défense des chômeurs – Confédération générale du travail*)
CNPF	National Council of French Employers (*Conseil national du patronat français*, now Medef)
DA	Confederation of Danish Employers (*Dansk Arbejdsgiverforening*)
DI	Confederation of Danish Industry (*Dansk Industri*)
ECU	'Everyone can be useful' (*Alle kan gøre nytte*), Danish reform programme

FO	Workers Force (*Force ouvrière*)
KL	Local Government Denmark (*Kommunernes Landsforening*)
LA	Liberal Alliance (*Liberal Alliance*)
LCR	Communist Revolutionary League (*La ligue communiste révolutionnaire*)
LO	Danish Confederation of Trade Unions (*Landsorganisationen*)
Medef	Movement of the Enterprises of France (*Mouvement des entreprises de France*)
MNCP	National Movement of Unemployed and Precarious Workers (*Mouvement national des chômeurs et précaires*)
MoDem	Democratic Movement (*Mouvement démocrate*)
PAP	Personalised action project (*Projet d'action personalisé*)
PARE	aid plan for the return to employment (*plan d'aide au retour à l'emploi*)
PCF	French Communist Party (*Parti communiste français*)
PPE	premium for employment (*prime pour l'emploi*)
Radikale Venstre	Danish Social Liberal Party
RMI	minimum insertion income (*revenu minimum d'insertion*)
RSA	active solidarity income (*revenue de solidarité active*)
SF	Socialist People's Party (*Socialistisk Folkeparti*)
TEPA	law in favour of work, employment and purchasing power (*loi en faveur du travail, de l'emploi et du pouvoir d'achat*)
UMP	Union for a Popular Movement (*Union pour un mouvement populaire*)
Unedic	National Professional Union for Employment in Industry and Trade (*Union nationale interprofessionnelle pour l'emploi dans l'industrie et le commerce*)
UPA	Professional Artisan Union (*Union Professionnelle Artisanale*)
Venstre	Danish Liberal Party
WISE	work integration social enterprise

Series preface

Heejung Chung (University of Kent, UK)
Alexandra Kaasch (University of Bielefeld, Germany)
Stefan Kühner (Lingnan University, Hong Kong)

In a world that is rapidly changing, increasingly connected and uncertain, there is a need to develop a shared applied policy analysis of welfare regimes around the globe. *Research in Comparative and Global Social Policy* is a series of books that addresses broad questions around how nation states and transnational policy actors manage globally shared challenges. In so doing, the book series includes a wide array of contributions, which discuss comparative social policy history, development and reform within a broad international context. Initially conceived during a meeting of the UK Social Policy Association Executive Committee in 2016, the book series invites innovative research by leading experts on all world regions and global social policy actors and aims to fulfil the following objectives: it encourages cross-disciplinary approaches that develop theoretical frameworks reaching across individual world regions and global actors; it seeks to provide evidence-based good practice examples that cross the bridge between academic research and practice; not least, it aims to provide a platform in which a wide range of innovative methodological approaches, be they national case studies, larger-N comparative studies, or global social policy studies, can be introduced to aid the evaluation, design and implementation of future social policies.

Magnus Paulsen Hansen's monograph contributes significantly to our understanding of social policy ideas, politics and policies in Europe by turning the eye on the ways in which activation policies are legitimised by political actors. We get critical insights into the function of ideas and morality in the setting of particular labour market policies towards unemployed people. While providing in-depth case studies on Denmark and France, the implications of Hansen's analysis make an important and much broader contribution to our general understanding of the moral economy of activation. By illustrating the composite and heterogeneous set of ideas that constitutes the moral economy of activation, Hansen's innovative approach shows us how the testing of unemployed people is an ever-present element in public debate and jobcentre practice. At a more abstract level, the book illustrates why continued and increased activation is still high on the political agenda, and why instruments like basic income are not a straightforward alternative. Together with Nicolaisen and colleagues' edited collection in this series, *Dualisation of part-time work*, Hansen's book sets the scene for enhanced discussions on social and labour market policies combining comparative with more general ideational dimensions.

Preface

The seeds for the thoughts developed in this book go back to 2010 when the shockwaves of the financial crisis reached the Danish labour market and workers began to feel the effects of unemployment. A year later, a centre-left coalition led by the Social Democrats came to power, replacing a decade of centre-right government. To many, at the time, the change in government portended a paradigmatic return to demand-side, redistribution, and social security measures. However, the response to the crisis was rather a consolidation of present ideas and policies. In other words, post-crisis reforms strengthened the 'activating' instruments throughout the unemployment systems. Unemployment continued to be a matter of making the unemployed active. My initial ideas about capturing this 'strange non-death of activation' (Hansen and Leschke, 2017) were developed with Mathias Herup Nielsen, who later took these events as a point of departure for his own analysis (Nielsen, 2014). However, it was Ove K. Pedersen who offered me the possibility of turning my rather loose thoughts into a proper research project. I am extremely grateful for his wise counselling and support throughout the years, and for the opportunities he gave me for discussing my ideas – in particular for offering up his office as a rare, safe space for curious and creative thinking – all the way to the last draft of the manuscript. At the then Department of Business of Politics at Copenhagen Business School, Ivar Kjær, Stefano Ponte, John L. Campbell, Janine Leschke, Tim Holst Celik, Martin B. Carstensen and Juan Ignacio Staricco all contributed with sometimes critical, but always thoughtful, comments on earlier drafts. I would also like to thank the committee members, Caroline de la Porte, Kerstin Jacobsson, and Tom Boland for their thorough and perceptive assessment of the dissertation.

In France, the response to the financial crisis was also one of more 'active' reforms of the labour market. However, while the Danish centre-left government's policies of sanctions and control were generally supported by the population, the attempt by the then French president François Hollande to introduce supposed Danish-style labour market reforms was met with hostility, peaking with large-scale '*nuit debout*' protests in 2016. In 2013, I went to France not simply to explore the country's bumpy road towards activation, but to seek new theoretical avenues for its appraisal. Existing critiques of workfare/ activation in both public debate and in academia seemed to have run out of steam, and I had the, at the time mostly intuitive, sense that in the English-speaking world the new wave of French pragmatic sociology might have something to offer. It is thanks to Laurent Thévenot that I got the chance to learn such 'pragmatic' thinking from within. I feel fortunate that my truly memorable six-month attendance at the École des Hautes Études en Sciences Sociales in Paris following his intense weekly seminars has turned into an ongoing intellectual exchange as well as a lasting friendship.

Finally, I would like to thank my new colleagues and students at Roskilde University, especially the research group of the Roskilde School of Governance, for their constructive comments on the manuscript. In particular, I am grateful to Peter Triantafillou, who has patiently been on the sideline of the project from the very beginning, and recently had the courage to include me in new shared research endeavours.

Magnus Paulsen Hansen, March 2019

PART I

Modelling

---

activation (n.)
> The action or process of activating something; the state of being activated.
> Etymology: < activate *v.* + –ion *suffix*

activate (v.)
> To make (more) active; to move to activity; to initiate (a process). Also: to motivate.
> To become active; to operate or begin operating.
> To cause (a device, machine, etc.) to operate or begin operating.
> Etymology: < active adj. + -ate *suffix*

active (adj.)
> Capable of acting upon something; originating or communicating action; spontaneous, voluntary. Opposed to *passive*.
> In operation, working; effective, functional.
> Of a person: participating or engaging in a specified sphere of activity, esp. to a significant degree.
> In predicative use. Of an animal or person: engaging in one's typical activity or work at a specified time, under specified conditions, etc.
> Of or designating a current and fully participating member of a group or organisation.
> Etymology: < Anglo–Norman and Middle French, French *actif* (of a life or lifestyle) characterised by external acts of piety rather than by contemplation (1160 in Old French in *vie active*), (of a person) fond of activity, busy, energetic (*c*1370), (of a remedy) efficacious (1378), having the ability to act (14th cent.)[1]

The active turn(s)

Sanctions imposed on those who refuse a job within their qualifications are already better than a gradually decreasing allowance which punishes all the unemployed indifferently. And the instrument will make visible to the jobseeker that they often have capacities that they didn't expect. Regardless of personal preference for a profession, who knows whether the required qualities for practicing it are not similar to other professions? Who knows if a hairdresser would make a good assembly-line worker of electronic chips?

To me, making demands on people is a consequence of respecting them. The day we don't make demands, we don't respect people. And what is the alternative? That some of them get stuck and then we can meet again in 20 years and, once again, find a young woman near her 40s who has been sitting 18 years on benefits? That simply won't do.[2]

Towards the active society

Since the late 1980s, a spectre has been haunting Europe and beyond, the spectre of what may be called the 'active turn'. It transforms welfare states and labour market regulation gradually, but radically. Regardless of previous paths, be they Bismarckian, social democratic, residual or post-communist, welfare states, as well as their clients, are becoming increasingly 'activated'. Policies representing such transformation have been given many labels, from 'active social policies' (Bonoli, 2013), 'active labour market policies' (Daguerre, 2007; Bonoli, 2010) and 'activating labour market policies' (Dingeldey, 2009), to 'workfare' (Jessop, 1993; Lødemel and Trickey, 2001; Peck, 2001), 'welfare-to-work' (Dean, 2007) and 'activation' (Barbier, 2002; Barbier and Ludwig-Mayerhofer, 2004; Serrano Pascual, 2007; van Berkel et al, 2012).

Although the many labels expose a certain ambiguity in these transformations, what characterises all of them is a will to construct policies that somehow underpin a more 'active society', where 'active' usually entails paid work or activities such as jobseeking and training whose ultimate goal is paid work. The term derives from the late 1980s vision of the Organisation for Economic Co-operation and Development (OECD) vision of what kind of social policy it would take to bring its member states out of the economic downturn (Gass, 1988; OECD, 1989; see also Dean, 1995; Walters, 1997). Since then, the term has come to be used to describe a direction of change that is nevertheless qualified in many ways, and can be applied to nearly all social policies – from labour market policies to health, education, pensions, childcare and migration.

The following chapters show that below the 'fuzzy' and 'ill-defined' denominators of 'active' and 'activation' (Barbier, 2014), a plurality of different and often contradictory ideas compete to give it meaning and to guide policy change. The moral repertoire of activation consists of a composite, heterogeneous mix of ideas and programmes – modern and old, North American as well as European – deriving from a variety of disciplines from sociology, political science and economics to psychology and social work. In terms of instruments, activation thus includes myriad components, from job placement services and job-seeking obligations, education, training and workfare schemes to leave schemes, wage subsidies, taxation, adjustment of benefit levels, sanctions, control and individual contracts, all with the aim of somehow bringing unemployed people closer to the labour market. The transformation towards the active society entails uncertainty, tensions and critique, both *in between* 'active' ideas and in confrontation with ideas underpinning the creation of the postwar welfare states.

The active society is permanently under construction and has been for the past 25 years. It never quite works as expected and never quite fulfils its promises. It is a prism rather than a utopia. Looking through its lenses it can always be improved, always become more active. But why is it that the need to reform, despite radical changes, seems to persist? What is it that makes the 'active society' an attractive destination for the majority of political actors in Europe? As the two opening quotes in this chapter illustrate, making people active is saturated with moral issues. How do policies influence the way people behave and perceive themselves? When can certain actions be sanctioned or even punished, how should the state approach its citizens, when should it treat them equally and when should it differentiate between them? The active turn is therefore also saturated with myriad questions that put both policies *and* people to the **test**. Are you active? Why not? Could you be even more active? Are you in risk of becoming passive? How can we activate you?

This book investigates the transformation towards the 'active society' through the politics of **unemployment**. Unemployment is the labour market's 'other'. It is far from a naturally occurring phenomenon but an invented and plastic category created to enable political intervention (Salais et al, 1986; Baxandall, 2004), a paradoxical and contradictory result of historical struggles and attempts to control and govern the unemployed as well as the employed (Walters, 2000; Zimmermann, 2001). The category defines a population of unemployed people that can be qualified and categorised further, with thresholds set for the working population of the labour market and those who are not working but who for various reasons are not unemployed (children, elderly and ill people, and so on). The category makes the people behind the phenomenon, those who for one reason or another are not (or are only partly) selling their labour, 'governable'. However, the governing of unemployment not only concerns unemployed people, but also contains a spectacular dimension of sending signals to the rest of society by establishing why the population should work, what it takes to do this, and why someone fails to do it. The governing and testing of the unemployed is therefore embedded with both 'grey' numbers, bureaucracies, technicalities and rules, as well as 'colourful' moral issues of redemption, what characterises the good society and what does it takes to be part of it, and what makes a(n un)worthy citizen.

Meanwhile, unemployment continues to disturb the harmony of the active society – it is the thorn in the side that will not go away. Its numbers oscillate, but never completely vanish. At the same time, the presence of unemployed people reaffirms the need to make society even more active. The active society is permanently at war against unemployment. Unlike many other studies (for example, Martin and Grubb, 2001; Estevao, 2003; Eichhorst and Konle-Seidl, 2008; Martin, 2014), this book has no ambition to unmask its failure or provide solutions as to how to make policies more effective. Rather, it takes a step back and asks what enables and motivates political actors to criticise the existing arrangements as 'passive' and henceforth invent and justify ever more active policies. The perspective implies that the governing of unemployment does a lot more than just respond to a functional problem – it shapes the problem, and by doing so it shapes, or at least intends to shape, the lives and behaviour of those who fall either inside or outside the immense categories that are tied to this abstract and statistical artefact of unemployment. The book is an examination of the moral repertoires that political actors use to make sense of the problem of unemployment (and unemployed people) and which provides them with the yardsticks to judge between good and bad instruments and criticise or justify them accordingly, vis à vis each other and the public.

In the active society, unemployment is not merely an abstract number; it is a matter of making the unemployed active, whether this entails working inside or outside the ordinary labour market, participating in a job training course, educating oneself, getting up in the morning, searching for jobs, not receiving benefits, responding to incentives and so on. This cannot be reduced to an attempt to retrench or dismantle the welfare state, as in the UK in the 1980s (Pierson, 1994). The active society does not govern the unemployed less; it governs them differently. In other words, this is not simply 'Washington consensus-like', neoliberal, deregulatory laissez-faire in action. Rather, activation promotes more *intense* governing. It derives from the precondition that it is necessary to activ*ate* and thus entails a 'politics of behaviour' (Rose, 2000) that insists on emancipating the unemployed from the shackles of inactivity, even if it sometimes takes coercive measures to carry it through. It insists on 'targeting' and 'personalising' the governing to identify who the unemployed are, and for this purpose invents and reinvents instruments of profiling and continuous evaluation of the unemployed.

The ideas driving the political reforms position themselves at the party political centre, beyond 'left and right' (Giddens, 1994) as a new 'third way' or 'new centre' (Blair and Schroeder, 1998; Giddens, 1998). Activation thus seem to correlate with a pragmatic, managerial and 'realist' approach that refuses the teleological language of old ideologies and the clash of classes, and in this way imagines a kind of 'post-political' arena (Mouffe, 2000) in which interests and classes are aligned towards the same goals (Hansen and Triantafillou, 2011). Most influential international organisations, from the European Union (EU) (Belgian Presidency, 2010) and OECD (2015) to the International Labour Organization (Eichhorst and Rinne, 2014; Escudero et al, 2016) and the World Bank (Brown and Koettl, 2012; Angel-Urdinola et al, 2013), have thus embraced activation as part of the standard reform package of developed as well as developing countries over the world.

Of course, these dynamics are not entirely new; social democracy and the development of the welfare state has from the beginning been seen as a pragmatic 'middle way' between capitalism and revolutionary socialism (for example, Childs, 1936; Marshall, 1964). However, the locus of the active society is not in between socialism and capitalism, but displaced to somewhere between unfettered, deregulating and privatising neoliberalism and 'passive' postwar welfare states and labour market regulation. The significance of activation can, to some extent, be illustrated in numbers. For instance, the LABREF labour market reforms database survey of EU countries shows that activation is the most consistent and expanding reform track since 2000 compared with all other labour market policies (Turrini et al, 2015, p 11). Remarkably, activation reforms seem to appear regardless of whether or not unemployment is on the rise. Thus, while the 2008 financial crisis and following recession led many to expect a counter-movement', including 'the return of the master' (a reference to the economist John Maynard Keynes) (Skidelsky, 2009), the response all over Europe has rather been more of the same and a consolidation of the active turn (Lødemel and Moreira, 2014; Hansen and Leschke, 2017; Smith et al, 2018).

Worlds of welfare capitalism, worlds of activation?

It is now clear that the active turn has begun to radically challenge and displace the normative logics that Esping-Andersen once identified and used to differentiate between Western welfare states almost 30 years ago, in the tentative beginnings of the turn. While Esping-Andersen's classic *The three worlds of welfare capitalism* (1990) provided a static comparison and categorisation of welfare state institutions, it also suggested an explanatory theory of varieties by pointing to differences in early class structures and compromises. In a variety of historical institutionalist thinking (Skocpol and Pierson, 2002), these configurations had set out the ideological *paths* for future reforms developing the postwar welfare states (Emmenegger et al, 2015). This idea of a rather stable and historically and geographically constrained set of reform paths became one of the dominating theories to explain the changes, or non-changes, preceding the oil and fiscal crises in the 1970s. First, it was used and developed further by Pierson to explain the relative incapacity of Margaret Thatcher's government to 'dismantle' the 'resilient' British welfare state in the 1980s (Pierson, 1994). In the 2000s, the theory was then applied to the active turn. Barbier thus mapped various 'worlds of activation' (Barbier, 2002; Barbier and Ludwig-Mayerhofer, 2004), distinguishing between a 'liberal' and a 'social democratic world'. Both of these approaches were interpreted as path-dependent. The 'liberal' was, to put it simply, an intensification of what could already be attributed to Esping-Andersen's Anglo-Saxon world, whereas the latter was seen as a reinterpretation of old Scandinavian social democratic and universalistic values with an emphasis on skills development.

This diagnosis of essentially two distinct activation paths was reproduced in a vast array of studies in the 2000s, albeit with a variety of labels: defensive/offensive (Torfing, 1999), social disciplining/ social integration (Larsen et al, 2001), work first/human resource development (Trickey, 2001), sticks/carrots (Serrano Pascual, 2004), workfare/enabling (Dingeldey, 2007), authoritarian/egalitarian (Dean, 2007) and negative/positive (Taylor-Gooby, 2008). It is clear from the labels that, just like in Esping-Andersen's typology, there was a normative bias towards the latter approach. In that sense, the two activation paths reinterpreted Esping-Andersen's more or less implicit assumption of a 'good', a 'bad' and an 'ugly' path (Manow, 2004). The 'bad' is the 'individualistic' (Barbier) and quid pro quo (Torfing) approach that adopts 'conditional obedience' (Dean) and using 'organised systematic use of sanctions' (Barbier), 'restrictions on benefits' (Taylor-Gooby), 'sanctions' (Larsen et al) and 'motivation, control and punishment' (Torfing), whereas the 'good' is universalistic (Barbier), an enhancing human capital approach (Torfing, Dingeldey, Taylor-Gooby) based on reciprocity (Dingeldey, Barbier) and enabling active participation (Dingeldey) using positive support (Taylor-Gooby), and 'empowerment' (Torfing) and self-motivation rather than sanctions (Larsen et al). The 'ugly' in this perspective again became the Continental and Southern European countries but this time with a path leaving them 'frozen' and resisting reform pressures (Palier, 2000).[3]

However, this 'path-dependent continuity argument' (Palier, 2001) of change or non-change towards activation, and hence the usefulness of clustering countries into various distinct 'worlds', is increasingly being questioned. First, at the end of the 2010s, it is clear that there are no 'frozen' countries that seem to be able to resist the active turn. Regardless of the origin of existing paths, activation policies are on the rise, whereas there is no consistent pattern in other policy areas such as job protection and unemployment benefits. Further, past activation reforms do not seem to saturate the need for future reforms (Turrini et al, 2015, p 15).

Within the 'worlds of welfare' debate, a number of recent studies contend that the general picture of reforms since the 1990s is one of departure from their path and thus also from the path-dependency arguments of both Esping-Andersen and Paul Pierson (Palier, 2010a; Emmenegger et al, 2012; Natali and Bonoli, 2012).[4] In relation to the 'worlds of activation' debate, some scholars dealt with this categorisation problem by extending the number of activation worlds (Serrano Pascual, 2007), while others have more profoundly questioned the meaningfulness of putting countries into homogeneous and path-dependent boxes and instead approach contemporary social and employment systems as hybrids. Aurich (2008, p 312) sees 'new diversity and gradual developments that seem to indicate cross-convergence, rather than gradual convergence or persistent diversity'. The Danish policy development, for instance, contains a number of 'bad' Anglo-Saxon tendencies. Eichhorst and Konle-Seidl (2008, p 19) identify 'the emergence of a flexible and broadly similar repertoire of activation measures applied to an increasingly heterogeneous target group comprising a growing share of the working-age population in all countries'. This process of 'contingent convergence' leads them to conclude that 'established typologies of activation strategies have to be questioned' (Eichhorst and Konle-Seidl, p 19). Similarly, in Lødemel and Moreira's edited volume (Lødemel and Moreira, 2014), the existence of hybrids seem to be the norm rather than the exception in all country case studies. Following van Berkel and colleagues (2011), they thus opt for studies of the trajectory of changes rather than placing countries within static typologies.[5]

Despite the recognition of hybridity and contingent reform trajectories, activation literature has so far provided little insight into the dynamics behind the creation of these composite arrangements or how they are organised in practice. There is still a theoretical vacuum from the previous path-dependency explanations as well as from the idea of 'worlds of activation' in terms of understanding the composite nature of activation. Put simply, if policy makers are not constrained by a singular 'world', how do they arrive at certain policy compromises rather than others? Further, there is also a political dimension to this vacuum: while the idea of two distinct activation worlds is problematic in terms of explanation, the normative assumptions of a good and a bad approach are still very much alive in intellectual and political debates. I return to this at the end of this chapter.

Foregrounding morality as justification and critique

The pivot of the book is as that ideas play a sine qua non in the legitimation and shaping of the active turn, and that the role of morality is key to understanding why they do so. Rightly, ideas and morality are certainly not the only drivers and variables behind the active turn. Beyond ideas, one may mention the structural crisis of the 'Keynesian welfare national state' (Jessop, 1993, 2003) as well as how activation policies provides politicians 'affordable credit claiming' obtaining 'maximum visibility with minimum spending' (Bonoli, 2013). Without downplaying the importance of such drivers, they are merely drivers, and thus say little about the variety and actual timing and legitimation of activation.

Moving closer to the subject of this book, one finds a number of studies that provide ideational explanations, but without a moral element. Rather these studies, drawing on discourse analysis and governmentality approaches, trace the acceptance of the 'active turn' through its *non-morality* leading to its 'depoliticisation'.[6] Using discourse analysis, one such type of explanation points to the way reforms are framed as pragmatic and necessary solutions to inevitable changes such as globalisation (Mouffe, 2000; Andersson, 2009). Reforms are thus presented as 'modernisation' and 'progress' (Strand, 2016) in a setting in which national 'competitiveness' is vital (Pedersen, 2010). A second explanation has shown how the 'active turn' is underpinned by technocratic and scientific discourses of economics (Larsen and Andersen, 2009) using statistics and benchmarking (Salais, 2006; Bruno, 2009; Hansen and Triantafillou, 2011) developed and coordinated by transnational organisations such as the OECD (Triantafillou, 2011) and the EU (van Apeldoorn, 2003; Haahr, 2004; Triantafillou, 2009). The explanations are all extremely relevant to understanding the drivers and diffusion of the active turn. However, by pointing to expert-driven processes in international fora, the studies tend to exclude morality and public deliberation from the equation legitimation of transformation as a matter that goes above or beyond national constituencies. We thus get the impression of a rather smooth technocratic process, hereby disregarding the moral contentedness and composite content of national reforms.

The question then is where to situate morality, how to conceptualise it and in the end study it. There are at least three ways of addressing the role of morality and normative ideas in welfare states, using **philosophical/normative**, **cultural/ideological** or **technical/ institutional** approaches. First, morality can be approached as a matter of political philosophy. In this perspective, morality provides the philosophical principles to normatively judge, from the *outside* point of view of the intellectual, whether or to what extent policies and institutions are socially just and therefore legitimate. For instance, to what extent do policies 'decommodify' (Esping-Andersen 1990), provide 'equal opportunities' (Rawls, 1999; Esping-Andersen, 2007), redistribute (Korpi and Palme, 1998; Fraser and Honneth, 2004) or provide the right balance between individual rights and obligations toward the community (Etzioni, 1995)? In relation to activation, the question has thus been whether activation is compatible with notions such as social citizenship (Handler, 2004; Dwyer, 2010; Nothdurfter, 2016) or social investment (Morel et al, 2012b; Bonoli, 2013). However, this perspective does not lead us closer to answering the question of *how* ideas are actively put to use or how they become legitimated and contested in the actual politics of activation.

As opposed to the philosophical perspective, morality in the latter two perspectives is approached as a societal phenomenon to be studied. Here, the second perspective approaches morality as residing in culture and norms 'below' politics and policy making as a set of taken-for-granted values. This perspective is invigorated in a number of important strands, such as the 'worlds' of welfare theories mentioned earlier, that attach distinct normative ideas (conservatism/corporatism, liberalism, social democracy) to categorising welfare states and labour market regulation. It is also the approach of the many comparative studies of how stable values and attitudes among populations affect welfare institutions or vice versa (Svallfors, 2003; Larsen, 2008; van Oorschot et al, 2008). Finally, we find this perspective in the so-called 'discursive institutionalism' (Campbell and Pedersen, 2001; Hay, 2008; Schmidt, 2008) in comparative political economy, where morality is conceptualised as residing in 'public philosophies' (Schmidt, 2011) that play out on a 'deeper' taken-for-granted level constraining policy changes (Carstensen and Schmidt, 2016, p 329).[7] On 'top' of policy transformations, this literature thus operates with an *ideological* role of ideas, basically putting new wine in old bottles. Public legitimation of activation ideas is a matter how 'rhetorical strategies … connect new proposals to an existing value structure' (Cox, 2001, p 498) or how political actors are 'manipulating the symbols available in existing ideological repertoires' (Béland, 2005, p 12). Morality is therefore only indirectly connected to policy making in a rather passive way, assuming stable and homogenous, and hence, uncontested national value structures, the so-called 'public philosophies' (Carstensen and Hansen, 2018). There is really no moral politics of activation in this perspective. Meanwhile, recent studies have shown how the framing in mass media of issues such as 'deservingness' (Slothuus, 2007; Esmark and Schoop, 2017) shapes the values and attitudes of citizens and thereby creates pressures for reform (see Chung et al, 2018). It thus acknowledges the importance of a moral politics, but still in a rather unidirectional and instrumental way whereby politicians simply respond to public opinion to gain legitimacy. What informs and shapes 'deservingness' remains a black box.

Third, a number of, often Foucault-inspired, studies have approached morality as 'immanently' manifest in the everyday governing of the unemployed. Morality enters policies and institutions as 'governmental-ethical practices' and forms of 'subjectivation' (Dean, 1995, 1998; Walters, 1997; Villadsen, 2007; Lessenich, 2011) and can therefore be identified in local practices of activation (Larner, 2000; Garsten and Jacobsson, 2004; McDonald and Marston, 2005; Marston and McDonald, 2006; Caswell et al, 2010). The point that activation policies, through their everyday instruments, shape the self-identities, conduct and experience (Demazière, 2013; Boland and Griffin, 2015) of unemployed people and street-level workers is a key point of departure for the perspective of this book. However, in focusing on governmental techniques, this governmentality literature has little to say about the dynamics of policy making. By approaching governmental techniques as immanently 'self-legitimating' in the way they subjectivise, these studies tend to assume that activation policies are uncontested and 'holistic' in the way they produce *a* particular 'active' subject. In consequence, uncertainty and dispute over the active turn, and in particular the level of public justification and critique, have therefore remained more or less neglected.

To conclude, the aforementioned perspectives confine the site of ideas and morality to either **outside of**, **below**, **on top of** or **within** policy transformations and therefore fail to account for the justification of activation policies in contested arenas as well as of the resulting composite policies and instruments. In other words, existing perspectives underestimate the reflexive, public and moral justifications and compromises that have underpinned and gradually shaped the 'active turn'. They hence neglect the many uncertainties, options and (moral) dilemmas political actors face within the active turn. For example, who is in need of monetary incentives to work and who will be adversely affected by such incentives? How big should the incentives be are they to be increased by means of subsidies or by reducing benefits? Should the incentives encourage part-time work? Who is capable of taking an ordinary job – those who are sufficiently mobile or those who are not in need of education or 'unordinary' jobs? To what extent are sanctions and control measures necessary, and to whom should they apply?

The book develops a novel *political* approach by foregrounding morality as integral to making sense of and evaluating policies and subsequently for legitimating transformations. The book thus asks how it becomes possible for political actors to distinguish between good and bad policy *adjustments*, and legitimise them for other actors, when they cannot simply rely on taken-for-granted values or paradigms. Account for the multiple ideas are put together and result in composite policy arrangements. Morality is neither below or outside policy making, but in the *foreground*, permeating sense making and in the end justifying policy. The book take its primary theoretical inspiration from 'French pragmatic sociology' – a strand founded in the late 1980s by Luc Boltanski and Laurent Thévenot, who initially developed a theory of the plurality of 'orders of worth' that enable people to justify and criticise in everyday situations of dispute – so-called 'test situations' (Boltanski and Thévenot, 1987, 2006). The theory entails an original conception of morality as well as of processes of legitimation that encompass the coexistence of a plurality of ideas and the tensions and uncertainty that this entails as well as the critical and reflexive competences of actors that this demands (Wagner, 1999; Eulriet, 2008; Blokker, 2011; Carstensen and Hansen, 2018).

From worlds to cities

To operationalise the aforementioned perspective, the book invokes and reinterprets the pragmatic sociological concept of 'city' (Boltanski and Thévenot, 1987, 2006). Unlike 'worlds' (or 'public philosophies') that derive their power from a shared set of institutionalised and taken-for-granted norms, 'cities' embody a 'repertoire of evaluation' (Lamont and Thévenot, 2000a; Carstensen and Hansen, 2018) that equips actors with the means to justify and criticise in situations of uncertainty and dispute. Cities thus take departure in reflexive and critical capacities of actors rather than at their sub-conscious level of being taken for-granted. The metaphor of 'city' is a(n inadequate) translation of the French *cité* referring to the Greek city state, or *polis*, in which the life of its inhabitants was put to the test by certain stable moral principles of good governing and conduct. We can thus imagine a number of controversies and tests *within* a city around how to govern it according to its moral principle. However, unlike worlds, cities are prepared to engage in disputes with other cities. The repertoires of cities can thus be combined and used by actors to reach tension-filled compromises. The result of this politics is a policy reality that is a *composite* rather than something that coherently corresponds to a 'world'.

Moving from this abstract conception of ideas to the specific problem of the book, the aim is to map the variety of **cities of unemployment**. Each city of unemployment is centred around a yardstick and a number of 'valorised' objects and subjects that enable actors to evaluate and put policies to the test, and in the end justify policy changes. These entail specific understandings of the causes and problems of unemployment, of the needs and desires of the (un)employed, and finally of what a socially just society entails and requires from the individual member and from the collective. Cities of unemployment thus guide actors in pointing out what is relevant to understanding the problem and suggesting certain measures to be strengthened over others in this highly complex assemblage of policies and instruments.

The book's main research questions are to ask which cities of unemployment are mobilised by political actors in activation reform processes, how the cities are mobilised to justify and criticise, and how the morality of cities 'sediments', or settles, into instruments and institutions governing the unemployed. In other words, *what is the moral economy of activation?*[8] This requires a meticulous analysis of the dynamics between the transformation of the governing of unemployment and political actors' justification and critique of this. The findings of the book are based on a comparative analysis of four case studies of activation reform processes, two in France and two in Denmark, two of involving unemployment insurance systems, and two involving social assistance systems.

Beyond 'good', 'bad' and 'ugly' activation

Alongside the explanatory aims of the book, there is a more political aim, entailing a wish to create space for new and innovative critical interventions. In doing so, the book differs radically from the current, dominant, normative intellectual positions. The intellectual landscape today is characterised by two kinds of criticism that could respectively by labelled **progressive** and **regressive**.

The *progressive* position is closely related to the aforementioned idea of two distinct activation paths, a 'good' and a 'bad', and an 'ugly' path of non-change. Deriving from 'third way' ideas (Giddens, 1998), this position, often identified as 'social investment' (Morel et al, 2012b) whereby Denmark and the rest of the Nordic countries are represented as 'good' examples to follow, is present in academia (for example, Sapir, 2006; Thelen, 2014) and in both international (Hansen and Triantafillou, 2011) and national policy debates, with the French president Emmanuel Macron's embrace of Scandinavian flexicurity as one of the latest examples. The problem with this position lies in its dichotomy between social investment on the one hand and neoliberalism on the other (see, for example, Morel et al, 2012a, pp 12–13). This division of 'good' and bad' may appear reasonable at an abstract level, but at a more concrete level the picture, even for the Nordic countries, is much more blurred. While the social investment state is presented as a place of 'empowerment', 'social inclusion' and 'equality of opportunities' (Palier and Hay, 2017), this perspective neglects the concrete (often coercive) measures it takes to ensure this. Further, it rarely considers the way that this perspective has in practice always blended with other ideas and programmes.

According to the *regressive* position, reforms from the 1980s onwards are basically a long regression departing from the key elements of the postwar welfare state. What was 'ugly' in the progressive perspective is thus considered 'good' in the regressive, whereas activation is simply 'bad'. For instance, this position points to the way 'conditionality' undermines social citizenship (Handler, 2004; Dwyer, 2010; Betzelt and Bothfeld, 2011; Nothdurfter, 2016), class consciousness and equality (Streeck, 2013; Zamora, 2017) and Keynesian demand-side policies (Blyth, 2013). Such analyses have forcefully pointed to some of the moral sacrifices that accompany activation. Meanwhile, the position also entails certain analytical shortcomings. By claiming a privileged, normative position of social justice that denounces the object of critique as im*moral*, activation is mainly described by what it is *not*. Therefore it has been prone to addressing how in fact a mix of ideas have underpinned and shaped activation reforms. The outcome of this position is often to invoke a nostalgic longing for the 'golden age' (Celik, 2016), where the blame is put on the 'new' idea, be it 'neoliberalism' (Wacquant, 2009) or 'market fundamentalism' (Block and Somers, 2003), terms that, as the coming chapters show, cannot fully capture the nature of the active turn.

While this book is clearly motivated by an uneasiness concerning ongoing transformations within (un)employment policies, it, as opposed to the two positions presented earlier, deliberately abstains from normative aspirations to compare such transformations with moral philosophical standards or unmask the discrepancy between promises made and reality. Rather, the aim is to develop a **non-normative critique** free from any constraints of what 'ought to' be or judgements of what is best, just, legitimate and so on, but nonetheless critical of frozen and excessive uses of power in whatever clothes it may put on (Hansen, 2016; see also Triantafillou, 2012; Koopman, 2013).[9] The reason for a non-normative, but critical, positioning is on the one hand pragmatic and methodological. In order to map the cities of unemployment as they unfold in the reform processes, it is necessary to turn the focus away from what they *do not do* through normative comparison, towards what they actually *do* and what realities they produce and shape. Part of this endeavour entails avoiding the temptation to reduce all the 'bad' elements to one common denominator – 'it's neoliberalism, stupid!' – a term both the progressive and nostalgic positions agree to denounce, although they take it for very different things (Hansen, 2015, p 305). The second reason relates to the kind of critical research needed to *repoliticise* the active turn and its moral consequences. By showing what the justifications of the active turn *do*, the analysis provides 'tactical pointers'(Foucault, 1984) showing both the ways critique is shaped by the dynamics of the active turn and how the transformations are based on fragile and diverse moral compromises. Hence, the book aims to open pathways towards thinking about and developing alternatives to the current and dominant moral economy of activation.

Structure and summary

The book is divided into three parts. Part I presents the steps towards composing a model of justification, critique and compromises as well as a typology of cities of unemployment. Chapter 2 introduces the meta-concepts inspired from French pragmatic sociology in order to develop an analytical model to map the plurality of moral and normative structures that are used to justify and criticise policies in public debate and lead to reforms in the governing of unemployment. Finally, the chapter presents how the model is operationalised through choices of case selection, data selection and coding procedures.

Chapter 3 presents the mapping of seven cities of unemployment that have been mobilised by political actors in the four reform processes. The cities are, on the one hand, mapped and composed on the basis of condensing the coded material of the four cases, and, on the other hand, they also provide the typology that is used in Part II to analyse the disputes and compromises in the reform processes. The presentation of each city is structured around four key dimensions: first, the overall principle and normative foundations of a city; second, the way in which the city qualifies the reality of unemployment and how policies are 'put to the test'; third, the way in which the role of governing in the city is presented, that is, what it takes to govern best, what kind of governing should be avoided, and when it is necessary (and legitimate) to use means of coercion; and fourth, the implications of being unemployed in each city. In other words, what characterises the unemployed moral subject and what makes the unemployed more or less worthy?

In the city of **demand**, unemployment is a consequence of economic fluctuations and stagnation. Governing is a matter of increasing demand for labour and increasing consumption. The unemployed are thus both workers temporarily on standby and consumers. In the city of **redistribution**, unemployment is a symptom of hegemonic interests groups and material inequality. Governing thus aims to distribute wealth and work better. The unemployed person is a citizen at risk of exploitation. In the city of **insurance**, unemployment is a social risk that should be collectivised. The unemployed are thus injured parties and entitled to compensation. In the city of **incentives**, unemployment is caused by insufficient financial incentives to work. Governing aims to generate incentives for the economic men to choose work rather than unemployment. In the **paternal** city, unemployment is a symptom of irresponsible behaviour and governing and it is thus a matter of making the unemployed take control of themselves through discipline and by setting requirements. In the city of **investment**, unemployment is the result of lacking societal investments in the human capital of the unemployed. Governing is a matter of investing in the skills of the unemployed to enhance their opportunities. Finally, in the city of **activity**, unemployment is the result of the insufficient adaptability of the labour market as well as the unemployed. The unemployed are in need of activity, if not work then jobseeking, and risk becoming lazy. In this way, the mapping of the cities exposes the politics and morality at stake in the transformations.

Part II comprises Chapters 4, 5, 6 and 7, and presents the findings of the four selected reforms. Although the reforms all exemplify the 'active turn', each has its particular political context, dynamics, scandals and controversies. The chapters all follow the same basic structure. Each chapter begins by providing a historical contextualisation of the reform. Through readings of secondary literature, the aim of these sections is to understand the previous compromises between cities of unemployment and morality in the French and Danish systems for the insured and uninsured unemployed. The sections are followed by a systematic analysis of the justification and critique in the reform processes. Each chapter ends with a detailed analysis of how compromises sediment into actual policy changes resulting from each reform followed by a brief outlook on major changes in the system preceding the reform.

Chapter 4 presents the reform process of the so-called PARE (aid plan for the return to employment) of the French unemployment insurance system in 2000. The instruments of PARE include an individual contract that obliges unemployed people to engage in 'personalised' job-seeking activities in order to access to support such as training courses. Further, PARE strengthened requirements to accept job offers from the job exchange service as well as sanctions for refusals and contractual infringements. The trade unions were divided in their stance towards this, causing intense debate, especially on the use of sanctions. The reform illustrates how the addition of a rather simple instrument radically changed the moral status of the unemployed.

Chapter 5 analyses the reform process ending with the Active Labour Market Policy Act (1992–93) of the Danish unemployment insurance system. The chapter explains how a number of instruments that were initially qualified to keep the existing normative principles alive were requalified and reshaped to activation. The reform introduced an individual contract similar to PARE but combined with a number of different instruments: leave schemes to ease access to the labour market, job training for the unemployed and job offers that the unemployed, after a period of time, would have to accept in order to continue to receive compensation.

Chapter 6 presents the reform process of the RSA (active solidarity income) in replacing the existing French system for the uninsured unemployed that had been in place since 1988. The reform process was launched at the end of 2007 and adopted at the end of 2008 once the financial crisis started to reach across the Atlantic. RSA entailed a negative tax scheme to increase incentives for recipients to take low-paid, part-time work, while also introducing a number of instruments and obligations with the aim of increasing the mobility of the unemployed. The result was a displacement of the compromise of the previous scheme and a radical requalification of the relationship between poverty and work.

Chapter 7 analyses the 'Everyone can be useful' reform implemented in Denmark in 2011–13. This reform transformed the system of social assistance in several ways. It reduced benefits and installed an 'education injunction' for young recipients, required all 'able' recipients to work for their benefit, strengthened sanctions, introduced new instruments aimed at 'vulnerable' recipients and young single parents, and created a complex system of 'triage' in order to categorise recipients according to a variety of instruments. The reform process involved two public scandals in which two individual recipients came to exemplify the dysfunctions of the system. In different ways, these scandals put to the test the question of whether the system was in fact 'active'. Chapter 7 further analyses the problem of profiling recipients, as well as how so-called 'utility jobs' became a panacea for all able recipients.

The comparative and conclusive Part III discusses patterns cutting across all four cases. Chapter 8 answers the question of what constitutes the moral repertoire of activation. All reforms are driven in particular by justifications from the **paternal, mobility, investment** and **incentives** cities, which are tied together in multiple ways. The other three cities do not vanish completely, but in the qualification of the unemployed they are increasingly marginalised and morally denounced as 'passive'. In all four reforms, the justification of coercive measures towards the unemployed is central. The chapter outlines how coercion plays a particular role in the moral economy of activation that challenges the idea, mentioned earlier, that it is possible to distinguish between non-coercive 'good' activation based on 'social investment' and coercive 'bad' activation based on neoliberalism. The mapping of the moral economy of activation thus prompts us to consider the explanatory and normative implications of both concepts.

Chapter 9 teases out the key dynamics driving the active turn. The composite and tension-filled repertoire installs a multicausal and behavioural problematisation of unemployment where there is constant room for improvement and adjustments. At the level of public debate, this manifests in a permanent testing of policy instruments' behavioural effect. At the level of the everyday governing of the unemployed, the tensions between the different cities of the active turn are mitigated in categorisations and various and continuous tests that evaluate the behaviour of the unemployed. The tests, such as profiling, screening, interviews and contracts, thus continuously ask what kind of subject the unemployed person is (that is, which city they live in), how worthy they are and what instruments make them more worthy (in other words, closer to working). The chapter then points to the implications for the way in which the voice of the unemployed is qualified. The book ends with a discussion of the extent to which the ideas of (universal) basic income and social economy/enterprises that have received growing attention in international policy debates contain credible alternatives to the moral economy of activation.

Notes

[1] Excerpts from *Oxford English dictionary*.

[2] Two quotes from public debates on activation reforms – the former from 2000 in France (see Chapter 4), the latter from 2011 in Denmark (see Chapter 7).

[3] The same normative distinction also appears in Sapir's (2006) influential paper on the reforms of European social models, comparing countries on social and economic performance. The Nordic countries scored high on

both (the 'good'), the Anglo-Saxon high on economic and low on social (the 'bad'), the Continental high on social but low on economic (the 'ugly') and the Mediterranean low on both (even more 'ugly').

4   It is worth noting that several scholars have criticised Esping-Andersen's idea of worlds for assuming too much internal consistency even in the period before the first activation reforms (for example, Kasza 2002; Salais, 2005). I find this more radical critique to be in accordance with and to underpin the theoretical premises of this book, taking departure in a 'composite reality'.

5   Bonoli (2013, p 24) has addressed this problem differently by suggesting an analysis of actual activation instruments, broadening the variety into four types of active labour market policy: incentive reinforcement, employment assistance, occupation and upskilling.

6   Biebricher (2008) shows how the moral element as well as the concept of struggle, which was central to Foucault's own genealogical analyses, is toned down in Foucault's (2008) governmentality lectures and subsequently in most governmentality studies.

7   Similar terms in use are 'public sentiments' (Campbell, 2004), 'Zeitgeist' (Mehta, 2011) and 'background ideas' (Schmidt, 2008).

8   Since E.P. Thompson's coining of the concept (1971), 'moral economy' has been invoked in multiple ways. Here I use 'economy' in the sense of the *Collins dictionary* definition of 'orderly interplay between the parts of a system or structure'. I thus take the moral economy of activation to be the repertoire of cities of unemployment that actors mobilise when justifying activation policies.

9   It is thus a matter of neither adhering to a neutral position of 'speaking truth to power' by means of evidence, facts and solutions (for example, Wildawsky, 1987) nor to a Weberian value-free position. French pragmatic sociology (FPS) has sometimes adhered to this idea. In order to take the critical operations conducted by the actors as their object, sociologists, according to Boltanski, have to give up the possibility of producing their own critiques (Boltanski, 2012, p 80). FPS was thus positioned 'scientifically' as aiming to produce 'original constructs' and offer 'better descriptions' (Boltanski, 2012, pp 23, 90). For a repositioning of FPS into a 'non-normative critique', see Hansen (2016).

2

Tests, compromises and policy change

The purpose of this chapter is to develop an analytical model that encapsulates the way political actors justify and criticise policy reforms when they are situated in an arena of coexisting ideas and uncertainty with regard to how to 'activate'. Further, the analytical model should encompass how these deliberations result in compromises and changes in policies and what the moral consequences of these changes are. Chapter 1 argued that existing theoretical perspectives, from historical institutionalist theories of path dependency to ideational perspectives of discursive institutionalism and governmentality studies, originate in a reality where the legitimation of activation resides in *shared* and taken-for-granted values, public philosophies, worlds, governmentalities and so on. In the case of historical institutionalism and governmentality studies, they have thus paid little attention to public conflicts, deliberations and legitimation. Discursive institutionalism and discourse analyses *do*, but in these cases they are presented as an arena for 'rhetorical strategies' (Cox, 2001) and 'weapons of mass persuasion' (Béland, 2005, p 12) used by 'framers' such as 'spin doctors' and 'campaign managers' (Campbell, 2004, p 103; see also Schmidt, 2006, p 254 onwards). This results in a rather 'populist' conception of public deliberation with preference for the 'heroic' politics of party leaders and elections and thus a certain neglect, or lack of understanding, of the kind of grey reform politics that is the concern of this book (Panizza and Miorelli, 2013). The following sections show how in French pragmatic sociology (FPS) concepts of tests, justification, critique and compromises propose a different approach that takes public deliberation and legitimisation of 'grey' reforms more seriously.

FPS has entered a number of fields, from organisation studies (Jagd, 2011; Patriotta et al, 2011; Dansou and Langley, 2012; Cloutier and Langley, 2013) and international political economy (Ponte and Gibbon, 2005; Cheyns, 2011) to economic sociology (Stark, 2009; Thévenot, 2015), urban studies (Blok and Meilvang, 2014; Holden and Scerri, 2015) and social theory (Honneth, 2010; Delanty, 2011). However, so far few have attempted to introduce FPS to studies in comparative political economy and the political science of legitimation of policy change.

The relevance of introducing FPS is related to its critique of the sociology of Pierre Bourdieu in the 1980s. Two former students of Bourdieu, Luc Boltanski and Laurent Thévenot, were faced with a similar problem and dearth of theory to that just mentioned. The social theory of Bourdieu distinguished between subjective reality, determined by the 'deeply internalised' habitus designating a 'unitarian way of life, that is a unity of personal choices, good and habits' *and* an objective reality of the oppressive and reproducing mechanisms distributing different forms of capital (Bourdieu, 1994, pp 23, 182). While the former was experienced by the actor, the latter was 'masked', resulting in 'collective misrecognition' that only the sociologist could unveil (Bourdieu, 1994, p 178 onwards; Celikates, 2012). Bourdieu's influential theory thus basically left no space for understanding actors' capacity to deliberate and criticise. Through exemplary studies of everyday conflicts, Boltanski and Thévenot (1981, 1987) were able to show that 'ordinary' people were sometimes placed in situations that required them to act in ways much closer to the competences that Bourdieu had confined to the sociologist. In these 'critical situations', people were acting as 'metaphysicians', capable of justifying and criticising by mobilising moral principles that resonated with grand political philosophies in order to settle disputes and reach agreement. Leading the research centre *Groupe de sociologie politique et morale*, Boltanski and Thévenot gradually developed concepts to capture the dynamics and tensions hitherto neglected. The first hallmark of this programme is *On justification*, which presents a model of the 'orders of worth' and the 'grammar' that actors follow in situations of conflict and dispute (Boltanski and Thévenot, 1991, 2006).[1] The following presents the key concepts of FPS while adapting them to the study of public justification and critique of policy reforms, and further relating them to the specific concern of this book – activation and unemployment.

Test situations, tests, testing, contesting

Contrary to the Bourdieusian theory of habitus, the ontological point of departure for pragmatic sociology is a world with uncertainty and tensions (Boltanski, 2011; Barthe et al, 2013) requiring reflexive coordination by actors (Thévenot, 2002a). The reality is regarded as fragile, heterogeneous and 'composite' (Thévenot, 2001a) rather than solid and coherent. FPS points to three reasons for this. The first is that human beings living together are confronted with the basic political and moral tension between commonality and difference in a community, between what makes human beings equal and what makes some more worthy than others (Boltanski and Thévenot, 2006, p 76). This tension is also at the core of the problem of unemployment, since the governing of unemployment is about how and to what extent the worthiness deriving from the dynamics of the labour market ought to be constitutive of the political community and thus of citizenship. The second reason derives from the way FPS has demonstrated that communities are in fact constituted by a *plurality* of formats to mitigate the aforementioned tension, resulting in a *composite* reality with tensions between these forms. Third, FPS points to a tension between formats and the 'flux' of reality that results in an ontological uncertainty and changeability with regard to what reality consists of, or in Boltanski's words, to 'the "whatness" of what is' (Boltanski, 2011, p 56).

A key concept in FPS for unfolding these tensions is the 'test'. FPS uses the multiplicity of meanings attached to the term (in French, *épreuve*) deliberately. First, test signifies a *situation* in which actors doubt or are in disagreement about 'what matters' (Boltanski, 2011, p 56) and thus in which the outcome is not entirely given. It is these test situations or 'critical moments' (Boltanski and Thévenot, 1999) that are the privileged research objects of FPS (Dansou and Langley, 2012), since this is where the aforementioned tensions surface. Thinking in terms of test situations thus provides a pathway to understanding how actors involved (politicians, interest groups, experts, unemployed people, and so on) find ways to handle the continuous uncertainty of how to organise the relationship between those who are regarded as employed and those who are not. This book focuses on a specific arena of test situations – that is, national public debates (primarily in newspapers) – but test situations occur, and could be studied, in many other places – in jobcentres in encounters between unemployed people and street-level bureaucrats, among experts and in the bureaucracies, on public squares, on social media and in private gatherings where unemployed people are required to justify their (lack of) status.

Second, 'test' refers to evaluative *action*, as in the verb 'to test' or to 'put to the test'. Test situations, in other words, require agency. When actors cannot rely on the-taken-for-granted, they must activate 'critical capacities' (Boltanski and Thévenot, 1999) of experiencing, thinking, creativity, coordination and, in the end, judgements. FPS is thus 'pragmatic' by being oriented towards practices and concrete situations and by taking as its point of departure people's own sense making in these situations. However, it is also pragmatic in the sense that 'to test' implies that some*thing* or some*one* 'real' is tested, which leads to con*test* – that is, justification or critique of concrete acts, things and so on. It is probably on this point that FPS differs the most from the conventional approaches of discourse analysis and framing within the so-called 'argumentative turn' (Fischer and Gottweiss, 2012). These perspectives point to the semantics, rhetoric and semiotics of deliberation in struggles over ascribing meaning to key 'nodal points' (Laclau and Mouffe, 1985) or 'frames' (Goffman, 1974). In the FPS perspective, the tension lies not only between various discourses but equally in their confrontation with reality in tests. Tests are uncertain, their outcome is not given. Semantic power over frames and nodal points thus matter less if they do not allow for political actors to put concrete policies to the test. This leads to the final components that actors need in order to test.

The third meaning of test signifies a yardstick that can lead to a number of concrete questions, such as a philosophical principle. FPS speaks of how yardsticks are prerequisites for establishing 'equivalence' (Thévenot, 1984), making it possible to see differences and similarities, or simply to recognise or disregard what is relevant in a particular situation. In this sense, it makes sense to speak of the test as an *idea*. This can be contrasted to the fourth and final significant meaning of test, which is test as a 'device' for testing. Following Boltanski, tests are in this case *institutions*. While the mobilisation of tests as 'ideas' requires the cognitive critical capacities of actors, test, in this latter institutional sense, is a 'bodiless being to which is delegated the task stating the whatness of what is' through repetitive tests (Boltanski, 2011, p 59). The tautological nature of institutions deprives them of the basic human capacities of doubt and reflexivity. The formation of institutions such as statistics, benchmarks, categories, definitions, indicators, standards and opinion polls are thus key research objects for FPS (Desrosières and Thévenot, 1988; Thévenot, 2009, 2011). Institutions of this kind are an integral and indispensable part of the governing of the unemployed: they set the boundaries between the employed and the unemployed, separate the unemployed into various categories, set criteria for receiving benefits, set benchmarks for jobcentre performance and so on. From the incomplete list of examples of institutions, it becomes clear that deliberation, in the perspective of FPS, never work as a 'free lunch', where political actors chose whatever test they find appealing. On the other hand, since institutions are not part of coherent and flawless whole, but are a tension-filled composite, actors are constantly confronted with the need to change institutional settings – adjust categories, create new performance indicators and profiling tools, order new annual reports and so on. Institutional tests thus both inform and format ongoing debates as well as being shaped and invented as outcomes of same debates.

Qualification of a moral reality

So far the concepts from FPS enable us to approach how actors in concrete situations (such as public debate on a specific reform) test things (such as policies and instruments) by means of yardsticks, and how these practices are formatted by institutionalised tests (such as statistics and existing categories). However, to understand the transfer from abstract yardsticks to the concrete tests of reality, Boltanski and Thévenot add a meta-layer of what they term **qualified** objects and subjects (Boltanski and Thévenot, 2006, pp 130–7). Since tests are always 'situated', yardsticks cannot simply be mobilised in the way that, for instance, a theory of principle-driven justice is applied to reality (Boltanski and Thévenot, 2000, p 216; 2006, pp 127–8). They need support in order to tie the yardsticks to the situation in order to prepare for evaluation (Thévenot, 2002b). For example, in order to evaluate to what extent unemployment benefits accommodate the insurance aim of compensation, political actors will make use of a number of objects and subjects that qualify the reality as one of social risks, solidarity, accidents, actuarial science, collective responsibility, victims, contributions, fraud and so on. But the exact same unemployment benefits could be evaluated on their capacity to provide incentives to work, if they were qualified in terms of unemployment traps, 'carrots', making work pay, perverse incentives and so on. Objects and subjects hence 'valorise' the reality (Boltanski and Thévenot, 2006, p 131) and bridge the questions of what reality *is* and the *moral* and political question of how it *ought* to be (Wagner, 1999, p 348; Boltanski, 2011, p 69).

There are test situations in which the scope of available qualified objects and subjects is rather narrow, such as in a trial in a courtroom. In the case of unemployment, it is much less straightforward as to what 'proof' can be drawn into test situations, such as reform debates. Statistics are obviously important, but which ones? Growth rate, unemployment rate, employment rate, consumption, poverty rate, wage levels, benefit levels, job turnover, education levels? And statistics are far from the only legitimate format. It could also be particular successful programmes and local experiments, stories in the news, documentaries, personal experiences, opinion polls, protests and so on. The governing of unemployment is thus characterised by a constant overload of information that forces actors to qualify reality by selecting what matters, since everything cannot be taken into account. In order to evaluate and make judgments, they are required to invest in some qualified objects and to sacrifice others (Thévenot, 1984). This is where FPS's distinct conception of ideas comes into the picture.

Cities of unemployment

Although 'ontological uncertainty' provides permanent scope for tests, tensions and critique, there are limits to the ways in which reality can be qualified and actions can be justified and criticised (Boltanski and Thévenot, 1987, 2006). FPS assumes that in specific places and periods there exists a contingent but limited number of legitimate and stable ideas that enable actors to qualify reality and establish equivalence (Blokker, 2011). In other words, it is possible to identify stable relationships, a 'grammar' in the lingua of FPS, between moral yardsticks and surrounding qualified objects and subjects. FPS has used a number of terms to conceptualise this understanding of ideas, from 'orders of worth' (Boltanski and Thévenot, 2006) and 'conventions of coordination' (Thévenot, 2001a) to 'regimes of justification' (Borghi, 2011) and 'repertoires of evaluation' (Lamont and Thévenot, 2000b).[2] This book uses the term 'city' that also figures in *On justification* to emphasise the governmental dimension that is more pertinent in the study of policy reforms than in everyday disputes. The original French term *cité* is more illustrative, since it refers to the Greek city-states and hence designates a society that is governed according to an overarching principle of justice.[3] I term them cities of **unemployment** to map the variety qualifying and evaluating the phenomenon of people who, for one reason or another, do not commodify their time and effort in the labour market (Polanyi, 1944).

Such cities thus qualify the phenomenon by identifying objects that influence it, by attaching particular behavioural characteristics to unemployed subjects and by providing tests by which one can evaluate and improve governing to make it more just and efficient. Cities hereby also 'valorise' the inhabitants as (more or less worthy) moral subjects. This, of course, includes the unemployed, but by specifying the level of worthiness of unemployed people as well as the thresholds between unemployment and employment, the cities are just as much about the employed as the unemployed. Finally, the cities also qualify all those who aspire to partake in the quest for governing the unemployed better. In other words, the cities expect particular capacities and knowledge in order to govern legitimately.

All cities thus need to comply with an overarching 'grammar'. They have (1) a yardstick that is supported by (2) a certain way of qualifying the phenomenon of unemployment that leads to (3) a policy test to judge policies worthy or less worthy, (4) a conception of what it takes to govern best as well what kind of governing should be avoided, and, finally, (5) a way of qualifying the unemployed – the path towards a state of worthiness, and, conversely, what conduct will make the unemployed less worthy. Integral to all cities is thus ideas of how and when to sanction those who do not comply with the moral standards, both in order to correct inappropriate behaviour as well as acting as a kind of punishment for not respecting the moral standards, and thus the 'worthy' of the city.

Cities are not ready-made prescriptions with a complete blueprint. They do not simply dictate to those who govern exactly what to change or what policy tool to introduce. Rather than answers they provide them with questions.[4] Cities do not operate in an environment in which they are completely taken for granted, but in one of uncertainty, tensions and contentedness. They instigate and *format* rather than exclude critique. They coexist, which means that they, unlike, for instance, Hall's Kuhnian 'paradigms' (Hall, 1993), can communicate with and relate to each other. In other words, they can be used to construct *compromises*.

Returning to the test situations, how can cities of unemployment then be mobilised by actors? There are basically two types of test situation – *within* and *in between* cities (Thévenot, 2002a; Stavo-Debauge, 2011). The first involves what can be termed 'reformative' or 'corrective' tests. For example, even when unemployment benefits are put to the test solely by an insurance yardstick, there can be great disputes about the levels of compensation and contribution, setting criteria for membership, how to organise funds and who organises them, what it takes to be entitled, how to deal with fraud and speculative behaviour and so on. Corrective tests, in which experts and intellectuals play a key role as 'grammarians', are thus key to developing and adapting the repertoire to provide political actors with effective means to develop policies that qualify for evaluation.

The second type of test can be termed 'radical', involving more than one city. Unlike reformative tests, radical tests not only put reality to the test but also the very yardsticks that underpin the cities. For example, the insurance yardstick can be radically challenged by a fundamentally different morality such as one that qualifies unemployment as a problem of economic incentives. There cannot be (full) compensation and monetary incentives at the same time.

Test situations with several cities thus test the balance and dominance of cities vis à vis each other. It is in pointing to the unexceptional occurrence of 'radical' test situations that one of the great theoretical innovations of FPS lies. It points to other dynamics of change than are acknowledged by existing perspectives. It implies that change is not a matter of one paradigm or ideology replacing the other, in which actors simply replace one set of taken-for-granted ideas with another, but of a *gradual* displacement in the reciprocal power relations between ideas in which actors are required to deal with the tensions and contradictions between ideas. This element differs substantially from Foucauldian governmentality studies. In focusing on the process of generating 'problematisations', 'governmental rationalities' and 'regimes of truth' (test as ideas), and techniques and modes of governing (test as institutions), governmentalities have paid less attention to the question of contentedness (test as situations and action). The FPS perspective thus accommodates recent criticisms towards governmentality studies of downplaying 'the politics of governance, including the politics of managing factional interests, unforeseen crises, and of countering competing problematisations and resistances' and of assuming 'too much coherence and order in the present' (Brady, 2014, p 24; see also Valverde, 1996; Biebricher, 2008; Collier, 2012; Hansen, 2015).[5]

From test situations to policy change

The dynamic of contentedness and composite arrangements is encapsulated in the FPS concept of **compromise**. Compromises, here, are not a balancing of interests, but designate the way in which two or more yardsticks are made compatible by establishing 'composite' arrangements that assuage the tension between them (Boltanski and Thévenot 2006, p 277 onwards). For example, a compromise between insurance and incentives could be to establish an upper limit of, say, 90% of compensation to ensure incentives. This example illustrates that compromises are fragile, since they never completely satisfy the yardstick of one city of unemployment. It is not given how the compromise should be settled. The percentage could be higher or lower, or could be arranged in different ways such as to gradually reduce the rate of compensation as time goes by. Further, compromises risk being challenged by tests based on cities that are not recognised in the original compromise, for instance, criticising the aforementioned compromise for neglecting the problem of (lack of) skills in relation to unemployment. Repeated testing by mobilising cities and assembling them in compromises is thus integral to the political actors' search for and justification of policy changes. In other words, tests and compromises 'sediment' (Salais, 2011), and result in composite and contradictory layering of different cities over time (Thévenot, 2011). While these enduring tensions between contending cities of unemployment enable actors to resolve tensions at any given point, it likewise creates impetus for future reform efforts as these unstable compromises bring up new test situations that need to be resolved (Carstensen and Hansen, 2018).

This model is illustrated in Figure 2.1. The main research object is illustrated as the 'evaluation' sphere, where multiple cities of unemployment are mobilised and put together in compromises where policies and policy changes are justified and criticised – that is, 'put to the test'. However, these processes do not occur in a vacuum – in other words, the bubble is highly permeable. First, actors engaging in justification and critique are dependent on various 'proofs' to qualify and contest arguments. Proof can take numerous forms: some of the feedback is highly institutionalised, such as statistics, measuring the achievement of objectives, benchmarking and multiplying ideas and perceptions in the media and so on, whereas other forms find less institutionalised ways to reach the 'sphere' of evaluation, such as public scandals and everyday experiences of unemployment, and the instruments governing it, that sediment into the (public) memory (compare Berger and Luckmann, 1966).

The rightward-pointing arrows illustrate the sedimentations of ongoing debates and evaluations. Sedimentations are not only changes in policies, but can also lead to institutional changes; for instance, classification systems are modified or new strategies are launched that

Figure 2.1: A model of tests and policy change

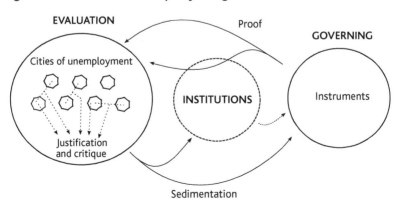

then have implications for the feedback. In the 'sphere' of governing, tests are thus *devices* used to classify and valorise the unemployed.

The FPS perspective of a composite reality and plurality of coexisting, legitimate, moral repertoires provides a framework that circumvents the explanatory limitations of theories of path dependency and 'public philosophies' that dominate debates within historical as well as discursive institutionalism, as presented in Chapter 1. Historical institutionalist scholars have departed from 'punctuated equilibria' explanations and started to address 'incremental' and 'cumulative' dynamics of change, such as 'institutional drift' and 'layering' (Hacker, 2004; Streeck and Thelen, 2005). Parallel to, and sometimes inspired by, these debates within historical institutionalism, discursive institutionalism has departed from a conception of ideas as the consecutive replacement of one 'policy paradigm' with another, where crises mark the passage from one to the next (for example, Hall, 1993; Blyth, 2002). Instead, it has emphasised the role of agency such as 'brokers' and '*bricoleurs*' (Campbell, 2004) in driving incremental ideational changes (Béland and Cox, 2010; Carstensen and Schmidt, 2016). However, unlike the model presented in this chapter, both strands have kept the level of morality and values stable and coherent, in the former case as 'worlds' and in the latter case as 'public philosophies' (Carstensen and Hansen, 2018). Table 2.1 summarises some of the key differences between FPS and existing analytical perspectives.

Methods

Case and data selection

The comparative analysis is based on four case studies of activation reform processes, two in France and two in Denmark, two involving unemployment insurance systems, and two involving social assistance systems. The cases and data are selected on mainly three criteria. First, the *exploratory* endeavour of the study, applying a novel theoretical framework with the aim of mapping the role of ideas and morality in the active turn, calls for diversity within and between cases. The study contains cases from two different 'worlds of welfare' and from both systems of unemployment insurance and assistance. The chosen reforms also provide examples of tipping-point reforms taking the first steps towards activation, as well as intensifying reforms of systems that were set on the activation path. Finally, the reforms vary in terms of occurring in a context of economic upturns as well as downturns.

Table 2.1: Conceptions of political ideas and morality

	Discursive institutionalism	Governmentality	Discourse analysis	FPS
Ideas	Public philosophies	Governmental rationalities, regimes of truth	Discourses, ideologies, frames	Orders of worth, repertoires of evaluation, cities of unemployment
Legitimacy	Shared 'Zeitgeist'	Scientific, everyday	Persuasion	Qualifying reality, justification
Enactment	Cultural	Technical	Rhetorical, populist	Evaluative
Morality	Coherent set of values (taken-for-granted)	Subjectivation (taken-for-granted)	Political ideologies, antagonistic	Plurality, worth, put to the test
Agency	Actors connecting programmes and policy ideas with public philosophies	Intellectuals and experts inventing new governmentalities and technologies of the self	Organic intellectuals engaged in party programmes and manifestos	Actors criticising policies and justifying changes

Further, there is diversity within cases by examining statements inductively in over 1,300 newspaper articles from when reform programmes are announced until they are adopted.[6] Since all statements of justification and critique are analysed and coded, the study gives a broader spectrum of ideas than a study of expert discourses or intellectual ideas. The limited number of cases, however, most likely does not represent the full repertoire of activation, but it provides a sound starting point for studies of similar dynamics in other settings. Another limitation is that, in order to focus on *policy* reforms, the study only loosely relates to the issues of changes in governance, such as privatisation, marketisation and (de)centralisation (see, for example, van Berkel and Borghi, 2008; van Berkel et al, 2012; Lødemel and Moreira, 2014).

Second, the case design is developed to provide insight into the *dynamics* of justification, critique and ongoing test situations and compromises. This is the reason for focusing on public debate over large-scale, and hence contested, reforms. Further, it is the reason why I choose to focus on the public debate in newspaper articles, since this is a genre where the tensions and dynamics between ideas, actors and the reforms are visible. The data thus have a high degree of intertextuality (Justesen and Mik-Meyer, 2012, p 122), where actors constantly make references to, and are confronted with, other statements. The data are thus appropriate for grasping how the reform process is a dynamical sequence of test situations, such as criticism by political actors, media stories that rise to public scandals and problems of local implementation, evaluation of experiments, protests and so on. The small-n case study is a prerequisite for studying the reforms as processes and understanding the way in which justification and critique result in ongoing 'test situations' that affect the dynamic and outcome of the process. The processual perspective further makes it a study, not simply of discourses, ideologies and narratives, but of the role of ideas and morality in conjunction with concrete policy changes (as compared with the sedimentation and feedback in Figure 2.1).

Finally, the dynamical aspect is highlighted by choosing 'least likely' countries in the sense that they were seen as resilient to a key feature of activation – the use of coercion. As mentioned earlier, Denmark was placed and used as example of a distinct 'soft' and universal type of activation. France, on the other hand, with its republican conception of citizenship, which implies that the state is indebted to its citizens (to provide a secure life), was seen as 'inconsistent' with the idea that citizens have obligations to the state (Barbier and Théret, 2001, p 177). The country was thus 'bound to experience limited pressure for job search, and the absence of a consistent punitive orientation' (Enjolras et al, 2000; Barbier and Fargion, 2004, p 457; see also Barbier, 2007).

Third, the study is set up to identify **sedimentation**, that is, the dynamics and direction of gradual policy change. This book thus carefully situates the case studies historically by examining past reform trajectories of national systems as well as policy developments from the adoption of reform to recent changes. Furthermore, it pays attention to how actual policy changes are integrated into existing policy frameworks.

Finally, to clarify, the explanatory purpose of comparing reforms in France and Denmark is not to track and trace universal independent variables in order to provide the final explanans to the question of *why* activation reforms happen. The aim is much more modest. On the other hand, the cases *do* have relevance beyond their particularity. The aim of the book can thus be described as to 'cast different perspectives on a problematized phenomenon' (Glynos and Howarth, 2007, p 207) by providing insight to the *what* and *how* of (the moral economy of) activation. The small-n but in-depth study of 'maximum variation' and 'least likely' cases can provide methodological tools, concepts and knowledge about dynamics that can be used to better understand the unfolding of the active turn in other settings.

Analysing and coding in two steps

The analysis of the primary data of newspaper articles, consisting of more than 3,000 statements, was conducted in two steps using the software nVivo. In each step, the data were supplemented with various secondary data in order to triangulate and substantiate the findings. The purpose of the first step was to develop a grammar or typology of all cities of unemployment that were mobilised in debates. The coding of the data was a process of gradually developing the typology. Starting with a tentative model based on conceptions of unemployment in the history of economic and welfare state ideas present in normative literature on the welfare state and current debates, the typology was substantially reconfigured throughout the coding process.[7]

The second step and reading of the material had a completely different objective. The focus was no longer on internal coherence within each city, but rather on tension, conflict and process. In other words, the second reading analysed the process of political actors mobilising cities of unemployment in test situations within each of the four cases (of which the findings are presented in Chapters 4, 5, 6, and 7). It thus asked the question of how the coexistence of the seven cities of unemployment resulted in test situations and compromises. In order to achieve this, I depend on other types of data. In order to understand the context of the reform, I rely heavily on secondary literature on the history of Danish and French labour market policies, and more specifically on the history of the systems that each reform transforms. Further, the reading involved a lot of 'snowballing' connected to specific test situations: looking into parliamentary debates, governmental reports, intellectual works, green papers and policy documents. Finally, in order to engage more directly with the question of sedimentation, the policy output of the reforms was analysed in detail in documents and laws related to the adoption of reforms.

Notes

[1] The most notable contributions to FPS since *On justification* are Boltanski and Chiapello's historical extension of the framework in 'The new spirit of capitalism' (2005) and Laurent Thévenot's extension into varieties of 'regimes of engagement' (Thévenot, 2001b, 2006, 2007) and 'grammars of voicing concern' (Thévenot, 2014). For overviews of FPS see Bénatouïl (1999), Blokker (2011) and Silber (2016).

[2] Boltanski and Thévenot initially mapped six 'orders of worth' mobilised in everyday situations of dispute that they associated with canonical

texts from political philosophy. The six orders of worth are: **inspiration** (St. Augustine), **domestic** (Jacques-Bénigne Bossuet), **fame** (Thomas Hobbes), **civic** (Jean-Jacques Rousseau), **market** (Adam Smith) and **industrial** (Henri de Saint-Simon) (Boltanski and Thévenot, 2006). They thus operate with sharp division between the micro-perspective of short-term, everyday situations and macro-moral construct of *longue durée* (Meilvang et al, 2018). In order to operationalise a meso-historical scale of years and decades (Meilvang et al, 2018), the model in this book develops moral constructs (cities of unemployment) that is better adapted to capture the tensions and changes of activation reforms.

[3] Further, because 'city' speaks intuitively to Esping-Andersen's concept of world, suggesting a less monolithic and holistic concept. In *On justification*, *cité* is translated to 'polity' (Boltanski and Thévenot, 2006) whereas it appears as 'city' in Boltanski and Chiapello's *New spirit of capitalism* (Boltanski and Chiapello, 2005).

[4] On this point, cities are thus like Foucault's concept of **problematisation**, 'turning a given into a question' (Foucault, 2003, p 24).

[5] Most governmentality studies have thus neglected Foucault's own call for thinking of governmental practices as a 'composite reality' (Foucault, 2007, p 144).

[6] I collected articles (in the national databases, Europresse.com and Infomedia) from the three largest, national, non-tabloid and non-specialised newspapers in each country (*Le Monde*, *Libération*, and *Figaro* in France, *Jyllandsposten*, *Berlingske Tidende*, and *Politiken* in Denmark). Articles were collected from the day the reform was announced until one month after it was agreed (280-450 articles per case), which all in all gives a broad selection of the most important voices in the debate, and makes it possible to study how the reform process evolved. For search criteria, see Hansen (2017, Appendix A).

[7] For more detail on this process, see Hansen (2017, Appendix B).

3

Cities of unemployment

This chapter presents the grammar of seven 'cities of unemployment', which are mapped and composed on the basis of condensing the coded material of the four cases. The chapter is structured around four key dimensions. First, it outlines the overall principle and normative foundations. Second, it describes how the city *qualifies* the reality of unemployment and how policies are put to the test. Third, the role of *governing* in the city is presented: what does it take to govern best and what kind of governing should be avoided, and when is it necessary (and legitimate) for the 'governor' to exercise authority by means of coercion? Last, the chapter examines the implications of being unemployed in each city, in other words, what characterises the unemployed *subject* and what is the path towards a state of worthiness? And on the other hand, what conduct makes the unemployed individual less worthy?

While all the cities provide answers to these questions, their radically different qualifications imply that they sometimes (prefer to) operate on different levels, from macroeconomic policy and taxation to workfare schemes and the counselling of the unemployed individual. Along this line of reasoning, the cities may appear 'incomparable' and, hence, unfit for a typology such as that presented here. However, as the chapter shows, the cities all induce different moral subjects that are mutually exclusive. This means that although it is possible to identify more or less stable compromises (such as the golden age compromise) with what appears as a stable division of labour between various cities, they are *compromises* with in-built tensions. To understand the tensions and compromises, it is first necessary to bracket and categorise the processes of justification and critique into the various normative yardsticks forged by a city of governing, tests and subjects. This is the aim of the chapter.

In order to tie the grammar of the cities of unemployment to intellectual ideas the primary source of the statements from the four cases is occasionally supplemented by secondary literature from canonical texts of 'grammarians' (Boltanski and Thévenot, 2006, p 71).

The rest of the chapter presents a condensed extract of the justification and critique taking place 'inside' the walls of each city of unemployment in selected debates on Danish and French reforms of their unemployment systems.[1] All cities are present in all cases, but with variations between reforms and countries. I hence treat the cities as transcendental, rather than national. Although the governing of unemployment has been and remains primarily a national issue for which national policy makers are held accountable, the occurrence of all cities of unemployment in both countries confirms that ideas do not respect national borders to the same extent. Governing unemployment has always been a comparative endeavour where policy makers, since the very first insurance scheme in Ghent in 1900, have sought inspiration from other countries (Rodgers, 1998; Edling, 2008).[2] Ideas are thus not confined by 'worlds' of welfare. Finally, the chapter concludes with a summary of the grammar of the cities (see Table 3.1, p 58).

City of demand

The, evidently, Keynesian starting point in this city is that market mechanisms, even in equilibrium, do not lead to full employment (Galbraith, 1987, p 233). Unemployment is first a question of where the economy is situated in the business cycle between 'upturns' and downturns. 'In a free market economy, the economic trends fluctuate (in more or less good times) – and with them so does employment' (Hansen, 2017). Second, however, unemployment is not to be considered 'inherent in nature'. It can and should be minimised politically. The state is the primary actor since, being subject to the market mechanisms, neither the unemployed nor the employers have the capacity to exit economic stagnation by themselves 'when the market mechanisms do not work'. If the economy is in a recession, resulting in a lack of demand for labour, it is the responsibility of the state to intervene more or less directly in the economy in order to balance the supply and demand for labour by either raising demand, or reducing the supply. Conversely, if unemployment is low, governmental interventions should either decrease demand or increase the supply of labour.

The city aims towards a society where 'full employment is re-established' and where the 'wheels are turning'. It is a place where 'everyone who wants to can get a job' and do 'useful work'. Everyone has a 'right to work' as it is 'unworthy to begin life by being brushed aside as a redundant'. In this way, the city aspires to an ever 'growing economy' that 'restores trust' and promotes 'progress', 'enterprise' and 'optimism'. Finally, it is a society in which people consume, since consumption is 'the main engine of growth'.

Although the city tends to take (macroeconomic) actions outside what is conventionally considered part of the unemployment system, it does have the means to *qualify* and evaluate certain parts of the system and the unemployed. Unemployment benefits, for instance, have an 'impact' on consumption or the 'purchasing power' of the population. Benefits thus serve as countercyclical 'automatic stabilisers'.[3] They 'maintain consumption' in times of high unemployment, and are 'automatically' reduced as unemployment decreases. Benefits, thus, also mitigate the effects of stagnation on the level of unemployment.

Although governmental intervention is needed at both ends of the business cycle, it most often justifies its relevance in 'recessions' and 'crises', since these are the situations in which the morality of the city is really put to the test. It is therefore important to qualify the situation as one with little or 'simply no jobs to get' in order to justify intervention. Proof varies from observing 'the ever-thinner job advertisement supplement' and the '150 rejections I have received during the last two years' to references to the 'stagnation of the job market' and that '65,000 young people under 30 have lost their job in the first two years of the crisis'.

Policies are *tested* according to whether they 'create jobs', or 'stimulate the demand for jobs'. 'Without job creation all politics is uphill.' Hence, 'economic results' should not be 'assessed on their own', but as the 'basis for fighting unemployment'. Likewise, rather than caring about benefit expenditures, one should 'spend the energy on creating jobs, then the unemployment benefit expenditures will decrease automatically'.

Governing comes with a responsibility for countering the negative tendencies of the market. It is up to the state to 'accept its responsibility for the high unemployment levels', since 'only the economic policy influences whether consumption and, hence, production must be raised or lowered'. Countering also means to "lift the lid" and invest, even if it is with borrowed money' when few have the means to spend (and vice versa). Likewise, the government should 'courageously' hire when businesses do not. Being cautious with timing and adjusting the policies according to the phase of the business cycle is of great importance.[4] A particular phase calls for the 'right medicine' at the right dose, since too much can cause 'overheating of the economy'. Policies therefore tend to be 'temporary' and are supposed to act on the situation 'right now'. It is, for instance, unwise to reduce benefits in 'a period of feeble growth' or when the economic situation is 'unfavourable to long-term saving'. On the other hand, one can 'profit from the prosperous economic situation'. Once the business cycle reverses, for example, 'once growth comes', countercyclical actions will be unnecessary. These changes in action can be built into policies so that expansionary actions will 'automatically' decrease on exiting the current phase. Government should then 'pull back, because the hole will be filled up by businesses'.

Governing implies being 'pragmatic' beyond the disturbances of 'ideology'. Rather it is matter of 'learning' from history's previous recessions, and carrying through new 'new deals'. There is, however, also a lot of bad governing that cannot stand the test, but are based on an 'ideological doctrine', 'blunted by overspending, 'unreflective' and only addressing 'symptoms'. In situations of recession, inappropriate actions include 'austerity policies' and 'cuts in government spending', which do nothing but 'strengthen the supply of labour, that is, creating more unemployed people'. In the same manner, taxation that decreases the disposable income of the population 'has a negative impact on consumption, and hence on growth'.

Coercion against the unemployed is generally considered inappropriate in downturns, since it 'is not fair to punish them for the fact that there are no jobs at the moment'. By contrast, 'it is the duty of the municipality to find a job for the individual'. In addition, 'private and public employers must be compelled to solve the unemployment problem'. However, governing the unemployed is, as mentioned earlier, dependent on timing. In times of no demand, the 'number of whiplashes' and 'sticks' and 'carrots' are inconsequential. In downturns, there might be a 'negligible group of unemployed who do not want to work. And as long as there aren't jobs for everyone, these people should be left alone.' However, 'if there is labour scarcity, one can always tighten the rules so that the jobless are once again on standby'.

Which *subjects* inhabit the city? As in Keynes' theory of effective demand (Keynes, 2006), the population is both a variable in the production and in the consumption function. This creates a split subject with worth as both worker and consumer, which applies to both the employed and unemployed. The employed individual is in a desirable state both in terms of contributing to growth by working and, as a consequence, usually 'ameliorating purchasing power'. Most problematic in terms of unemployment is when the prospect of unemployment leads the employed subject into 'fear-motivated money saving that could have been used for consumption'. In this sense, and in general, it is important to strengthen the interest of the employed 'in getting the unemployed employed'.

The unemployed individual is on the one hand a potential worker when 'there is no need for people at the moment'. Unemployment is 'a result of the crisis'; the unemployed person 'actually wants to work' and would 'almost take any kind of job', which, however, is 'practically impossible, even if one offers oneself at a bargain price'. Unemployed people should 'be put to work', but only by creating demand, which makes employers less 'picky'. The unemployed person is thus a worker who is involuntarily put on standby and remains 'prepared' for better times. Concurrently with being a potential worker, the unemployed person is a particularly worthy consumer imbued with a 'purchasing power … with no propensity to save'.

City of insurance

Unemployment, in this city, entails the *risk* of losing the economic means of self-support. When these risks occur, they are as *accidents*, out of the hands of the individual. Thus, 'it is out of the question to blame the unemployed'. Rather, a 'dismissal on economic grounds is a serious occupational injury'. Since risks are inherently social, the question is not who is responsible, but how the (insured) unemployed should be compensated.[5] Insurance is a means of sharing burdens collectively[6] and unemployment benefits are therefore 'a substitute for missing earned income, not alms or poor relief'. The 'social safety net' provides individual security or 'protection', which is the basic common good in this city. Those who are least worthy are in situations of economic 'precariousness' characterised by 'insecurity and stress'. The principle of insurance is hence about 'ameliorating unemployment benefits and noticeably increasing the number of indemnified unemployed persons'.

The collective sharing of risks, however, does not exempt the individual from all responsibility. The insurance subject has to recognise a priori belonging to a community of shared risks, and hence the subject's own share of collective responsibility. Responsibility, in other words, is a matter of showing *solidarity* with those who are hit by the accident of unemployment. This implies that the principle of compensation is underpinned and preconditioned by a principle of solidarity that is qualified by a set of membership rules. 'Indemnification' is thus 'an outstanding debt, that is, the counter-demand of the paid membership fees'. This sets the criteria for what it takes to be a member with a right to compensation as well as for worthy moral conduct, since the right should only be exercised if the situation is that of an accident, that is, if the event of becoming unemployed is 'involuntary'. Within the city the possibility of abuse is ever present, which again leads to issues of control and sanctions to ensure that only those who are technically entitled to benefit from the insurance are granted compensation. However, employers can also infringe on the insurance principle by 'speculating' on the compensation by temporarily laying off people.

The city is not concerned with social causes of unemployment. Rather, unemployment is *qualified* as an inevitable consequence of the collective striving for goods,[7] such as 'technological advances'. What matters is how these risks are managed and whether risks are 'securitised rather than made more precarious'. This takes vigilance, since 'precariousness has a tendency to aggravate'. The qualification of unemployment is a combination of moral critique and technical solutions. Regarding the former it is, for instance, a 'scorn against … [the] unemployed to claim that unemployment is a problem they created themselves' and attention is put on the way work is 'made precarious by part-time constraints or temping jobs', generating 'pessimism' and a sense of 'social insecurity'. The diagnosis of a rising 'precariat' (Standing, 2011) can thus be situated within this city. Regarding the latter, the city relies on actuarial sciences to calculate risks and fees and grant rights of membership and compensation.[8] This is only possible because the distribution of accidents follows certain mathematical laws that can be calculated by means of statistics;[9] for instance, how to distinguish between different risk groups accruing to industries? Or what are the consequences when earning rights are modified? For instance, what is the effect on the 'proportion of compensated unemployed people' of extending unemployment rights to workers having worked at least four months during the past 14 months (as against four months during the past eight months)?

When policies are put to the *test*, the question concerns the extent of (economic) compensation for the social risk of unemployment. Contrary to the city of **redistribution**, the aim is not equality in the population as such, but that the transition from employment to unemployment is insignificant with regard to the 'conditions of life', leading to an equality between unemployed and employed people with similar social risks, thereby 'preventing comedown' for the individual. Although the prime concern is evidently unemployment, the test potentially applies to all kinds of accidents and illnesses related to the labour market, such as compensation for reduced working capacity due to disabilities. Policies thus do not stand the test if 'their compensation will be reduced'. Further, the test also applies to the general conditions of the labour market, for instance in terms of employment conditions, asking whether unemployment instruments promote 'precarious' or more 'durable' employment relations.

Governing is a matter for all those who contribute to social risks. Contrary to the city of **redistribution**, which points to certain exploiting classes or privileged groups, there is a shared responsibility. On the one hand, the co-responsibility of social risks naturalises the causes as mere accidents. Since the risks are collectively constructed, no one is essentially to blame; hence, both the 'alarming criminalisation of unemployment' and the 'suspicious attitude of unemployment as self-inflicted' are denounced. On the one hand, co-responsibility leads to constant uncertainty with regard to the distribution of responsibility in terms of contributions from employees as well as employers. On the other hand, co-responsibility also induces a common interest in reducing risks such as instances of fraud or levels of unemployment. While the issue of unemployment provides scope for compromises with other cities, that of fraud and 'speculation' provides scope for coercive measures of control, such as 'regular control of abuses' *within* the city.

The *subjects* are bearers of social risks, making them, in a Durkheimian sense, dependent on one another. They basically feel either secure or 'insecure' and 'uncertain', with an inherent preference for the former. The feeling is dependent on whether and to what extent subjects are compensated for the *chances* of unemployment. Although unemployed people in principle are 'unlucky' 'victims', the city relies on a certain spirit of solidarity, or temperance, ensuring that rights are only claimed when needed. Subjects must therefore know and act according to the intentions behind the rights. If people are not to abuse the rights, which may appear as 'cheating' or 'fraud', they must 'understand the nooks and corners of the unemployment benefit system'. However, there are also those who know this, but 'cheat' anyway. It is, for instance, a 'moral' problem when 'people make demands that they are well aware the social assistance act is not designed for'.

Returning to the issue of coercion, there is a delicate tension and threshold between the two types of subject of the city. On the one hand, the solidary (insured) unemployed subject holds a right to compensation and hence to be left alone. Adding further duties (apart from paying fees) or 'threatening the unemployed with sanctions' equals 'rendering the unemployed responsible for his or her situation'. On the other hand, there is the unsolidary, 'speculative' unemployed subject, who takes advantage of rights without being exposed to accidents, or chooses not to subscribe and contribute to the compensation of those exposed.

City of redistribution

The rather pessimistic premise of this city is a society in which the hegemony of certain groups and the domination and exploitation of others leads to material *inequality*. Material equality is thus both the desired end and the primary means to counter domination and exploitation. Contrary to other cities for which some degree of redistribution may be recognised, it is not subordinated to other principles, such as the ability to play the game of the labour market (**incentives**), the compensation of risks (**insurance**) or equal opportunities (**investment**). Inequality is, in other words, *the* independent variable that ensures a well-functioning and just society (Wilkinson and Pickett, 2009). 'If you do not want to share, the consequences are increasing inequality, anger, frustration and despair, and in the end insecurity', always resulting in the same situation, whereby 'the weakest are affected adversely'. Material inequality is directly tied to various reinforcing dynamics related to capitalist societies, such as the concentration of profit and property (Piketty, 2008) or commodification (Polanyi, 1944; Esping-Andersen, 1990). Intervention is, therefore, needed to limit employers and other elite groups in 'imposing the dictum of the demands of the market'.

Redistribution is the prime means of counterbalancing these dynamics so that 'capital is genuinely harnessed' and all groups benefit from the wealth produced. In relation to unemployment, redistribution is not only a matter of balancing the relative strength between capital and labour through taxes and wages; it is also a matter of distributing work and redistributing wealth through unemployment benefits. Whereas solidarity in the city of **insurance** implies the sharing of risks, here it is about 'sharing out' the production of wealth as well as the 'sharing of time in life', entailing a more direct confrontation with 'capitalism' and the 'economic logic'. Unemployment is hence not an evil in itself. The possibility of more leisure time can be a good that comes with being unemployed. Hence, it benefits both the working population and the unemployed to 'distribute work and leisure time better'. People *do* 'commit suicide due to unemployment – however, not because they had psychological problems or had problems with killing time, etc, but solely because of economic reasons owing to too low benefits'.

Proof of the need for redistribution surrounds the identification of (increasing) impoverishment and 'pauperisation', such as the 'number of young homeless people'. When policies are qualified and *tested*, it is a matter of whether they lead to a concentration, or rather, privatisation of property, or a socialisation. Redistribution is a way of socialising property to the benefit of the non-owners (Castel, 1995). This results in an inherently critical attitude towards 'unsocial cutbacks' and 'gigantic cost-saving programmes providing tax reliefs for the employed and with an extra profit for those with the highest incomes and largest houses'. Embedded in the issue of socialisation is not just the distributional effect of policies, but also the way in which are financed and the role they play in budgetary struggles such as 'in conjunction with an increasingly polarised redistributive system [in which] some contribute massively, whereas others benefit massively' or how cuts in benefits cause recipients to experience a deterioration in 'their conditions of life ... in order to make room for reliefs in top taxes'. The zero-sum game also qualifies the issue of the distribution of work. Getting a job for the insured unemployed will result in 'the cuckoo in the nest effect, pushing the marginalised on cash benefits even further back in the queue of unemployment'. Likewise, 'inciting the unemployed to accept a job will only rob Peter to pay Paul.'

While the city of **insurance** sees the negative consequences of a capitalist society as a shared responsibility, that of redistribution blames agents with egoistic interests for abusing and exploiting their privileged position, for example, employers 'forcing down wages outcompeting those that play by the rules'. The same critique applies to workers who, in order to keep their jobs, take a pay cut, which, however, 'will spread to the rest of society leading to a society with far greater inequality'. The same also goes for the unemployed person whose labour (by means of subsidies) starts competing with the regular labour force. In the city of **redistribution** this person is exploited; here, the person becomes a 'scab'.

The influence of private interests often manifests itself in 'secret reunions'. There is a certain *civic* demand of representation that suspects the governing 'elites' of becoming 'rootless', thereby losing 'the ability to receive reports from below'. In the same civic spirit, the city grants more legitimacy to those representing the many as opposed to those representing the few. However, representing the many can also be denounced by unmasking unions engaged in the 'betrayal of unemployed persons'. The clash of interests between the many and the few sometimes leads to a confrontational struggle in which employers can never be found in 'the same boat as the workers'. They are 'not social partners' but 'social adversaries'.

While there is mistrust towards *governing* authorities for serving the interests of the few, it is the same state that 'should pursue a redistributive policy' by being 'the guarantor of social cohesion and the common good'. However, to ensure support for redistributive policies, it is problematic to simply distribute from rich to poor and disregard the group in between. 'The more benefits one removes, the larger the risk that substantial parts of the population loses ownership.... One risks short-circuiting the acceptance of the middle class to contribute to the community, if it does not experience getting a little back'. The question of whether the benefits and services provided should be 'targeted' or 'universal' is thus key in this city, leading to a preference for the latter (compare Korpi and Palme, 1998). Ultimately, the city imagines a place in which class struggles and private interests are suspended. In line with the universal spirit, the 'division of unemployed persons in groups' is denounced while advocating a 'unified system'. The use of coercion against the unemployed is denounced because it forces people to accept the exploiting structures that produce inequality, such as the 'pressure on the candidates to accept pauperising jobs'. Sanctions, however, *can* be introduced against those who benefit from those structures, such as 'employers that will profit from the [scheme] in order to multiply the number of unworthy jobs'. Further, the important function of taxation as the prerequisite of redistribution legitimises the need for control, for instance of people (including the unemployed), who 'earn their money from moonlighting'. The logic goes, 'if you introduce a tax, you also introduce control, otherwise it does not make sense. If there is a speed limit on the motorway, someone has to see if it is respected'.

The universalist preference fits with the overall aim of less material inequality in so far as the unemployed are considered neither *subjects* of alms (**paternal**) nor victims hit by chance (**insurance**). They are rather *citizens* who, due to power struggles, are exploited, oppressed or 'indignant'. Echoing T.H. Marshall (1964), it is a citizenship that is not simply liberal, but social (Handler, 2004; Dwyer, 2010). Inequality is 'unworthy against our fellow citizens, making their existence more economically miserable and humiliating for them'. Redistribution thus plays the role of restoring 'dignity'. By being 'equal fellow citizens', the city grants unemployed people a legitimate political voice that can be used to denounce the political process if neglects 'the ones that each day feel their self-esteem go down while they're watching longingly all those taking the train or the car to the "heavenly" job'. The issue of dignity opens up scope for criticising 'control of the way of life of claimants', as well as for instruments that 'disenchant' the unemployed.

City of incentives

The principle of the city of incentives is perhaps the most straightforward and directly applicable of all the cities: it 'believes in economic incentives' and aims to 'render the return to employment more incentivising' and 'attractive'. Hence, it seeks to ensure that every unemployed person has an incentive to work so that there is no longer the 'absurd moment in which one regrets working because it implies losing revenues'. With its roots in neoclassical thinking, labour supply always tends to generate its own demand in this city. A lack of incentives decreases the disposable supply of labour, which again increases wage levels, thus decreasing productivity and the competitiveness of firms.

More incentives do increase inequality, but 'it is only by allowing the rich to become richer that one gives the poor the desire to become rich one day too'. And in the end, 'we all become richer when people enter the labour market'. As much as they target the unemployed, incentives also send signals to the employed that guarantee reasons for remaining in the job. In a system with a lack of incentives, 'one is punished' if taking a job will 'undermine trust to the system, and create undue suspicion towards the recipients'. If incentives are back in place, 'there will be nothing to worry about, since you know you will gain more money when working'.

The lack of incentives is put to the *test* in a number of ways. For instance, it is a 'sign of failure' that immigrant workers are taking the 'least attractive jobs, while there are thousands on benefits'. But a single person can also be exemplary, for example where an unemployed person 'openly admit[s] saying no to all jobs with a salary of less [than] the daily allowance'. In the city of incentives, unemployment benefits as such are not approached in absolute terms; what matters is the relationship between benefits and the productive population of the city (Oliviennes, 1994). It thus addresses 'problems of interaction' between benefits and the labour market', asking whether 'it is more profitable to work than staying on benefits'.

In hindering people from playing the economic game of the labour market,[10] the city of incentives thus identifies 'poverty traps', 'inactivity traps', 'financial brakes' or 'perverted effects' that 'disable the poor by confining them in "traps"'. Although benefits are always regarded with suspicion, they are not to be eradicated completely. Poverty is generally considered inappropriate, since it hinders people from even responding to incentives. Reducing benefits can have a 'motivational effect' on some, but for others it will only have 'poverty-creating effect that demotivates participating actively'. Hence, increasing incentives should never 'have the consequence that people are put on the street and hereby further societal exclusion'.

It is the responsibility of *governing* authorities to strike the right balance between the monetary thresholds of 'poor versus able to get along' and 'unemployed versus employed', with the latter always getting first priority because the benefit itself so easily becomes part of the problem. The governor thus acts on the 'motivation effect' of each individual. This makes the governing much more complicated and interventionist than a matter of deregulation or dismantling.

There is a certain suspicious attitude when evaluating the governing of the unemployed, since it always has a potential effect of being too 'generous' and thereby 'excluding people from employment'. Governing thus precludes all 'measures that reduce the supply of labour'. 'Unemployment-inducing system errors' (levels of benefits or high taxes on wages) are 'our time's cynical crime'.

The use of explicit coercion in this city is limited, since whether the individual wants to behave rationally and respond to incentives is 'optional' and based on 'voluntary adherence'. It is in this sense, and only in this sense, that the city is liberal by formally leaving the choice of working or not open to the unemployed. It does not formally 'oblige' the unemployed to work (Stoleru, 1974, p 140 onwards). However, while direct coercion is irrational in the city, governing through incentives nonetheless works on the motivational threshold of pleasure and pain. Whether instruments are considered 'carrots', 'bonuses' or 'monetary stimuli', or 'sticks', 'whiplashes', 'sanctions', 'nudges' or 'squeezing the wallet' really only depends on what side of the threshold it addresses. Regardless of whether the unemployed choose to act according to the incentivising environment, it is not supposed to be pleasurable for those who 'do not play the game'.

The *subjects* in the city are all *homines oeconomici*, responsive to, and acting on, economic stimuli. They seek out opportunities where the monetary reward is highest for as little effort as possible. This is, in the end, what 'motivates' them to take a job or do nothing. The reasons for being unemployed thus lie outside the individual. 'One cannot blame the persons involved for thinking economically rationally.' If it implies being unemployed, 'why should one work?' The unemployed person simply says 'if I resume work, I lose', which means that people would be 'idiots if they go from an economically safe life (based on support and benefits) to a more doubtful situation on the labour market'. The unemployed must 'never be tempted to depart from the right track'. It is thus important that unemployed people know about and 'appropriate' incentivising schemes.

The 'motivation effect' is not only targeted at the unemployed subject; if there are no incentives to work, the employed subject 'feels foolish'. 'Why slave when there is nothing to strive for? We might as well wallow in misery.' Incentivising is the guarantee for those who 'get up early to work', as well as a message to those who don't: 'one does not work for nothing'. Incentives to work thus 'moralise' the labour market, which correlates with the city of **activity**'s appreciation of (work) activity.

The paternal city

The paternal city's pivot is 'larger personal responsibility for the welfare of each individual', that is, a city in which 'everybody must be able to support oneself'. 'The capacity to support oneself must be promoted because it strengthens people's satisfaction with their lives – and that is more important than the economic bottom line.' The dystopian alternative is 'the risk of creating a large assisted population'. Instead, the city 'must transfer the responsibility of people's lives back to those who can carry that responsibility'. Being *competent* in the behavioural sense of the term is hence a precondition of becoming worthy.

Being (ir)responsible is closely linked to the inner characteristics and self-perception of the individual, although this is heavily influenced by external factors. Following this logic, unemployment is an outcome of a lack of responsible behaviour by the unemployed person, which again can be influenced by, and may even be a result of, political intervention. Policies are *tested* on whether they 'responsibilise' or 'deresponsibilise' the behaviour of the unemployed and the labour force in general. Putting policies to the test may result in the identification of a 'stifling effect that works counter to self-worth, participation and initiative, which are exactly the qualities that make a human being capable of fending for himself'.

The city shares the problematic of the heritage of inner behavioural characteristics with social Darwinist ideas (for example, Herbert Spencer), but at the same time it recognises that the characteristics can be changeable and politically produced, for instance, by the 'practitioner's language'. Since the city is deeply concerned with the self-perception of the individual, it has a direct interest in how self-perception is affected by the way the risk of unemployment is qualified by governing authorities and society. If there is a social risk in the city, it is the 'social risk … of dependence'. The societal acceptance of such attitudes hence bears the risk of spreading a 'culture of dependency' or a 'relief culture'. One can thus only be 'appalled by a new generation of young people that experiences no connection between work and money [and by] the way the breadwinner has become such a vague concept'.

Governing unemployment by upbringing is a matter for the pater, not the mater. It always involves the danger of misguided kindness and 'playing good Samaritans'. This resembles the city of **incentives**, but here it is not a matter of leading the economic man in inappropriate directions, but simply a matter of inhibiting the unemployed subject from becoming competent in the way a child becomes an adult. Contrary to a 'maternal' education, the pater educates by providing 'structure' and 'making demands' in order for the unemployed to 'learn or learn again the rules of the world of work'. By contrast, 'maternal' state intervention serves as a key explanation of unemployment. By 'paying the bill' and initiating 'some polite services', the state in reality deprives 'the individual from creating his or her own existence'. The city denounces the 'all-powerful nannies of the unemployed – employment arrangements, activation services, wage subsidies'. The same goes for simply allocating money to the unemployed, which is qualified as doing a 'disservice' because it does not provide people with more 'freedom' or 'responsibility'. The unemployment system is therefore 'not supposed to be a comfortable place to be. It is a misunderstanding that employment initiatives should involve lemon pies and wickerwork'. An effect of this misunderstood care is that people who would otherwise be able to provide for themselves remain provided for.

Benefits should therefore be restricted to 'he who cannot provide for himself and who's provision does not lie with anyone else'. Rather than redistribution or compensation, benefits are seen as *charity* depending on the threshold of can/cannot provide, ensuring those who cannot a 'worthy and adequate provision'. The threshold of can/cannot induces a continuing test (and intellectual controversy) within the city to explain the threshold. Is the cannots' incompetence inherited (Hernstein and Murray, 1994) or caused by inappropriate governing? (Mead, 1997a). Although the former case (genetically inheritance) legitimises elements of charity, laissez faire is continually problematised, first, because the worthiness is never really located on the 'cannot' side of the threshold and, second, because people will not automatically or voluntarily pass the threshold. 'It is no good lugging a big and growing group of people incapable of taking care of themselves, let alone of others.' Incentives, for instance, 'have not shown much power to alter the behaviour of the unemployed' (Mead, 1997b, p 24), since 'you can neither wave financial carrots nor kick them into work or education by reducing or completely removing their benefits since a lot of people in this group have not the least idea of how to administer money'.

The city posits a variety of instruments that are enacted to (re)install the responsible behaviour of the unemployed to make them leave the system 'with a straightened backbone'. Governing, in other words, aims to correct the lack of upbringing and virtue of the unemployed. On the one hand, upbringing necessitates the participation of the unemployed. 'We know it from bringing up our own children. It is not right to not include our children in the cleaning and cooking in our homes.' On the other hand, the use of coercion is completely integral to bringing up the unemployed. The use of coercion and discipline is a *means* of making the unemployed pass the threshold of incompetent/ competent. Instruments thus have 'an upbringing effect, which makes it clear the municipality is not a gift shop'.

The justification for the use of coercion relies on the *subjectivity* of the unemployed. The lack of competence of the unemployed implies that the hierarchy of unemployed people and authorities is not simply a matter of who is responsible, but a matter of who knows what is best for the unemployed. The unemployed have a 'gap' between behaviour and intention and are thus in need of direction and supervision (Mead, 1997b, p 6). 'We think it's what you need, and you probably will too.' The unemployed person is therefore someone who is to be 'persuaded' in order to change their false self-perception. For example, it is important that unemployed people are 'met by positive demands and expectations, which can strengthen their self-esteem and ambitions'.[11] The city therefore provides room for the identification and testing of a variety of behavioural 'gaps' that load the unemployed with incompetence.

It is the same behavioural gap or false self-consciousness of the unemployed that is applied in behavioural economics to evaluate labour market policies (for example, Babcock et al, 2012; Holmlund, 2015). Behavioural economics criticises policies of incentives relying on the rational, since the lack of self-control of the unemployed leads to 'inconsistent preferences', which makes them 'procrastinate … against their own, long-run self-interest' (Babcock et al, 2012, p 4). The result is 'potential conflicts between an unemployed individual's current and future selves', which again generates 'a situation where stronger work and job seeking requirements that appear overly paternalistic in the usual model of *homo economics* may actually benefit the program participants themselves by helping them overcome self-control problems' (Babcock et al, 2012, p 4). The use of coercion is thus a means to free unemployed people from their behavioural deficiencies, which, evidently, are especially predominant among young people.

Coercion is integral to persuasion, or rather legitimate when persuasion fails. It can be 'good and necessary' because 'pacification can be invalidating and if a person has arrived at the conviction about oneself that he or she is not good at anything, we cannot simply accept that and say "well, that's up to you!"'. The pater's knowledge about the recipient is thus authoritative. 'Being one of these experts I actually think that I sometimes know best and must try to stop an unhappy comedown which the person considered cannot see right now.' The pedagogy of the city is thus to learn the hard way. 'One has to realise that changes only come if you make an effort yourself. How can such a change of attitude be implemented? How should the citizens (that is, those who are leaning too much on the state) learn this? The answer is: the requirement of quid pro quo in order to receive public aid…. The individual must get an offer that cannot be refused (if you want to survive). With such a Sicilian offer, well-known from the mafia, the beneficiary will, at the same time, experience the dignity that comes from making demands on someone.' 'Youth unemployment is one of our greatest societal problems and now we have come to a point where we have to put the whip into service. There are some young people who need a caring push in order to get away from the computer screen.'

Second, besides being a means, coercion (and the discipline it implies) is also a kind of valorised good. A stable society necessitates respect for the authorities and discipline, since 'requiring something from people is the implication of respecting them. The day we don't make demands, we don't respect people'. The lack of thus relational good is often tied to a dystopian diagnosis in which the 'young ones … have no discipline, no respect' and 'miss the consciousness of the necessity of working in order to survive'. Paternal subjects 'don't ask for help'; rather, they say, 'it's okay because it's my own fault so I have to learn it the hard way'. The worthiness of being disciplined and respectful is thus a prerequisite for becoming a citizen. Benefits provide people with 'the means to survive, not to be a citizen. Since Tocqueville it is well known that assistance leads to enslavement'.

City of investment

The city of investment is situated in an economy that is increasingly globalised, post-industrial and knowledge-based (for example, Esping-Andersen, 1999), changing the conditions of the labour market and society in general.[12] It is a setting in which 'skills' or 'human capital' are predominantly the precondition for being 'employable'. It is a labour market in which 'almost no jobs are created for people without education' and that demands 'intensified requirements to the qualifications of the labour force'. In this city, even the 'big bosses recognise that if oil and raw materials rarefy, their principal concern will be to find and fasten human resources'. This demand for improving skills is 'lifelong'.

The importance of skills raises an issue of social justice permeating this city. The necessity of education tends to 'exclude' a number of people and groups in society from participating in the 'community' of the labour market. The city thus 'strives for equal opportunities for all'. It is a 'collective responsibility' that 'the nation must invest in order to enable all those who live from benefits or odd jobs to finally get their heads above water, to make up new projects, to rediscover their dignity'. Rather than a logic of 'assistance' composed of a 'safety net', the city is founded on 'emancipation' in the shape of a 'trampoline' or a 'stepping stone', 'enhancing people's life chances'. This morality is not far from Rawls' maxim that 'those who are at the same level of talent and ability, and have the same willingness to use them, should have the same prospects of success regardless of their initial place in the social system' (Rawls, 1999, p 54). These ideas tend to align with ideas of 'social investment strategies' (Giddens, 1998) that have paved the way for a vast literature that addresses how and when to invest in 'human capital' in order to enhance the opportunities available to, and the capabilities of, the population (for example, Esping-Andersen, 2002, 2007; Taylor-Gooby, 2008; Abrahamson, 2010; Jenson, 2010; Morel et al, 2012).

Enhancing opportunities and employability for the marginalised is a win–win situation for society: socially, it hinders the 'polarisation between groups' and prevents 'society from breaking down' by replacing 'the class struggle' with a 'struggle of ranks'. It 'finally effaces the social division that undermines national cohesion'. Economically, upskilling 'strengthens employment and competitiveness in the long run', since 'competitiveness is not just about taxes and wages but also about a good primary school, education for the children of blue-collar workers, research that makes us smarter, an efficient public sector, training of the jobless'. Furthermore, although investments are 'costly, the investment is small compared to a life on benefits and enhanced risk of disease and social problems'. Without any viable opportunities, they may 'mark society by means of vandalism, violence or threats'.

Society is generally *qualified* as divided between those who are included (in the labour market) and those who are more or less permanently excluded while living 'alongside society'. Hence, society 'does not live up to … the principle of equal opportunities'. It is an 'hourglass society in which the dividing line between those on top and the lost generations that are expelled in the bottom becomes more and more pronounced'; a 'waste of a lot of resources, both human and economic'.

The fact that certain groups have become more or less permanently 'excluded' or 'marginalised' can be explained by the undesirable cumulative dynamics within and between social groups. The groups located outside the labour market are *excluded* by the lack of a 'spacious labour market' where, for instance, corporations invoke 'stereotypes' of the unemployed as 'unemployable', or by 'the reluctance to deal with' the way the labour market 'disqualifies' particular groups such as people with disabilities or older people. Meanwhile, exclusion is also a product of dynamics within the unemployed group such as 'laws of social inheritance', and the fact that those 'with 'benefits parents' have a 'higher risk of themselves becoming recipients of benefits'.

Qualification in terms of risks and opportunities prepares policies for *tests*. While the notion of 'active' plays an important role in the city of **activity** in the sense of movement, activity and work, in the city of investment it relates to the question of how to prioritise and 'activate expenses'. In this sense, governing is either 'passive' and 'unproductive' or 'active' and always aims for 'utilisation that is more effective and active'. In these cases, government expenditure should no longer be 'considered expenses but investments'. In the end, 'they won't cost society a thing, among other things because the preventive strategy against long-term unemployment works and saves a lot of money'. The policy test is thus essentially asking whether a given arrangement has 'improved their employability'. Is the unemployed person 'given better opportunities for perfecting her skills and hereby improving her position on the labour market'?

What does it take to 'fight against exclusion'? First, *governing* entails awareness of the risks and opportunities, that is, the employability of the population, in order to 'prevent' these negative dynamics from growing. The 'hard core of unemployment' must be tackled by getting long-term unemployed people 'back on the ladder in order to avoid the group from amassing by detecting very fast the least employable'. Second, the governor must be able to disregard (and sacrifice) the immediate effects of policy instruments, whether they be redistributive or budgetary, and think 'long term', just 'like when investing in shares'. 'Invest in human resources rather than repair.'

Third, since each unemployed person has a particular set of (or lack of) skills, governing must 'personalise', 'individualise', 'target' and 'tailor' its instruments. To govern means that there 'is no standard menu, no fast food for returning to employment, but a personalised action plan'.[13] Personalised governing is closely related to variation in potential and in its realisation. Unemployed people 'constitute a more and more fragmented population with a variety of paths and needs'.

The fragmentation of unemployed people entails that in order to ensure equal opportunities, individuals in this group should be treated *differently*, and ideally as differently as possible. Governors therefore need to 'listen to the needs of each individual'. This takes a 'systemic effort' in which 'all good capacities work together'. Accordingly, the effort must not only be 'specialist', based on 'genuine social work', but also 'interdisciplinary' across 'occupational groups and administrative departments so that case workers, teachers and health visitors are not sitting in each their silo speaking each their language'. Finally, governors, when listening to the needs of the unemployed, should have eyes on opportunities and 'resources rather than limitations'. It is about 'making the dreams come alive'. Hence, despite the fact that unemployed people are not really to blame for their situation, the social worker ought not to 'feel sorry for' them.

Tailored treatment may involve rights that are universal in principle, but whether the unemployed individual is granted those rights is conditional on specific needs. The right to investment hence takes a particular form. While in the city of **insurance**, for instance, the right is conditional on the duty to pay a membership fee, the duty is not really a duty here. When governors speak of 'rights and duties', the two things are aligned, or rather fused towards the joint goal of increasing the employability of each unemployed person and the population in general.

Coercion can thus be justified as a means to make people increase their 'human capital' and make use of their opportunities. 'We give them an obligation to get an education. Conversely they get the right to complete an education.' Coercion is thus a necessary means to make sure that unemployed people first accept, and then manage, the investment properly. For instance, the governing authority has the possibility of 'suspending the unemployment benefit, if the jobseeker does not pursue the training that is offered to him with diligence'. Coercive measures are not only targeted at the unemployed individual, but are also used as a means of *prevention*. When 'too many young people are decoupled from the machinery of society', a 'penal action' thus 'may be used … so [the very young] understand the value of education'.

Subjects find themselves with various degrees of potential that are also realised to various degrees. The point of departure is that unemployed people 'can do more than we get to see just now', but also that it is naïve to believe a 'decent and full life' is a matter of getting' sufficiently high benefits'. Worthiness comes with realising potential. Unemployed as well as employed people should always 'become smarter', and so it is wiser, in the long run, 'to work for a low salary in a place where you learn something, than … for a high salary with something that is of no use later'. A worthy individual is thus not only someone with skills and employability, but also someone with an inexhaustible will to 'acquire new skills'. The unemployed person should thus see herself as a kind of enterprise, constantly 'seizing chances' for accumulating capital and improving the chances of selling its commodity, namely her skills. It is in this sense that the unemployed individual is turned into 'an actor in the construction of his or her own project'.

City of activity

The city of activity concentrates all attention to the question of (in)activity. It 'encourages activity' while denouncing everything that 'keeps [persons] in inactivity'. The difference between passive and active 'is what makes all the difference'. It thus echoes and reignites the Calvinist ethic to whom '[n]ot leisure and enjoyment, but only activity serves to increase the glory of God'.[14] Activity thus is a matter of 'maintaining social cohesion, that is, avoiding the harmful consequences of inactivity: the despair, the social violence and the insecurity'. The most worthy state of activity is work. 'The exit route is work, again work, always work.' Regaining activity is a matter of 'getting a place within the community of workers'. Likewise, it 'would do every child good to experience their parents saying "I am going to work" with pride in their voices'. **Mobility** underpins activity as the necessary capacity of people to move to where the work is located.

This city *qualifies* the labour market, and the policies surrounding it, in terms of flexibility and barriers. A policy could hence be justified for 'accelerating the flow of resumptions of employment by the unemployed'. The mobility of the labour force is deemed increasingly important due to structural changes affecting the labour market. For instance, 'globalisation does not kill jobs, but it imposes changes and adaptations'. The mobility and 'flexibility of the labour force' can be limited by a number of barriers, such as 'means of transport, health condition or difficulties of childcare'. Policies are hence *tested* in terms of their ability to enable flow, or 'rotation', in the labour force and thus reduce 'frictional unemployment' while avoiding 'bottleneck problems'. 'The goal is to galvanise the labour market by privileging the adjustment of offer and demand.'

Due to the variety of barriers, it takes intervention to match the supply and demand of labour effectively. One example is the labour exchange services bringing unemployed people into contact with employers.[15] *Governing*, in this case, aims to 'match businesses' and public authorities' need for labour' by providing job offers to unemployed people, accelerating and improving the efficiency of the jobseeking process, and knowing the needs of employers in order to avoid 'mismatches'. Further, governing implies ensuring flow among those already in the labour market, making it accessible, for example, by means of 'job-rotation arrangements', 'leave-of-absence schemes', temporary work arrangements, childcare provisions, and investments in transportation and infrastructure. Importantly, governing implies making sure that unemployed people are 'at the disposal of the labour market'. A prerequisite for this is that unemployed people are 'active'. This is important because of a self-reinforcing risk of being passive, 'getting stuck' and 'taking root'. For this reason, it is imperative 'to stir the cooking pot of unemployment'. 'Activating' the unemployed involves making sure they are 'active', 'positive' and 'serious' in their job searches and 'efficiently and permanently looking for a job'. However, if there are, for whatever reason, no jobs for unemployed people, being active might as well entail working in 'artificial jobs' within the benefit system. Whatever the instrument, the governing authority thus aims for 'rehabilitating work'.

Governing is a matter of eradicating structural as well as individual barriers to becoming active. However, structural causes inevitably magnify explanations that point to the unemployed individual, since below the structural barriers lurks the issue of *idleness* – the question of whether an unemployed person 'is willing to take on a job'. When the unemployed individual is on the worthy side of the threshold, being one of 'those who want' a job, governing is a matter of 'more targeted actions in order to find the job openings' that reassure the individual that 'society is held liable to provide a job'. However, if the unemployed individual does not want a job, their inactivity becomes an occasion for punishment since it breaches the city's valorisation of activity and work. 'The necessity of accepting a job [is] the central measure of national solidarity.'

Coercion thus becomes a means to 'fight the attitude: "I don't want to take a vacant job"'. It is 'normal to sanction unemployed persons … whose jobseeking is not genuine and serious'. The prospect of forcing unemployed people to work for benefits serves a double purpose, both punishing them for inadequate jobseeking efforts, and making them more worthy by making them active. As in the Calvinist ethic, work is both redemption and a sacrifice of (immediate) pleasures, such as relaxation or even pay.

In this city, the least worthy of all *subjects* are idle – the antithesis to the active. Idle people are perceived as being struck by 'the danger of relaxation'; their 'unwillingness to work is symptomatic of the lack of grace'.[16] Although those who are 'not set for work' may be in a minority, 'it's a minority that shocks', since such individuals are seen as 'recalcitrant', deliberately preferring 'to laze around at society's expense'. The idle person also 'lacks professional flexibility as well as a desire to travel to where the job is'. The outcome of this is an immobile subject that has come to a standstill. 'Too many [benefits] recipients live their lives as Robinson Crusoe stranded in a two-roomed apartment with TV dinners and shitty TV.'

If the unworthy unemployed are lazy, the worthy unemployed person is rather a 'jobseeker', or is 'available'. As opposed to the 'riskophobic' subjects of **insurance**, they are the 'riskophiles'. Although they may face structural barriers and limited opportunities, they should not dwell on such matters as doing so will only make them less flexible. The worthy unemployed person is above all someone who is willing to do (whatever kind of) work is available, believing that 'it is almost of no importance what I do as long as I have my hands full. I don't want to laze the day away'.

The worthy unemployed person is 'proactive', 'searching uninvited' and 'appearing in person' at potential workplaces, as well as 'flexible', 'being ready to move to another part of the country to get a job and take a job in a supermarket even if you want to work in a clothes shop'. Governors in the city of activity thus become 'steely when someone questions whether a jobless academic should clear up the woods or whether an immigrant woman give a hand in a public kitchen'.

The grammar

The grammar of the seven cities is condensed and presented in Table 3.1. The table outlines the key principles of each city, the ways in which it qualifies unemployment and tests policies, how it should be governed, when and why coercion is necessary and legitimate, and, finally, the characteristics associated with its unemployed subjects and their resultant state of worth.

What can be concluded from the grammar of cities of unemployment? First of all it implies that there is a *plurality* of repertoires of evaluation that share some degree of legitimacy in contemporary debates in France and Denmark in the sense that they can be mobilised in criticism and justification. Although this says little, if anything, about the content and direction of policy transformations (the concern of Part II of this book), it does say something about the legitimation of reform. It confirms that ideas in public debates do not simply work as a coherent set of norms, paradigms or 'public philosophies' that are taken for granted throughout society and hence inform and shape policy changes in a quasi-unconscious manner. Furthermore, it challenges the existing theories of transformations presented in Chapter 1, by showing first that there is greater plurality and a larger degree of coexistence and tension in the processes of transformation; second, that the repertoire of ideas is present in all four reforms, in both France and Denmark, and thus does not designate a specific deterministic path for a country, or cluster of countries; and third, that the justified use of coercion cannot, unlike much of the comparative literature, be confined to a singular idea or 'bad' approach, but rather is present in all cities in different ways. In other words, it cannot be reduced to a distinct, punitive, neoliberal variety of activation. We return to this argument in Chapter 8.

The second conclusion is that the grammar brings to light the politics and morality embedded in the justification, as well as the governing, of the unemployed. It shows that there is a lot more at stake in the debates than *ideology* masking interests and dodgy intentions, or simply finding technical solutions to existing problems. What is at stake is moral – tensions between substantially different ideas about what society and people are made of and in what direction both should be heading in terms of governance and behaviour. The morality of the cities therefore leads not only to seven rational ways in which to govern unemployment, but also to seven paths towards making society and unemployed subjects more worthy, as well as seven ways to justify the use of coercion. The point of mapping the seven cities

Table 3.1: Cities of unemployment

	Demand	Redistribution	Insurance	Incentives	Paternal	Investment	Activity
Qualification	Stagnation	Struggle between interests, distribution of work and property	Collective responsibility, a matter of chance (un)luck	Unemployment traps	Irresponsible behaviour, absent societal upbringing	Lack of social investment, (un) equal opportunities	Barriers to labour market, insufficient activation of unemployed
Test, whether policies are...	... leading to job creation?	... increasing or decreasing material inequality?	... compensating people when unemployed?	... generating incentives to stay unemployed?	... making people competent?	... increasing the employability of the labour force?	... making the labour force mobile and active?
Governing	Boost demand through public intervention to achieve full employment	Strengthen social citizenship through redistribution. Share profit and work	Collectivise and depoliticise social risks by granting security. Ensure solidarity	Ensure incentives to work, maximise supply of labour, society that makes work pay	Set requirements and discipline, increase responsibility and charity	Invest in skills of the unemployed. Reintegrate unemployed people into society	Maximise and ease transitions, activity and adaptability
Coercion needed to...	... intervene in job creation	... socialise property, counter greed and self-interest	... ensure solidarity, stop fraud	... ensure sufficient incentives	... induce self-awareness	... signal the worth of education	... increase availability of workforce
Unemployed subject	*Consumer* Willing to work, exemplary consumer	*Citizen* In risk of exploitation, disenchanted	*Victim* Exposed to an accident	*Economic man* Rationally choosing not to work	*Dependent* No self-control or self-awareness	*Unemployable* Lack of human capital due to social heritage	*Stranded* Inflexible, in danger of taking root, lazy
Worth	Consumption	Dignity	Security	Opportunism	Self-control	Release of potential	Work

of unemployment is not to show that some of them, or all of them, are false or illegitimate; it is rather the opposite, that in their capacity to put policies and unemployed people to the test, these cities are (inconveniently) true and real. In the same way, coercion is not a phenomenon that is hidden behind ideologies – it is *legitimised*, and thus contains a moral economy.

Now that a grammar of a plurality of coexisting cities of unemployment has been developed, it is possible to move on to the key empirical questions of the book. What constitutes the moral economy of activation? How is it mobilised in practice to test policies and justify reforms? And how are different cities tied together in compromises resulting in concrete adjustments and the introduction of new activation instruments?

Flexicurity: an illustrative example of compromises in the plural

In order to illustrate how the analytical framework is put into action, this section provides an example of how the concept of flexicurity can entail various compromises between the cities of unemployment. Since the concept of flexicurity was first coined in the mid-1990s to describe Dutch labour market reforms, it has circulated among scholars in debates on how to define the concept and among policy makers eager to make use of the concept, with more or less success, to justify reform programmes. It has thus from the beginning been used as an 'evaluative device' to put policies to the test (Hansen and Triantafillou, 2011).

The first, and most intuitive, compromise of flexicurity is between the worth of mobility of labour of the city of **activity** and the worth of security of the city of **insurance**. This compromise can be conceived in quite different ways. It can be conceived first as a bargaining of interests between employers wanting flexible means to adjust and workers wanting stable incomes. Workers thus demand compensation in order to accept liberal labour law and vice versa for employers (see Wilthagen and Tros, 2004). But the compromise can also be conceived in ways that blur lines between interests and cities of unemployment. Flexicurity scholars have, for instance, suggested that high compensation rates can work as a mobility-enhancing instrument in itself by creating a more risk-willing labour force where employees do not cling to their jobs but constantly seek new opportunities (see, for example, Kristensen, 2013). Here, although social protection measures are recognised, **insurance** is subordinated and put to the test as a means to enhance mobility. Further interests are no longer antagonistic, since both workers and employers benefit from the same instrument.

This type of win–win qualification appears in most flexicurity compromises that involve other cities of unemployment. Take, for instance, the idea that flexicurity entails a transition from 'job security' to 'employment security'. In this qualification, **insurance** instruments are no longer important. Rather, 'employment security' relies on instrument deemed worthy in the city of **investment**. 'Flexicure' policies are those that enhance the 'employability' of the worker, such as training and 'lifelong learning'. Here, flexibility and security-enhancing policies are inseparable (see Hansen and Triantafillou, 2011).

Finally, flexicurity can be conceived in ways that basically include all measures that aim to reintegrate unemployed people into employment. An example is Kongshøj Madsen's conception of the Danish labour market as a 'golden triangle' of 'generous welfare systems', 'flexible labour markets' and 'active labour market policies' (Madsen, 2002). While the former two reproduce the **insurance–activity** compromise mentioned earlier, the latter opens a black box of questions and tests similar to the ones addressed in the coming chapters. Here, Kongshøj Madsen mentions various 'effects' such as 'motivation', 'training' and 'locking-in'. Motivation effects could be related to monetary **incentives** and enhanced by lowering unemployment benefits, but they could also be related to training and activation instruments, since 'an unemployed person seeks work more actively in the period immediately before she or he has to participate in a mandatory activation programme' (Madsen, 2002, p 7). This is no longer the economic individual of **incentives**, but the idle person of the city of **activity**. However, this creates a 'dilemma', and tension, between **activity** and **investment**, since if 'it is wished to increase the motivation effect, there may be a temptation to change the content of activation programmes to make them less attractive to participants. But this would also probably imply that the quality of the programmes themselves would be lowered in terms of their training content and other activities to improve the skills of the participants' (Madsen, 2002, p 9). The same tension exists within the 'locking-in' effect, which suggests that job-search activities (**activity**) are reduced during the period that an individual takes part in training (**investment**).

Notes

[1]   Exact references to quotations can be found in Hansen (2017).

2   The European Employment Strategy and the Open Method of Coordination of the European Union and the Organisation for Economic Co-operation and Development have provided such fora in recent times (de la Porte et al, 2001; Esmark, 2011; Hansen and Triantafillou, 2011; Triantafillou, 2011).

3   Compare Zimmermann (2006, p 33).

4   It is in this sense that Keynesians speak of a 'discretionary policy' (Sandmo, 2011, p 419).

5   On the social character of risks in insurance, see Ewald (1990). The origins of the insurance principle are closely tied to the problems of handling work accidents in the late 19th century (Ewald, 1986; Defert, 1991), providing the techniques that were later used to establish the first unemployment insurance schemes (see, for example, Zimmermann, 2001).

6   Compare Ewald (1991, p 205 onwards).

7   Compare Lehtonen and Liukko (2011, p 35).

8   See Ewald (1986) and Lehtonen and Liukko (2011).

9   See, for example, Defert (1991).

10 On the game metaphor in relation to the negative tax, see Foucault (2008, p 201).

11 While the virtues of the city may appear archaic, the basic premise of a behavioural gap and a subject with no self-control can also be found in contemporary techniques of social work that aim at 'empowering' or encouraging the 'self-mastery' of the unemployed. For analyses of such techniques in social policies, see Cruikshank (1993) and Villadsen (2007).

12 Compare Andersson (2009).

13 This resembles what Robert Castel has termed a 'logic of positive discrimination' (Castel, 1995, p 676).

14 Weber (2003, p 157). On the Protestant view of the unemployed specifically, see Zoberman (2011, p 89 onwards).

15 On the historical origin and dissemination of the exchange services, see Garraty (1978, p 130) and Edling (2008).

16 Weber (2003, pp 157, 159).

PART II

Activation reforms

4

From looking backwards to forwards: unemployment insurance, France, 2000

In early 2000, the major French employers' organisation Medef launched a programme of social reform that coincided with the triannual negotiations of the convention of the unemployment insurance system. This process, which was not without controversy, led to the introduction of PARE, the 'aid plan for the return to employment'. Figure 4.1 provides an overview of the key events during the debate up to the ratification of PARE.

The instruments of PARE included an individual contract that would oblige the unemployed to engage in 'personalised' jobseeking activities while gaining access to support such as training courses. Further, PARE strengthened requirements for jobseekers to accept job offers from the job exchange service as well as introducing sanctions for refusing jobs and for contractual infringements. The trade unions were divided in their stance towards this, causing intense debate that finally resulted in the adoption of the reform with the support of the government. The instruments of PARE did not replace the existing scheme, but the introduction of various tests fundamentally changed the way the unemployed were qualified morally. Hence, PARE marks a tipping point (in favour of activation) in the governing of insured unemployed people in France.

The chapter is structured as follows. The first two sections introduce the historical creation and development of the French unemployment insurance system. The aim is to provide a brief picture of the compromises that have shaped the system and have 'sedimented' in its institutions and instruments, and to consider the effect of intellectual movements on perceptions of the problem of unemployment. The following four sections present the justifications, test situations and compromises that characterised the reform debate, while the final section analyses the institutional and instrumental changes adopted in the legal convention and briefly addresses subsequent reforms.[1]

Figure 4.1: Timeline of the PARE reform process

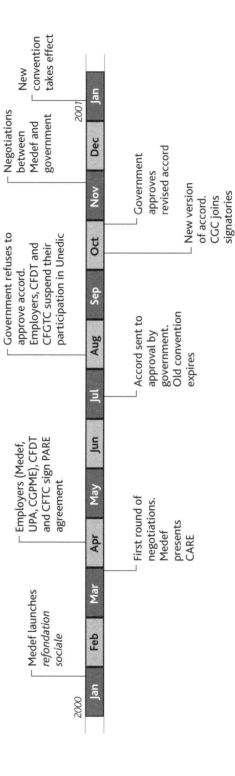

Creation and reforms of French unemployment insurance

It was not until 1958 that a nationally governed system of unemployment insurance was established in France. Since the end of the 19th century, unemployment was handled by local insurance funds organised by workers and employers, and delimited by professional borders alongside local, but publicly funded, schemes of 'assistance' involving extensive control and workfare schemes to counter 'voluntary idleness' (Daniel and Tuchszirer, 1999, pp 85, 161). Even though the insurance schemes had been subsidised by the state since 1905, they played a marginal role (Daniel and Tuchszirer, 1999, p 89).

The major postwar reforms initiating the French welfare state were heavily based on a Bismarckian approach (Palier, 2002, pp 73–7) residing in the city of **insurance**. The established social security schemes concerning work accidents, pensions, invalidity and family matters were all contribution-based and founded on the principle of lost income (that is, compensation). Social security hence tied entitlements to the worker (in practice, the male breadwinner), rather than the citizen, ensuring horizontal solidarity within social groups, rather than **redistribution** between them (Palier, 2002, p 105). Curiously, in the foundational 'social security plan' of 1945, unemployment was not directly addressed as an **insurance** problem, one of the reasons being that the main labour market problem at the time was labour shortage. However, unemployment *was* a matter of concern to postwar reformers, but predominantly viewed as a conjectural **demand** issue of how to avoid future crises and ensure 'full employment' (Daniel and Tuchszirer, 1999, p 162). According to the plan's founding father Pierre Laroque, it would enable 'the constant and as perfect as possible adaptation of offers and demand of labour' by combining counter-cyclical **demand** policies with a focus on 'professions', 'occupational training' (**investment**) and 'placement' (**activity**) (Laroque, cited in Palier, 2002, p 94).

The success of the full employment strategy characterising the *trente glorieuses*[2] hence pushed demands for a nationally coordinated system based on **insurance** into the background (Daniel and Tuchszirer, 1999).[3] The risk of unemployment was simply too marginal. However, at the end of the 1950s economic growth decreased, fuelling fear of a coming recession (Daniel and Tuchszirer, 1999, p 185). As a result, a compulsory system of unemployment insurance was established in 1958 by the major social partners – the employers' organisation CNPF (now Medef) and the labour unions FO, a reformist defector fraction of the revolutionary CGT labour union, the Christian labour union CFTC and finally the CGC, which represented the particularly French managerial class of *cadres*. The aim was both, in accordance with **insurance**, to provide employees with 'stable resources' in case of unemployment and, in accordance with **activity**, to 'facilitate redeployment' (Daniel and Tuchszirer, 1999, p 187).

The scheme was placed within the new corporatist body of Unedic in which the employers and employees' representatives negotiated the unemployment insurance agreement every second or third year. Below Unedic, a number of local offices, so-called Assedics, were set up to collect contributions (from employers and employees, and from 1979, also from the state (Tuchszirer, 2001]) and pay out compensation. Although Unedic was established outside the system of social security, the state was always involved as a third party with authority to intervene in the negotiations (Daniel and Tuchszirer 1999, pp 185–6). In 1967, the close ties with the state intensified when the government established the ANPE, which worked alongside Unedic with the specific aim of facilitating the transmission of information between employers and unemployed people (Daniel and Tuchszirer 1999, p 225 onwards). ANPE thus strengthened the **activity** element, of matching supply and demand of labour, in the scheme. Until the early 1980s, the involvement of the state resulted in constant improvement of the social rights attached to the unemployment insurance system (Tuchszirer, 2001), which reached a coverage rate of 76% in 1976 (Daniel and Tuchszirer, 1999, p 249).

In the 1980s, well past the *trente glorieuses* of close-to-full employment, the rising number of unemployed people put Unedic under continual financial pressure. While the financial crisis was more or less constant well into the 1990s, actors mobilised a variety of cities of unemployment to interpret and handle the impending deficit. First, within **insurance** thinking, contributions were raised in order to increase resources and balance funds, although this resulted in prohibitively expensive fees in some cases (Daniel and Tuchszirer, 1999, p 257 onwards). However, the financial difficulties also spurred a critique of the logic of **insurance** from the so-called 'second left', a movement within the Socialist Party and around the newly established labour union CFDT.[4] The historian Pierre Rosanvallon was central to the intellectual development of these criticisms (Béland, 2007a). In the 1970s and 1980s, the 'second left' was anti-statist (as opposed to the CGT and FO), advocating radical democratisation of workplaces and governing beyond the welfare state, designating a key role for the labour market parties (Rosanvallon, 1976, 1981). Later, the critique became less anti-statist and turned into a critique of a particular 'passive' way of spending resources while advocating an 'active welfare state' (Rosanvallon, 1995). In the 1980s and 1990s, **investment**-inspired policies were introduced along these lines to 'activate the expenses' of the unemployment insurance system, such as the so-called 'conventions of conversion', offering vocational training, internships and preparation for job interviews for people hit laid off for economic reasons (Daniel and Tuchszirer, 1999, pp 320–4).

In 1982, the criteria for compensation were changed. In line with **activity** worthiness, insurance benefits came to depend on the period of contribution, thus valorising past work efforts, rather than on the circumstances related to the event of unemployment (Tuchszirer, 2001). Out of these institutional changes, combined with economic stagnation, a new group of unemployed 'ex-contributors' came to the fore. These people were not entitled to compensation because long-term unemployment meant that they had not made sufficient contributions. In 1984, this group was separated from Unedic and included in a state-governed 'regime of solidarity' that was placed between the system of unemployment insurance and that of assistance, and offered conditional, means-tested, lump-sum benefits to some of those who were no longer entitled to insurance benefits (Eydoux and Béraud, 2011, p 44 onwards). The new group of unemployed and the regime of solidarity thus spurred uncertainty and tension about how to organise the unemployed 'inbetweens' and who should organise them. This tension was to resurface during the debate on PARE.

In the same period, a number of evaluations mobilised the city of **incentives**, testing the 'generosity' of the compensation as disincentivising work (Béraud and Eydoux, 2011, p 132) as well as highlighting the negative impact of (employers') contributions on businesses' competitiveness and hence employment (Palier, 2005, p 136). As a result, entitlement conditions were hardened and the duration of compensation was reduced (Béraud and Eydoux, 2011, p 132). The most important change was the introduction of the 'unique diminishing allowance' (AUD) which replaced the existing 'basic allowance' 1992. The AUD reduced the level of compensation every four months (thereby strengthening monetary **incentives**), while the entitlement period was reduced to 30 months (Palier, 2010c, p 84). While AUD was supported by the employers and the CFDT, the CGT, together with the FO, refused to sign the accord, thus marking another line of tension that would re-emerge in the debate on PARE.

AUD succeeded in balancing the Unedic budget of the funds, but it also reduced the number of unemployed people being compensated. This bolstered the demand for policy reform to target the groups that were no longer entitled to unemployment insurance due to long-term unemployment, as well as the rise of work forms (such as fixed-term contracts) that did not grant the same entitlements as traditional permanent contracts (Palier, 2002, pp 224–5). Importantly, this spurred the creation of a national, tax-funded, 'minimum integration income' scheme (RMI) in 1988. The RMI replaced the old system of social assistance and aimed to reinclude in its remit the rising group of people hit by the dynamics of social exclusion.[5]

Another outcome of the increasing number of unemployed people who found themselves outside of the unemployment insurance system safety net was the mobilisation of the unemployed in various protest movements and organisations (Chabanet, 2012). Some were supported by labour unions such as the CGT-chômeurs and AC !, while others, importantly, MNCP and Apeis, came from civil society movements. None of the organisations was, however, legally recognised by Unedic.

Launch of Medef's 'social restructuring'

It was the French employers' organisation Medef that launched the debate leading to the introduction of PARE. The initiative grew out of a major restructuring of CNPF in the late 1990s, renaming itself Medef and launching a large-scale political programme named 'social restructuring' (*refondation sociale*). The new offensive arose from a profound discontent with the government, culminating with the passing of the so-called 'Aubry Act' in 2000. Named after the then Socialist minister of employment and solidarity Martine Aubry, the Act, from a **redistribution** perspective, aimed to distribute the total pool of labour, reducing the working week to 35 hours and thereby creating jobs for the unemployed. To Medef, the Act was authoritarian and harmful to French enterprises in particular, because it was partly financed by the social protection funds of social partners (Palier, 2002, p 404).

At the beginning of 2000, Medef convinced the other social partners to gather and discuss the eight items of its programme. The first item concerned unemployment insurance (Palier, 2002, p 407). The ideas informing 'social restructuring' were developed by Medef's new vice-president Denis Kessler together with his adviser François Ewald, Michel Foucault's former assistant, whose work on insurance and the welfare state (Ewald, 1986) had somehow curiously led him into the private insurance industry (see Behrent, 2010).

The programme had certain affinities with the 'second left', such as its scepticism towards state intervention, seeking to reclaim some of the initiative from the state to the social partners (Vail, 2008, p 343). The choice was between 'reorganization or statification' (Medef, cited in Palier 2002, p 405). 'Social restructuring' also contained an **investment** critique of existing policies. In a state of globalisation, the nation state today, according to Medef's president Ernest Antione Seillière, 'does not function as a reducer of risks …, but as a producer of risks' (Seillère, cited in Ewald, 2000, p 4). The **insurance** instruments of the current system, adapted to 'the risk for an employee of finding himself deprived from revenue (accident, illness, old age)' were undermined and inappropriate, since they were 'progressively substituted by the risk of not being "employable", of not being able to integrate' (Ewald and Kessler, 2000, p 71). Further, the **investment** critique ruled out **redistribution** measures, since '[t]oday's biggest injustice relies less in the unequal distribution of revenues than in the inequality when confronted with risk' (Ewald and Kessler, 2000, p 71).

At the same time, Medef made clear references to the city of **activity**, qualifying unemployment as a flexibility problem of the supply of labour not adapting to demand. It was concerned with 'developing the suppleness of companies', encouraging the removal of 'recruitment obstacles' and 'dismantling French rigidities', causing 'labour shortages in certain sectors' and excluding 'persons far from the labour market' from getting 'experience'. 'Social restructuring' thus aimed to 'galvanise the labour market by favouring the adjustment of supply and demand'.

The employers' proposal

Medef's policy proposal coincided with negotiations concerning the renewal of the unemployment insurance convention, which was about to expire on 1 July 2000. Because Medef threatened to leave Unedic, the whole institution of unemployment insurance was therefore put to the test. Without a renewal, Unedic would have no mandate to manage the system.

Medef's calls for reform were supported by the two other (minor) employers' organisations, the craftsmen's union UPA and the small and medium-sized enterprises' CGPME. The cornerstone of the proposal was the so-called 'aid contract for return to employment' (CARE), an individual arrangement specifying 'the reciprocal commitments of the regime of compensation and the jobseeker' that each unemployed person would sign, and keep, in order to be compensated. The contract combined **investment** and **activity** elements while clearly privileging the latter. The contract included an assessment of the unemployed person's 'competences and aptitudes', leading to a 'plan for personalised support' that outlined the job categories corresponding to existing competences or the training needed to access an available job (**investment**). After signing the contract, the unemployed person would meet for an interview every two weeks to follow up on the plan and check whether they had participated in 'the effective and permanent search for a job' (**activity**). From the other side, Unedic committed to proposing a job offer (**activity**), or if necessary, a qualifying training course (**investment**). In order to further favour mobility, the unemployed person would get an additional benefit if taking a job in another business area. If 'within a certain period' the unemployed person had not received any offers of employment, Unedic would facilitate a job by contributing to the salary paid by the participating employer (activity). This instrument also had **investment** aims. Since 'one jobseeker out of two does not have an education', the job offers included 'short-term training programmes'.

When launching CARE, Medef was very explicit about the binding and ultimately coercive nature of the contract. While Medef promised to 'adjust the gradual decrease of the allowance' of AUD, it demanded a revision of the 'consequences for the terms and conditions of the compensation' if the obligations of the contract were not met. Basically this strengthened obligations relating to a problem within the city of **activity**: according to Medef, '[t]here are vacant jobs. The jobseekers have to take them'. The sanctions would apply in cases where jobseekers fail to attend their assessment; refuse to undertake any training course offered; fail to follow the course 'with diligence'; undertake non-declared remunerated work; or refuse a job offer corresponding to their current 'professional competences [with remuneration] in accordance with a salary normally practised in the profession and in the region'.

Despite the details regarding the obligations of the unemployed, many questions were left unanswered in Medef's proposal. Who, for instance, would carry out the sanctions and training – Assedic, governed by the social partners, or the ANPE? How to fund the cost for training as well as adjust the AUD? What would be the content of sanctions in case of non-compliance with CARE?

The unions' critique of the CARE

The negotiations in 2000 were characterised by optimism with regard to the performance of the economy and its impact on unemployment. After the previous round of negotiations, unemployment was decreasing, approaching the symbolic threshold of 10%. Qualifying the situation according to **demand**, Unedic consequently anticipated a correlation between growth, job creation and decreasing unemployment in the coming years. The expected growth rates in 2000 (3.6%) and 2001 (3.1%) would allow for the creation of 801,000 positions and 613,000 fewer unemployed people. However, the government explained the decreasing unemployment as a consequence of reduced working time as enshrined in the 'Aubry Act' (**redistribution**) and the 'fights against exclusion' such as the 'conventions of conversion' (**investment**).

For the trade unions, decreasing unemployment, and as a result of this, the surplus of unemployment insurance funds, provided a justification for using the surplus in accordance with **insurance** to 'better compensate the employees who are subject to precariousness', as well as increasing the 'proportion of unemployed benefitting from an allowance from Unedic', which was limited to 40%. The CFDT thus proposed to extend the period during which compensation entitlement accrued from the existing criteria of four months' work during the previous eight months. Those who had previously been included in the solidarity regime could thus be integrated into the unemployment insurance system.

In addition to modifying the compensation criteria for unemployment insurance, the city of **insurance** was used to mobilise criticism of Medef's CARE programme. The FO stated that 'Unedic is not the property of the employers' since it was 'financed by social contributions from employees and businesses … that are constitutive of the right to compensation'. The CFDT argued that 'there are already sanctions when only 41% of unemployed are compensated by Unedic'. The communists also mobilised arguments around the city of **insurance**, in this case to criticise CARE for resting 'on a logic of suspicion through which the unemployed are once again considered responsible for their own situation'.

But criticisms were also based on **redistribution**, qualifying the proposal as a class struggle of (rich) employers against the poor, thereby undermining citizenship. The communists continued their arguments thus: 'Masked as modernisation, Medef reinvents the old conflation: unemployed = 2nd class citizen = social delinquent'. CARE represented 'social racism against the unemployed and poor' and used Medef's president as an inequality test:

> You know, when five million people have trouble reaching the SMIC,[6] Mr Seillière, and when you earn more than 55 times the SMIC, when you have 2,200 times the yearly

SMIC in stock options, you understand, Mr Seilllière, that inequality is something that exists.

In the case of the CGT, the **redistribution** qualification led to calls for 'guaranteeing a decent revenue for all unemployed', removing AUD, and a 'modulation of employers' contribution in order to better responsibilise businesses'. The CGT's critique of the interests of businesses was also a critique of the **activity** requirements of mobility to adapt to 'the needs of businesses' and hence 'be young, pretty, dynamic, intelligent, in good health and qualified'. FO called CARE a 'one-sided contract' and accused Medef for wanting to base Unedic on a 'logic of profitability intensified by the labour market'. Similarly, mobilising the **redistribution** argument, AC !, one of the organisations representing unemployed people, criticised the employers for wanting to 'take control of the placement of the unemployed and impose its own terms on the workforce'.

Although critical of CARE, trade unions also mobilised **investment** tests similar to those that Medef had used to justify it. To the CGT, for instance, 'reforming the conditions of security and mobility from passive protection to active security is an inspiring programme'. However, the CGT criticised CARE on these measures for not being a 'process of integration but an additional instrument of exclusion and selection' (**investment**). In place of CARE, the CGT proposed to limit the recourse to fixed-term contracts while developing qualification contracts for people under 25 years without an education. Likewise, while the CFDT predicted 'many frictions with Medef', it also, ironically, accused it of 'hi-jacking the ideas that CFDT [had] defended for a long time', notably 'the active policies against unemployment' needed to avoid the risk of a 'hard core of unemployed subsisting like a cyst in the society of full employment'.

Curiously, trade unions, when evaluating AUD, also mobilised **incentives** tests. According to CFDT, 'compensation should play an active role to redeploy the unemployed, and gradually decreasing [the benefit] is one way, among others, to encourage it'. Although the CGT wanted to put an end to AUD, it proposed to use the surplus of the funds to let every unemployed person be compensated at 85% of the SMIC in order to 'make unemployment expensive', hereby 'settling on another dynamic of employment'.

An offer you can refuse? Sanctions put to the test

In the negotiations in May 2000, trade unions appeared to unite around a critique of Medef's CARE. First, all of them refused 'to enter a process of sanctioning the unemployed'. In a first attempt to reach a compromise, the CFDT, CFTC, CGC and FO jointly proposed to rename *le* CARE to *la* CARE by replacing 'contract' with the less binding 'convention'. Whereas a contract defined the basic relationship between employer and employee, as well as between insurer and insured, a convention would be adopted voluntarily.[7]

Underneath the compromise, however, different qualifications seemed to underpin the engagement of the coalition of unions. The CFDT thought that unions and employers 'could converge' if the aim of CARE was to 'put everyone's feet back on the ladder', but not if it was 'to sanction the unemployed'. The union criticised CARE by mobilising **activity**. Testing the population in terms of the latter, CFDT president Nicole Notat 'knew of few unemployed people who did not aspire to work.... In the rare opposite cases, these tendencies are anticipated in the current system'. On the contrary, most unemployed people were valorised beings with a work ethic: 'The interest of everyone is to seize new chances, not to settle oneself in unemployment'.

A way of circumventing the problem of sanctions, according to the coalition of unions, was to legitimise the **activity** elements of CARE by rewarding those engaging in the scheme, thus suggesting a kind of compromise between **activity** and **insurance**. CARE could in fact be accepted by the unions 'when it is not simply a matter of cutting the allowances of the recalcitrant unemployed, but a matter of ameliorating those for the unemployed who are making the necessary efforts to find a job'. CARE should thus be 'an optional convention that the unemployed are incited to subscribe to'. By introducing a 'bonus' for those engaging in CARE, 'the coercive dimension is eliminated'. In this way, CARE was not sacrificing the **insurance** logic, but was simply adding an extra, optional layer and category of unemployment next to those 'solely being compensated'. Notat thus questioned polemically 'whether the unemployment insurance system must be strictly oriented towards cold compensation or if, on the contrary, it should be combined with accompanying rights oriented towards the return to employment'.

Meanwhile, the FO, which co-authored the joint statement, took a much less accommodating stance towards combining the **activity** element of CARE with **insurance**. FO denounced the fact that 'the unemployed must engage in an "active" search for a job, at the risk of suspension or removal of allowances' as 'STO' (compulsory work service), a term that was used for the French workers who were forced by the Vichy government to go to work in factories in Germany during the Second World War.

The CGT, the only union that was not a signatory of the joint statement, took a similar principled stance. Unlike the CFDT, the CGT saw CARE as a sacrifice of **insurance**, since requiring jobseekers to accept a job proposal in order not to lose their allowance was 'making the contributor pay for what ought to be paid by the contributions of businesses and employees'. Thus, CARE would be the 'death certificate of the unemployment insurance system from 1958'. The **insurance**-based critique was backed by a **redistribution** element relating to interests and representation. Medef was accused of greed and self-interest, since the surplus in the funds was not used to extend the number of compensated unemployed, but rather to reduce contributions. Employers would gain 42 billion francs while the unemployed would gain nothing 'You could say: Medef: 42, unemployed: 0'.

Allying themselves with the CGT, the associations representing unemployed people organised protests around the country, 'making the voice of those affected by the reform heard' and calling the other trade unions to 'turn down the accord of shame'. One of the associations, the CGT-chômeurs accused the CFDT of 'declaring war on the unemployed' (**redistribution**). Denouncing **activity** by mobilising **redistribution**, they argued that Unedic 'will no longer be a system of compensation but a system that hunts delinquents, that is, the unemployed, so as to punish them if they do not accept the jobs that businesses propose whatever the social conditions of those jobs'. The movement had support from several intellectuals, including Pierre Bourdieu, who greeted the protests, and Robert Castel, another prominent sociologist who supported the protests, regretfully arguing how CARE would sacrifice the **insurance** conception of risk and responsibility:

> It implicates a complete transformation of the conception of unemployment. Until now, even though compensation was imperfect, it allowed you to touch a deferred wage when you were unfortunately deprived of unemployment. When thrown out, the employee was not held responsible for the situation. The logic of the system of unemployment compensation came close to the [logic] of retirement: by

working you acquire rights which allow you to continue a decent life, even though you quit the professional world because of age or because of a dismissal. CARE radically calls this logic into question.

Another sociologist saw Medef's project as part of a 'global tendency to recommodify what struggles and the social state had achieved to withdraw from the market' (**redistribution**). Furthermore, the national movement for unemployed workers, MNCP, mobilising both **insurance**'s valorising of security and **redistribution**'s critique of inequality and capitalist power, argued that 'if the battle against unemployment is won without twisting the neck of precariousness and poverty, it will be a Pyrrhic victory'. The MNCP called for the government to intervene in order to restrict Medef's ambition to 'impose the dictum of the market'.

The first round of negotiations ended in an agreement between the employers and the CFDT and CFTC, only two of the five unions, and in terms of representation, only around one third of union votes. To accommodate the criticism of the CFDT, CARE was renamed 'aid plan for the return to employment' (PARE). Jobseekers no longer had to engage in a 'contract' but a 'project' named PAP (personalised action project), which was considered less obligatory since it no longer derived from civil law.

Despite the semantic change, the content of PAP remained more or less the same. PAP would still be based on a 'contractualisation' and sanctions would be enacted following refusals to take a proposed job, from a 20% reduction in the first instance to a complete removal of entitlement after the fourth refusal. Although the parties agreed to suspend the periodic reduction of AUD for those engaging in PAP, there was still uncertainty over whether the scheme should be facultative and over the role of the ANPE (Lyon-Caen, 2001, p 379). Finally, the CGC joined the non-signatories (the FO and CGT), calling the new scheme 'an electroshock of the poor'.

Testing limitations and authority to coerce

Despite opposition from the non-signatories, in June 2000 the agreement was sent for approval to the government, which had to ratify the convention in law.[8] However, the government, represented by the minister of employment and solidarity Martine Aubry, was highly critical of the proposal (see, for example, Aubry and Fabius, 2000). Finally, after three weeks of intense debate, the government rejected the accord. The rejection was celebrated by the FO, CGT and organisations representing the unemployed as a 'victory of democracy'. In a public letter, about 50 leading figures from various factions of parties, unions and civil society from the left[9] urged the government to ensure better compensation for unemployed people (**insurance**), 'the effective equality of rights for everyone' and the 'freedom to choose employment and training in place of a principle of imposed employment' (**redistribution**). They also recommended that the government include all concerned actors in the debate, including the organisations for the unemployed and 'democratically elected representatives'.

Part of the criticism was supported by the government. Aubry questioned the agreement basing her argument on the already existing **insurance** criticism regarding the limited number of compensated unemployed people. According to Aubry, the agreement's extension of the period during which compensation entitlement accrued from the existing four months' work during the previous eight months to 14 months was 'weak', costing only 4 billion out of the expected surplus of 75 billion francs. The minister noted that the proportion of those compensated had dropped from 52% to 42% over the previous ten years, and that the extension would cause an increase of only 0.2%.

However, it turned out that not all of the government's criticism coincided with the alliance of the left. While the government strengthened the weight of **insurance** in the financial allocation of the convention, it did not mobilise any substantive critique based on **redistribution**. Rather, it stressed **activity** and **investment** in the conditions of PAP. Aubry criticised PARE both for treating people unequally as well for treating people *too* equally. In the former case, Aubry accused PARE of creating a system 'in two speeds', where 'the unemployed who are the least cut off from the world of work', that is, those entitled to unemployment insurance, 'are benefitting from the best job offers', whereas the 'long-term unemployed …, in large numbers, tip into the [systems of] solidarity and assistance of the state'.[10] Combining two cities, the minister criticised PARE for excluding services of mobility to the most mobile (**activity**) while also in a more profound way discriminating by excluding a group of people from the services of the ANPE, 'a public organization and guarantor of equal opportunities before the return to employment' (**investment**). In any case, Aubry hereby also criticised the exclusive membership criteria (**insurance**) for privileging insiders.

The latter critique of PARE of being *too* equal was purely based on **investment** and addressed the question of what would be a worthy job offer to an unemployed person. In the agreement, job offers should not correspond to the jobseekers' official qualifications (based on diplomas) but merely their 'competences' and, after 12 months of unemployment, simply their 'aptitudes'. Aubry thus criticised PARE for *not* subordinating the demands of **activity** to what makes people worthy in the city of **investment**, that is, skills. 'Under these conditions', the minister remarked with contempt, Aubry herself (holding highly esteemed degrees in economics and political science) 'was fit for being a cashier'. For the same reasons, the CGC, representing the highly educated management group of *cadres*, wanted to insert the notion of 'classification' in order to be certain that one cannot 'downgrade an employee'.

In terms of the use of coercion towards unemployed people, the government took a more accommodating stance towards PARE. Whereas the **insurance**- and **redistribution**-based criticisms of FO and CGT denounced the use of coercion per se, the question for the government and CGC was rather *when* it was legitimate. Mobilising the city of activity argument in her justification, Aubry recapped that as a minister in 1992 she had already introduced the possibility of sanctioning unemployed people if their jobseeking was inadequate or if they refused a job proposal, and hence saw it as 'normal to sanction the unemployed'.[11] However, in order for sanctions to be 'impartial, the decisions should remain the responsibility of the state', that is, the ANPE.

In July 2000, as a response to the government's rejection of the agreement, the signatories (employers, the CFDT and CFTC) decided to leave the institutions of Unedic. Meanwhile, the government had provisionally extended the convention relating to the unemployment insurance system to the end of 2000. Despite their symbolic act, the signatories also accommodated the government's criticism. While Medef led bilateral negotiations with the government (Lyon-Caen, 2001, p 380), CFDT justified PARE and the stance of the signatories in public. To accommodate the **insurance**-based criticism, the signatories emphasised the significance of removing the gradually diminishing benefit of AUD. Yet, **insurance** in itself was disqualified as completely inadequate, and almost inhuman, leading to a situation where 'the unemployed were left alone with their difficulties'. The idea that Unedic should be limited to its function as an insurance provider 'was a static conception of the mission of system of unemployment insurance that contributed to exclusion' and thus the system could not simply be a 'counter for allowances'.

Regarding the authority to decide on sanctions, the signatories simply agreed that this ought to be the responsibility of the ANPE. However, by turning the **investment** critique upside down, the signatories completely dismissed the accusation that PARE was leading to a system with 'two speeds'. Rather, the French system of unemployment insurance had 'in fact' been running at two speeds for the past 20 years. PARE had the effect of combating this situation rather than encouraging it. The signatories stressed that the PARE was also aimed at long-term unemployed people situated within the state-governed regime of solidarity, provided that the state contributed (financially).

Another important element of PARE that countered the danger of a 'two-speed' system was in fact its obligatory character. Here, CFDT's justification and response to previous criticism mobilised a new **paternal** qualification of the unemployed person as incompetent, possibly not knowing his or her own true interests:

> Many doubts would be raised if PARE had been optional. If guaranteeing compensation and services at the same time is good, it's good for everyone.... It is by leaving PARE optional that one approaches a system in two speeds: On the one side, the well educated and well informed unemployed profit from all their rights; on the other, those to whom entering a training course is not self-evident, or those who are already on the road to exclusion, continue to lose hope of their chances. But the content of PARE is adapted to the needs of each individual. There is no standard model for everyone.

In this context, the obligatory nature of PARE forces the hand of those who, irrationally, would not sign it if they had the choice. This demonstrates the need for a coercive element in the 'emancipatory approach' of PARE, an approach that 'turns the unemployed person, by the help of professionals, into an actor in the construction of his or her own project'. The **paternal** qualification is in this case closely tied to the city of **investment**'s need for targeted (that is, unequal and not standardised) treatment in order to ensure equal opportunities. It also addresses the criticism that PARE leads to excessive **activity** requirements of flexibility (for the skilled).

> Everyone knows that the [personalised] plan of a qualified computer engineer, a laid-off worker in the textile industry

or a young person without a professional project will not be identical. There will only be a presentation of job offers for the first, an evaluation of the level of competences … perhaps followed by a complementary training course for the second, and a complete assessment of competences for the third.

This justification thus combines the incompetent **paternal** subject and the unskilled **investment** subject, with the use of coercion serving to encourage the unknowing and unemployable unemployed to make use of rights that will provide them with better opportunities.

But the **paternal** subject could also be merged with the subjects of the city of **activity** for whom work *always* trumps inactivity. Henri Vacquin, a sociologist and consultant with close ties to the CFDT, made this clear in his justification of PARE.

> Sanctions imposed on those who refuse a job within their qualifications are already better than a gradually decreasing allowance which punishes all the unemployed indifferently. And the instrument will make visible to the jobseeker that they often have capacities that they didn't expect. Regardless of personal preference for a profession, who knows whether the required qualities for practising it are not similar to other professions? Who knows if a hairdresser would make a good assembly-line worker of electronic chips?… PARE is an act of mediation. If an employer seeks an assembly-line worker of chips, it's up to the mediator, ANPE, to get the hairdresser to understand that he or she is qualified for that position and will benefit from it.

While Vacquin denounced sanctions based on **incentives** as too 'indifferent', they were legitimate when based on the aim of 'getting the unemployed to understand' (**paternal**), which again would make them more flexible and willing to take on other kinds of jobs (**activity**).

During the final negotiations, the **investment**-based criticism led to changes to PARE, which ultimately made the CGC join the signatories. Besides replacing 'competences' and 'aptitudes' with 'validated qualifications' and 'professional capacities', the paternal qualification was integrated by taking into account the 'degree of autonomy' of unemployed people when considering sanctions.

The accord was finally approved by the government in October 2000, after several modifications and concessions accommodating its critique. The FO and CGT, however, were excluded from the negotiations and remained opposed to the final accord, condemning 'the obligatory PARE' for 'preparing for forced underpaid work' and conducting 'social eugenics'.

Sedimentation and subsequent changes

Having mapped the changes that PARE makes to the French contributions-based system, as well as the qualifications and justifications behind these changes, it is now possible to identify the sedimentation of the various cities into the assemblage of instruments governing unemployed people. The result is a complex patchwork of institutionalised tests that (e)valuate and categorise unemployed people according to several cities. Some of the tests set clear thresholds for qualification as worthy or not worthy, while others set up continua. Some look backwards in time, some plan ahead, and some do both. They also appear at different moments in the unemployed person's trajectory. The tests are described in Unedic's ratification of the new convention, which describes all the criteria for receiving allowances, including PARE (Unedic, 2000).[12] The trajectory of the unemployed person is illustrated in Figure 4.2.

In their initial Unedic assessment, the unemployed person is treated as a potential victim in need of compensation (**insurance**) as well as someone whose worthiness depends on past work activity (**activity**). Regarding **insurance**, an individual instance of unemployment is tested with a focus on a number of criteria that define 'involuntary' unemployment (art. 2). Furthermore, Unedic checks whether the individual concerned has paid contributions to the scheme. If the first criterion is not met, the social assistance regime takes over (at the time RMI, today the RSA, or active solidarity income). If the second criterion is not met, the unemployed person may be eligible for an allowance from the solidarity regime. When it comes to **activity**, the unemployed person is tested with respect to past 'affiliation periods', which are calculated by the number of working hours in the period leading up to the event of unemployment (art. 3). In the new convention, the basic criterion of four months of work during the previous eight months was changed to four months during the previous 18 months, thereby addressing **insurance**-based criticisms and extending the number of compensated persons. The test determines whether the unemployed person is eligible for compensation, or,

Figure 4.2: Trajectory of tests for unemployed people under PARE

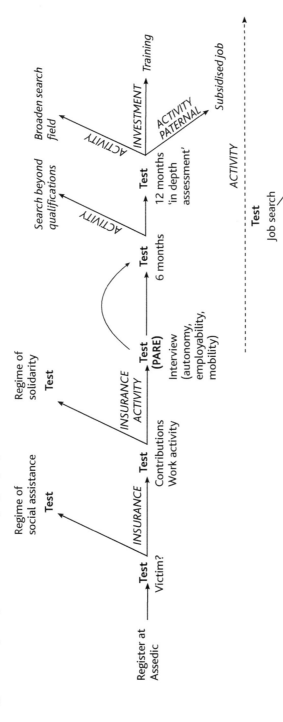

instead, should apply through the solidarity regime. If eligibility is proven, the 'duration of compensation' is dependent on the number of hours the unemployed person has worked, that is, on worthiness according to past **activity**. The more working hours accrued and the longer the period of work, the longer the duration of compensation (a five-step scale, from 122 to 1,825 days) (art. 12). Finally, the unemployed person is once again evaluated in the city of **insurance** by a number of rather complex tests based on past wage levels (the 'damage'), which set the entitled compensation (art. 21, 22, 23, 24). The unemployed person thus receives the 'return to employment allowance' (ARE) that replaces the previous gradually decreasing AUD.

Once eligible, the unemployed person's status as victim fades into the background as a number of new tests, related to PARE, begin the process of requalification according to the moral economy of activation by installing a number of continuous, forward-looking tests. The change is almost symbolically identifiable in Unedic's documentation. In the first part, which defines the aforementioned initial eligibility criteria, the unemployed person is designated an 'employee deprived of employment'. However, from the first paragraph introducing PARE, the person figures as the 'jobseeker' (art. 14, §1). In order to receive the allowance, the unemployed person must sign the 'personalised action project' (PAP), which establishes a new set of 'rights and obligations' for receiving benefits. The PAP is dependent on a test, an 'in-depth interview', which evaluates the subject according to three cities. The first is **paternal**. The interview is 'the occasion' for the agent from the ANPE to 'appreciate the degree of autonomy of the jobseeker in his or her search' (art. 14, §2) and take this into 'account' in the PAP (art. 15) in the sense that a low degree of autonomy involves more rights and obligations.

Meanwhile, in a test of **investment** evaluating the employability of the 'jobseeker', the interview must also 'take stock of qualifications and compare [them] to available or potential offers on the labour market' (art. 14, §2). If the subject's score is sufficiently high, they can remain in the city as the PAP will describe the job types that correspond to their qualifications (art. 15). However, if the score is low (again, the test is on a continuum), the PAP includes two paths: one based on **activity**, which suggests 'the job type(s) towards which he or her may like to convert', or one based on **investment**, which outlines the 'services and training' that are necessary to 'access a job in compliance with the project' (art. 15). Finally, the PAP must also take into account the subject's 'personal and family situation', which will set limits to their 'potential geographical mobility' (art. 16, §3). While this test sets limits to the city of **activity**, it also legitimises obligations to move if the personal situation does not inhibit it.

After signing the PAP, the unemployed person must be continually active in the city of **activity** and 'carry out positive actions of job seeking' and be 'available and genuinely involved in the move towards the return to employment' (art. 16, §3). On the other side of the threshold is the idle subject who does not search 'genuinely'. Non-compliance is followed up by sanctions (as outlined earlier in the signatories' proposal).

The period after signing the PAP is characterised by continuous, ever-intensive evaluation as well as by rights and obligations. Concurrently, as time passes, the jobseeker's 'degree of autonomy' decreases. In the first phase, the unemployed person is classed as capable of finding a job. It is not until six months after signing that person's PAP profile is officially established (art. 17, §1). In addition, the balance between **investment** and **activity** changes as time passes. At the beginning the unemployed person is merely obliged to accept a job offer that 'corresponds to current professional capacities, qualifications as a result of diplomas, knowledge and professional experience'. After six months, the job search and any offers need only 'be part of the field' of professional capacities (art. 17, §1,2). Finally, after 12 months, the ANPE should 'accentuate their efforts in order to redeploy those concerned or favour occupational integration and ensure that they acquire professional experience' possibly by means of 'regressive assistance' allocated to the employer (art. 17, §3). In addition, in order to broaden the jobseeker's 'field' of interests, an 'in-depth assessment of competences' is offered (art. 17, §1). Finally, 'if, despite all these measures, the beneficiary still has not found a job, allowances will be retained within the duration of the rights' (art. 17, §4). Time thus works as an automatic test gradually reassessing the unemployed person's eligibility.

PARE marks a radical change in the way that it, as time passes, transforms what initially is a homogenous group of compensated 'victims' into a disparate group of subjects, all of whom are nevertheless in need of some kind of activation. As shown earlier, it does not wipe out the insurance instruments, but rather works to limit their capacity to encompass unemployed people. Furthermore, it consolidates that the primary aim of the French unemployment system is to, somehow, bring the unemployed back into 'active society', even if it takes coercive measures. One of the immediate effects of PARE was thus a quadrupling of use of sanctions from 2001 to 2004 (Barbier, 2013, p 159).

At the same time, the reform changes the balance between various explanations of unemployment. Although PARE recognises that individual cases of unemployment may be due to 'involuntary' events, it gradually reinterprets and attributes the event to factors residing in the individual – lack of autonomy, mobility and employability. PARE thus opens a new arena of tests in which the distinction between collective and individual responsibility is much more blurred and subject to continual revision and testing. Is the unemployed person searching hard enough? Is the job search sufficiently broad? Are the placement agencies offering enough jobs? Is the jobseeker 'diligent' and autonomous, and are the training and services sufficiently targeted? The same goes, and this will become much clearer in the final two cases, for the evaluation of activation policies: is the policy not performing because of the policy itself or because unemployed subjects (or social workers) are unwilling to make proper use of them? These are tests that are much harder to answer than the **insurance** tests addressing the event of unemployment and they entail another logic. Whereas individual and collective responsibility in the insurance test are mutually exclusive, the tests surrounding activation measures seem to strengthen individual obligations concurrently with the number of services offered. Finally, since there are no 'standard' solutions, one of the answers to the blurred lines of responsibility – of 'rights and obligations' – are more precise instruments of categorisation of the unemployed.

Subsequent reforms of the unemployment insurance system tend to reinforce the dynamics that PARE set in motion. The 2005 law for 'social cohesion' strengthened flexibility requirements to accept training and job offers, as well as control and sanctions relating to the adequacy of jobseeking measures, causing significant increases in the number people being removed from the unemployment insurance system (Béraud and Eydoux, 2011, p 136). Due to increasing financial pressures on the system, the expansion of access to compensation that was part of the PARE compromise was withdrawn, while the duration of benefits was further reduced in the conventions of 2003 and 2006 (Béraud and Eydoux, 2011, p 133).

The convention of 2006 refined and intensified the tests of PARE and the PAP. Since then the PAP has been replaced by the 'personalised project for returning to employment' (PPAE) and by 'monthly personalised support' (SMP), through which unemployed people are now categorised according to three 'job-search support profiles': 'type 1' entails 'accelerated job seeking' for the immediately employable, 'type 2' is 'active research' for those considered as having an intermediate profile, and 'type 3', is the least autonomous and employable in need of 'accompanied job seeking' (Béraud and Eydoux, 2011, p 135).

Concurrently with these activation reforms, the areas of dissent among and between social partners have concerned issues of labour law, thus focusing less on unemployment itself and more on the question of how to govern the threshold between employment and unemployment. Subsequent reforms have consistently focused on the (lack of) flexibility (**activity**) of the labour force as a result of labour law, such as the relaxation of conditions for lay-offs and a decrease in contractual job security. However, massive protests in 2006 managed to bring to a halt the 'first employment contract' bill that aimed to make it easier to hire and, especially, fire young employees (Cole, 2008) and in 2007 the French president Nicolas Sarkozy was forced to drop a proposal for a 'unique employment contract' intended to remove a number of the rights connected to the CDI (indeterminate employment contract) (Lane, 2018, p 9).

In the same period, the concept of flexicurity entered French public debate, calling for reforms that would push for still more flexibility but now in combination with security measures in the **investment** understanding of employability and more modest attempts to extend **insurance** entitlements to more groups. For instance, the journalist Alain Lefebvre and philosopher Dominique Méda (2006) argued for the need to take inspiration from the flexicurity model of the Danish labour market, thus calling for workers to accept of a more flexible labour market in return for better training for unemployed people (Lane, 2018). In 2013, the Socialists, led by president François Hollande, passed a 'job securitisation law' that aimed to increase the mobility (**activity**) of workers by enabling the portability of rights (**insurance**); to ensure 'continuous education' by granting each worker a 'personal training account'; and to allow for local agreements between employers and employees on reductions in pay in return for a guarantee of no redundancies (Lane, 2018, p 10). Subsequent reforms have strengthened these logics. The 'El Khomri Act', which relaxed working time and lay-off regulations, was adopted in 2016 by the Socialist government, despite the mobilisation of the social protest movement *nuit debout* ('standing night') in the Place de la République in Paris and several other public places around France.

Notes

[1]   Exact references to quotations can be found in Hansen (2017).

[2]   The post-war economic prosperity period from 1945 to 1975.

3 Similar to the unfolding events of PARE, criticism and protests have resulted in postponing or bringing to a halt some reforms, but have not managed to provide an alternative reform path. The criticism thus remains defensive and reactive. Emmanuel Macron's presidency thus seems to indicate a consolidation and intensification of activation instruments, with explicit admiration for the flexicurity of the Danish labour market. The first reforms of the French unemployment insurance system in 2017 and 2018 thus aim to grant freelancers entitlement (**insurance**) and promise substantial spending on education and training for unemployed people (**investment**) in return for further flexibility in case of redundancies and more control and sanctions to ensure sufficient jobseeking and flexibility (**activity**). Thus, while **insurance** is used to justify an expansion of the scheme, the *content* and logic of it remain within, and in fact strengthen, the moral economy of activation. Although the recent rise of the *gilets jaunes* (yellow vests) protests is clearly nurtured by mass unemployment, it has not, so far, been able to transform indignation into an alternative system of tests and governance [into an alternative programme of tests and policies]. The introduction of a scheme based on insurance was also challenged by the actuarial problem of predicting the risk of unemployment (Daniel and Tuchszirer, 1999, p 187).

4 The CFDT was the newest of the five trade unions legally recognised by the state and emerged in 1964 from the Christian CFTC as a secular, non-communist alternative to the CGT. The five recognised unions participating in the Unedic negotiations are hence the FO, CGT, CFTC, CGC and CFDT.

5 On the particular discourse of 'social exclusion' in France, see Béland (2007). The trajectory of RMI is described in more detail in the context of RSA in Chapter 6.

6 The SMIC is the minimum wage, guaranteed and set by the state.

7 Not all opposed the use of sanctions, however. An unemployed person ironically noted: 'They want to reduce allowances? It's all the same to me because I don't receive them! If I have to sign a contract for someone to offer me a job, that's all I ask for'.

8 The negotiation and voting procedures are extremely complex and follow more or less official codes of conduct. Initially all social partners were required to ratify agreements, but since 1989 they need only be signed by a minority. However, non-signatories can demand a new round of negotiations. Furthermore, regardless of whether the accord has been unanimously agreed, the state (Council of State) ultimately has to approve it (Lyon-Caen, 2001, pp 378–9).

9 The signatories came from the socialist party, PCF, LCR (Communist Revolutionary League), CGT, CGC, the anti-globalisation trade union

SUD, a minority of the CFDT, and organisations representing the unemployed (MNCP, Apeis, CGT-chômeurs and AC !).

10 Likewise, FO had earlier warned against a 'risk of discrimination' between different groups of unemployed persons.

11 In practice, however, the sanctions were rarely used, and when they were, it was in cases of non-attendance because the unemployed person had found a job without giving notice. According to *Le Figaro*, the rare use of sanctions was a result of their disproportionate severity. It was in this light that FO and CGT's opposition to the sanctions of PARE should be understood. While PARE would make sanctions 'more gradual and less tough' this would also make them more 'realistic and applicable'.

12 Unedic (2000) '*Règlement annexé à la Convention du 1er janvier 2001 relative à l'aide au retour à l'emploi et à l'indemnisation du chômage*'. January 1st, Unedic.

5

Turning solutions into 'structural' problems: unemployment insurance, Denmark, 1992–93

The reform process resulting in the 'Active Labour Market Policy Act' (henceforth ALMPA) began with the adoption of an experimental and temporary law in 1992 that was set to expire at the end of 1993.[1] Whereas the French PARE was rooted in an explicit call for reform that was clearly confined to the unemployment system and the negotiation of its convention, ALMPA is an example of a more disordered process with a variety of parallel test situations in a number of instruments that somehow became tied together. Figure 5.1 provides an overview of the key events during the debate up to the passing of ALMPA.

ALMPA introduced an individual contract quite similar to PARE while combining it with a number of different instruments: leave schemes to ease access to the labour market, job training for unemployed people and employment offers that jobseekers, after a period of time, would have to accept in order to continue to receive compensation. Further, it changed the rules of entitlement. While the PARE reform process was mainly driven by the unions and employers' organisations, the ALMPA reform was orchestrated by the state. This different dynamic is the result of the particular history of the Danish unemployment insurance system, which is presented in the first two sections of the chapter. As in Chapter 4, historical sources are read with a view to understanding the tensions and compromises between cities of unemployment that have 'sedimented' into governance systems for insured unemployed people, thus providing the context for the process of ALMPA. The following four sections each present a test situation concerning a specific problem relating to the governing of the unemployment insurance system: wages, financing, subsidised jobs and leave schemes. Finally, the chapter concludes with an analysis of the changes that the ALMPA entailed and a brief look at subsequent changes to the system.[2]

Figure 5.1: Timeline of the ALMPA reform process

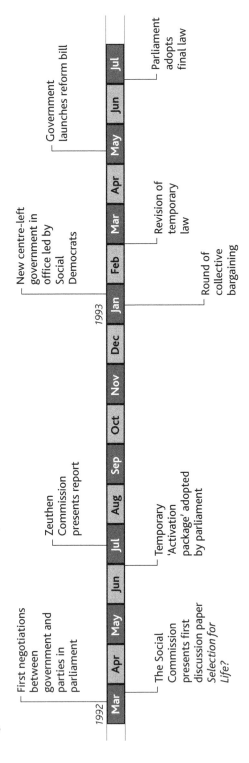

Creation and crises of the Danish unemployment insurance system

Unlike in France, where the creation of a national, contribution-based, unemployment insurance system was initiated by the state, the Danish equivalent was the direct result of pressure from the labour movement, which from the beginning was much more homogenous than in France, and closely allied with the Social Democratic Party. It is also 50 years older. The establishment in 1907 of the unemployment insurance system followed the recommendations of a government commission that was set up to satisfy demands from the rapidly growing Social Democratic Party (Christensen, 2011). Whereas the French system was orchestrated in a tripartite, corporatist manner, with equal representation of employees and employers, the employers only played a marginal role in the Danish set-up. Neither did they initially contribute to, or partake in the control of, the 'unemployment funds'; these were financed by workers, municipalities and the state. The funds, despite being legally independent, were in reality closely tied to the labour unions that would control the solidarity of **insurance**, organise the placement service (**activity**) and encourage workers to enrol in the voluntary scheme. To strengthen mobility of the labour force (**activity**), the funds and placement offices were delimited by professions rather than local borders (Christensen, 2011, p 517). Initially, the scheme was only intended to be a short-term instrument to compensate for the shortage in labour demand due to economic crises (**demand**). With confidence in the **demand** and placement (**activity**) instruments to control such crises, the maximum period of compensation was only set to 70 days annually (Christensen, 2011, p 519).

The economic crisis of the late 1920s resulted in the establishment of so-called 'help funds', similar to the French 'regime of solidarity' (see Chapter 4) established in the 1980s, which compensated unemployed people whose right to compensation had expired. As in France, the problem of insured unemployed people losing their right to compensation was a recurring issue in the numerous reforms of the Danish unemployment insurance system. The help funds, which were financed with contributions from the unemployment insurance fund as well as the state and the employers, were designed to prevent insured unemployed people from entering the system of poor relief (Christensen, 2011, p 535). The insurance scheme had a marginal **investment** element, since the help funds involved the possibility of training at the folk high schools[3] (Christensen, 2011, p. 557).

Up until the end of the Second World War, a number of corrective tests and reforms unfolded, mobilised from within the city of **insurance**. *Venstre*, which at the time was an agrarian party,[4] and the Confederation of Danish Employers (DA)[5] pushed for the use of individual control cards, popularly labelled 'dog tags', to ensure that people did not commit fraud by receiving unemployment benefits while working (Christensen, 2011, p 555; 2012a, pp 487, 499). Further, while in government, *Venstre* reduced the state subsidies while increasing the membership fees. The government justified the cutbacks as a way of strengthening the 'principle of insurance' in the scheme (Christensen, 2011, p 552). Finally, the help funds were increasingly aligned with the unemployment insurance system. Previously, the help funds were conditional and based on a definition of 'extraordinary unemployment', that is, unemployment in the sense of the city of **demand**, and had lower compensation rates. The definition of 'extraordinary' gradually widened and compensation rates increased, and finally the help funds were integrated in the unemployment insurance system in 1958 (Christensen, 2011, p 563 onwards).

While the postwar period was characterised by expanding rights to compensation, the **insurance** logic was simultaneously challenged from other cities of unemployment. Keynesian **demand** policies focusing on state-initiated job creation were on the rise in the decades after the war (Christensen, 2012b, pp 505–7). While these policies helped reduce financial pressure on the insurance scheme, they also gave rise to the idea that governing unemployment was the responsibility of the state (Christensen, 2012a, p 523), which in turn legitimised further financing by the state. State financing peaked in 1967 when membership fees were reduced to a symbolic contribution. The level of compensation improved, more groups were covered and the compensation period gradually increased (Christensen, 2013, p 538 onwards). However, the transition from a compensation to a tax-based scheme also decoupled the financing from the risk of unemployment, challenging the contributory solidarity logic of **insurance** (Christensen, 2012a, pp 520–2).

This decoupling provided further space for **activity** and **investment** uses of the funds and further involvement of the state in the organisation of instruments. This is partly why the unions and employers' organisations were marginal players in the reform of ALMPA. The developments were also fuelled by criticism of the compensatory way of handling unemployment residing in the city of **insurance**. For instance, the influential economist and social democrat Bent Rold Andersen criticised the unemployment system for not bringing people back into the labour market. The solution, according to Andersen, was to further integrate the contribution-based system into the welfare state (Christensen, 2012b, p 515). In the 1950s, **activity** strategies such as travel support, help with finding accommodation and moving jobs to the rural areas, combined with **demand** strategies of regional investment, were introduced to address so-called 'unemployment islands' (Christensen, 2012b, pp 500–1). In conjunction with enlarging the set of **activity**-enhancing instruments, in 1967 the state took over the placement service and control of unemployed people in the so-called 'placement service' that had hitherto been in the hands of the unemployment funds, in practice, the unions (Christensen, 2012b, pp 526–7). The **investment**-based tests of the postwar period, moreover, spurred the idea that the labour market, as a result of increasing mechanisation in the agrarian sector, would need fewer unskilled workers, which resulted in apprenticeship and training schemes targeting unskilled, unemployed workers (Christensen, 2012a, pp 505–9).

Oil crises, rising energy prices and inflation, a huge deficit on the balance of trade and rising unemployment provided the context for the debate and reform of the unemployment insurance system in the 1970s. However, unlike in France where the funds were mainly contribution-based, the predominantly tax-based funds in Denmark were not put under the same immediate financial pressure. Even though the system had lost a key **insurance** component (contribution-based), it was still qualified and problematised by means of the city of **insurance** as a way to compensate for loss of income in case of unemployment. However, just as the state's improvement of compensation provided space for other qualifications and instruments, the **insurance** debates and sedimentations of the 1970s and 1980s would later come to serve as a kind of Trojan horse.

Two examples of this dynamic are worth noting, since they came to set the scene for the final Bill of ALMPA. The first example relates to the possibility of the abuse of rights in the city of **insurance**. In the 1980s, suspicion of speculative behaviour by both employees and employers soared. On the one hand, employers were accused of exploiting the system by strategically laying people off during vacation periods and bad weather conditions. On the other hand, employees were suspected of permanently working part-time with a compensation supplement, while employees serving a notice period were suspected of only subscribing to the unemployment insurance once the notice was given (Jensen, 2008, p 262; Christensen, 2013, pp 552–4). In response, the period of membership required for benefit entitlement was extended, and contributions from both employees and employers were once again raised (Christensen, 2013, pp 552ff). However, such speculative behaviour also provided scope for **activity** critique, since extension of the vesting period accentuated the obligation to work a priori and be at the disposal of the labour market in order to receive unemployment benefits.

The second example illustrates an instrument that was mainly justified in accordance with **insurance**, but could be requalified in other cities. The Social Democrat proposal in 1978 for a so-called 'job offer plan' was justified as a way to prevent the growing number of long-term unemployed people who were about to lose their right to compensation from entering the state's cash-benefit system for uninsured unemployed people (Christensen, 2013, p 549). By being granted nine months of subsidised work, long-term unemployed people would regain their right to another two-and-a-half years of compensation, which would be succeeded by a second job offer (Kolstrup, 2013, p 201). This was the main function of such job offers up until the 1990s (Christensen, 2013, p 551).

However, the job offers contained other qualifications that would later be mobilised to criticise the same instrument. First, the most obvious was also the most implicit: by being given a job, unemployed people were put to work and hence deemed worthy in the city of **activity**. They would be 'activated', a term that would gradually become common in connection with the offers.[6] Second, the offers were also qualified in **paternal** terms. DA, the employers' confederation, supported the job offers, but only in their capacity as 'rehabilitation positions', implying incompetent unemployed people in need of basic competences (Christensen, 2013, p 550). Third, the job offers had a distinct **investment** element, since the jobs had to fit the qualifications of the unemployed person. This element was later strengthened by replacing the second job offer with a (re-)education offer (Kolstrup, 2013, p 201).

Fourth, the job offers were seen as a job creation strategy in accordance with the city of **demand** – hence the jobs should be 'productive and useful for society' (Christensen, 2013, p 557). Finally, the arrangement prepared the unemployment insurance system for a *redistributive* qualification that would later serve as both a justification of the unemployment insurance system and an object of critique. The jobs offered had to be paid according to collective agreements and, at the same time, they should be 'extraordinary' in order not to push wages down. However, the job offers also had an unintended consequence – that of extending the total compensation period to around nine years. This made it resemble something like the 'utopian' idea of a guaranteed 'basic income', which had gained intellectual and public impetus after the publication of the bestselling book *Revolt from the centre* (Meyer et al, 1978). Criticising one of the core dimensions in the city of **demand**, the three authors, a poet, a politician and a scientist, predicted the coming of the 'zero-growth society' and called for a 'society of economic equality' based on a minimum guaranteed basic income (Meyer et al, 1978; see also Petersen et al, 2013, p 100 onwards).

The job offers were, thus, embedded with tensions and radically different unemployed subjects: they should be productive (**demand**) but at the same time extraordinary, while rewarding equally with ordinary jobs (**redistribution**); they should provide the unemployed with new rights to compensation (**insurance**) while matching their qualifications and increase their employability (**investment**); and they should activate the inactive (**activity**) and rehabilitate the incompetent (**paternal**).

The black box of 'structural unemployment'

Apart from the specific **insurance**-related problems, the unemployment insurance system became part of a more general debate questioning the capacities and goals of the welfare state in relation to the labour market, which would frame the work of two government commissions leading up to the reform of ALMPA. In contrast with France, the Danish economy was booming in the mid-1980s, and unemployment only modestly decreased to around 8% in 1987, when the economy abruptly returned to recession.[7] 1987 was also a year with major wage rises. Leading economists were interpreting the events as a problem of 'structural unemployment' (Larsen and Andersen, 2009). This explanation entailed a radical test of Keynesian **demand** policies' narrow focus on conjectural unemployment. The reason why unemployment had remained relatively high was allegedly because the rate had approached the threshold of what two economists had earlier labelled the NIRU (non-inflationary rate of unemployment) (Modigliani and Papademos, 1975).[8] In a situation like this, demand- and consumption-oriented policies would only lead to increasing inflation and hence to a situation of coexisting economic stagnation, often labelled 'stagflation'. In 1989, the diagnosis became a central concern for the centre-right government in its White Paper on the 'structural problems of the labour market' (Torfing, 2004, p 181).

While the structural unemployment explanation was clear in its criticism of the city of **demand**, since existing unemployment was not conjectural (that is, caused by lack of demand for labour), job creation and consumption-oriented policies were basically useless, and there was no consensus about which 'structures' *were* causing it. Besides **demand**, the new qualification of unemployment rested beyond the scope of, and often in contradiction with, the cities of **insurance** and **redistribution**. Yet, as will be evident in the following sections, the **investment**, **incentives**, **activity** and **paternal** cities could all be mobilised to identify, and handle, unemployment-producing structures.

In 1991, two government commissions were set up to look into how to address the problem of structural unemployment. The first, named the Social Commission and chaired by Aase Olesen, the former minister of social affairs from the Social Liberal Party, *Radikale Venstre*,[9] was given the task of evaluating the role of benefit levels, including unemployment benefits, with the aim of getting more of the adult population included in the labour market. The second commission, the so-called Zeuthen Committee, would address the 'structural problems', specifically with regard to the unemployment insurance system concerning the 'activation' of unemployed people and the financing of the system.

Much of the existing analysis of the Danish labour market reforms has focused on the construction of this imperative to reform through the discourse of structural unemployment (Cox, 2001; Torfing, 2004; Larsen and Andersen, 2009). Without questioning its importance, it is only by analysing the process through which the broad discourse is qualified and turned into specific changes in instruments and institutions that the moral consequences and plurality of the shift become visible. Further, the idea of structural employment may have been a paradigm shift within economics, but in the politics of unemployment it entered a context of pre-existing critiques that also played their part in the reform process of ALMPA, such as the ideas of zero growth, sharing of labour and basic income mentioned earlier (**redistribution**). Furthermore, the diagnosis far from wiped out any mobilisation of **demand**-oriented justifications and instruments. Importantly, long before economists were convinced of the NIRU theory, numerous 'structural' explanations of unemployment were, as shown earlier, informing policy changes. The change, in other words, was a much more composite and gradual process. The following sections map four key test situations evolving from the debate surrounding the initial temporary law to the adoption of the final law around a year later, from how to explain the rising levels of unemployment to the three concrete tests involving financing, 'job offers' and 'job-rotation' schemes.

Qualifying labour and wages in- and outside the labour market

The story of the first test situation begins in spring 1992 when a temporary law to deal with record high unemployment rates was negotiated and adopted in parliament. **Demand** qualifications were not excluded from this debate, since all actors agreed that unlike the situation in 1987, current rates were not simply a matter of structural unemployment. For instance, an economist and member of the Social Commission estimated that 'the use of traditional economic policy could, as a matter of course, reduce unemployment from the current level, 11%, to somewhere between 7 and 8%'. Likewise, the centre-right and centre-left parties recognised **demand**-type unemployment. The Social Democrats advocated 'long-term investments in the societal infrastructure and expanded employment in selected parts of the public sector', whereas the centre-right government led by the Conservatives recommended increasing consumption through taxation and credit policies. One such policy, which was to become incorporated into the temporary law, was the creation of ten geographical so-called 'business zones' where businesses creating jobs would be enticed with favourable conditions, such as tax reductions and faster casework by public authorities, such as processing various applications, for the businesses that create jobs. The government justified the measure as a 'saline injection to particularly exposed areas' and emphasised that it was a 'temporary measure … to immediately add renewed growth'. Meanwhile, unions and Social Democrats were criticising the 'business oases' for making 'outlawing' employees by 'suspending all labour market laws so businesses can do as they please with employees and the environment', thus infringing the worth of citizenship and rights tied to **redistribution**.

The city of **redistribution** was also mobilised to justify another proposal to solve the lack of jobs, namely fairer work distribution. For instance, the newly established Unemployment Party argued that all the 'resources that were spent on the remedy of unemployment and repairing the damage' should rather be used for compensating the wage losses caused by work-time reduction (see also Jensen, 2008, p 303). Unlike in France, reduced working time would not be used as an instrument in Denmark. However, the temporary law did include an instrument that aimed to distribute work. The so-called 'job-rotation scheme' extended the rights of wage earners to take leave on the condition that an unemployed person replaced the leave taker. The leave, on the other hand, should be used for either education (**investment**) or childcare, thereby freeing scarce day-care resources to parents willing to work (**activity**).

Despite the economic crisis, the central concern of the debate, however, *was* the question of 'structural unemployment'. Concurrent with negotiations on the temporary law, the Social Commission would publish its first discussion paper, entitled *Sorting for life* (Socialkommissionen, 1992). The commission presented a somewhat sociological explanation that went well beyond its primary task of investigating the impact of benefits in terms of **incentives**. When presenting the report, Aase Olesen, the chair of the commission, spoke of a 'polarised society with a soaring group of marginalised and excluded people'. The commission qualified the group through the **investment**, **incentives** and **paternal** cities. First, excluded people had an educational deficit compared with their opposite number (**investment**). According to the commission, the risk of unemployment for the unskilled was twice as high as for those with a vocational education, and it thus concluded that 'a life with unemployment and benefits is inherited' (p 11). It also spoke of a 'lost generation' – young people in the early 1980s' recession that had never managed to get a hold in the labour market. Although members of this group were victims of stagnation, they had been failed by **demand** policies. The Social Democrats substantiated the heritage explanation: 'Elementary school teachers already speak of new behaviour from children from homes where none of the parents have ever had a job. It's a family pattern never seen before in history'. Thus, 'also, we must do something for their children'. In keeping with **investment** thinking, the commission proposed a special education for 'non-academic' students.

However, according to the commission, as well as the government and employers, the identification of an educational deficit was not necessarily an **investment** problem. Rather, it was both a problem of the level of benefits (**incentives**), and a **paternal** problem related to wage levels. With regard to the former, the question of whether benefits were reducing the incentive to work was extensively put to the test by the commission. The general conclusion, however, was that lack of **incentives** was not a problem for the large majority of the population receiving benefits. However, for certain 'marginal groups', young people and single parents, employment could result in reduced income. The government mobilised the findings as proof of an unemployment insurance system that was 'very generous' and where the 'high degree of coverage … deprives the lowest-paid [of] the economic incentives to work'. Unions, on the other hand, had little confidence in the city of incentives' premise of the 'economic man': to the Danish Confederation of Trade Unions (LO),[10] 'believing that by making the lives of people sufficiently miserable they will get themselves a job does not hold water'.

The problem with the **paternal** qualification did not (primarily) concern benefit levels, but rather the other side of the (un)employment threshold. According to the commission, if wage levels were too high young people would be 'tempted, after ending secondary school, by the fair wages of an unskilled worker and thereby [would] not even consider placing themselves in the danger zone of unemployment'. The commission thus associated the idea of the incompetent **paternal** subject in lack of self-control with the **investment** premise of education as a means of long-term employment security.

However, the **paternal** qualification also involved a more radical solution that would run counter to **investment**. The commission was highly sceptical of the capability of the education system to prevent exclusion and produce equal opportunity. While 80% of children from parents with superior positions would get an extended education and similar employment opportunities, the same would only apply to one third of children with unemployed parents. Thus, according to Olesen, the chair of the commission, 'even if you have the fortune to break from the family tradition and get an extended education, there's a still a larger risk of becoming unemployed if your parents don't have one. So even if you initially overcome the social inheritance, your parents still influence you'.

Further, the problem for this group was not simply *external* mechanisms of exclusion, but certain self-reinforcing mechanisms *within* the group. The commission had insisted on a 'no-work, no-money attitude' towards unemployed people, which, however, was somewhat ineffective as this group 'were incapable of taking care of themselves, let alone of others'. The commission hence proposed the **activity** solution of becoming active as a means to encourage responsibility in the **paternal** sense. Since the commission did not see any demand for this group on the labour market, there was no reason for them to be at its disposal. Further, the commission did not see much potential for investing in their employability. Hence, again combining **activity** and **paternal** elements, it proposed the establishment of a 'third labour market'. This neither private nor public labour market would encourage hitherto passively supported individuals to become active, thereby contributing to their own and society's welfare, gaining greater self-respect and relieving the system of a number of control functions, such as being at the disposal of the labour market. The jobs in this third labour market thus eliminated the need to test for potential idleness (**activity**). Similarly, an editorial in the centre-left newspaper *Politiken* called for a labour market operating at 'several speeds', with 'special zones' of 'jobs where the payroll costs and demands make room for the weakest'. Instead of improving their employability (the **investment** solution), unemployed people would get a job as well as a wage that would fit their low competence and function in non-market conditions. They *would* be active (**activity**) and even though their lack of competence made them less worthy than properly self-supporting persons, jobs for the 'weakest' did establish some degree of 'self-respect' by enabling these workers to use the (limited) competences they possessed (**paternal**). Later in the reform process, the new centre-left government argued for a similar instrument where 'groups without full work capacity' were offered 'minor tasks in well-defined employment areas without deductions in their benefits'. This instrument was a way of ensuring that everyone would 'have the chance of a life where you experience that there is a need for you and that you are good at something. But – the responsibility for how you want to live is your own'. The solution thus completely disregarded structural unemployment premise of limited supply of labour to the ordinary labour market. To proponents of the 'third labour market', the problem was not that unemployed people were excluded from the labour market, but simply that they were excluded from working (**activity**) and from being responsible in the sense of somehow providing for themselves (**paternal**).

The 'third labour market' solution was heavily criticised for the same reasons that its proponents advocated. The Economic Council, for instance, warned 'expressly' against a 'permanent "third labour market" where jobs are protected against the regular market economy'. 'Such an artificial labour market' would risk 'creating a situation where the two sides of industry neglect the real size of unemployment and hence agree on untenable wage increases'. In other words, the 'third labour market' would not reduce structural unemployment and lower the NIRU. Others disagreed that 'third labour market' could stand the **paternal** test and criticised it for not responsibilising unemployed people. For instance, a politician from the Social Liberal Party *Radikale Venstre* argued as follows:

> [People] with a lack of competences and opportunities for matching the requirement of the labour market of 37 hours of intensive and high-skilled work a week are put to one side. The situation now is so absurd that everybody talks about an alternative or third labour market – in reality a second-rate labour market where the deviants are placed under the responsibility of the public authorities.

The problem, however, was not the lack of competences as such (**investment**), but rather the **paternal** terms on which the measure was predicated. The lack of divergence in wage levels (a problem caused by **redistribution** measures of guaranteed wage levels) was preventing low-skilled jobs from being created, since they were deemed too costly. Wage levels, in other words, did not correspond to competences, thereby referring for public benefits a group of people who could have provided for themselves. An example of such an instrument, advocated by all the centre-right parties and the employers, was the so-called 'phase-in salary', a minor wage targeting unemployed youth in particular. Lower wages, corresponding to the (low) productivity of this group, was a means to provide low-skilled people with access to **paternal** worthiness. DA thus argued that 'the phase-in salary should be introduced for the sake of the weaker groups, such as the young or long-term unemployed with little attachment to the labour market – not for the sake of businesses'. It would underpin the idea of the responsible self-made person gaining worthiness (and monetary remuneration) through their own actions.

> What you are capable of, is decisive for what you get.... 'What you are capable of' is a combination of natural preconditions, wisdom and experiences. The latter is especially important when you want to carve a place on the labour market. Experiences grow and alongside you become more worthy to the enterprise that has bought your labour.

Proponents of both the 'third labour market' and the 'phase-in salary' typically wished to create non-skilled jobs for supposedly non-skilled, marginalised groups of unemployed people. As in the case of the aforementioned job-rotation scheme, training was only considered an instrument for wage earners. Both thus disregarded the possibility of **investment** in this group of unemployed people. For instance, the minister of education from *Venstre* criticised the 'misunderstanding that unemployment is the result of the unemployed not being sufficiently talented'. It was not 'education that creates jobs but rather the other way round'. The minister thus encouraged social partners to 'reduce the wage increases for vulnerable groups and limit educational and professional barriers as well as rigid wage systems'.

Mobilising the city of **redistribution**, the 'phase-in salary' was strongly criticised by Social Democrats, who 'refused to support a policy of increasing wage inequality'. According to LO, lowering 'the wage in the extreme and [taking] away all social goods, could create an underground economy that would flourish as nicely as in Hong Kong'. Aligning with the city of **investment**'s preference for skills, LO did not 'feel inclined to believe that shoe-shiner jobs and other unqualified jobs ought to contribute to solving the problems of Danish society'. As a way of accommodating this **redistribution**-based criticism of the 'phase-in salary' and making it more 'digestible', one economist proposed to use 'tax subsidies; when businesses pay salaries according to qualifications, the salary is replenished by the tax system so the result is a socially acceptable total income'.

Despite the fact that none of the exact proposals of the 'phase-in salary' or 'third labour market' was implemented, the temporary law introduced instruments that accommodated their logics. For instance, it gave employers the opportunity to get a long-term unemployed person 'on probation' for two weeks, while the said person would still receive unemployment benefits. In addition, all insured unemployed people under 25 would be offered a job after six months with a salary corresponding to their unemployment benefits, thus at a much lower rate than the negotiated minimum wage. The law also introduced a so-called 'foals' scheme', where young uninsured people would work in public jobs for a reduced training salary.

Financing put to the test

Alongside the more general debate initiated by the Social Commission, the Zeuthen Committee published recommendations that specifically targeted the 'structural problems' of the unemployment insurance system (Udredningsudvalget, 1992). Part of the work concerned the financing of the system. In line with the reasoning of the diagnosis of structural unemployment, the Zeuthen Committee was concerned with how to 'make unemployment more visible'. If the unions negotiating wages could more clearly see the negative consequences of (excessive) wage increases (inflation, reduced competitiveness for firms, and eventually unemployment), so the argument went, the wage levels could be stabilised.

While the committee addressed the problem of 'structural unemployment', its recommendations were curiously based on ideas and instruments from the city of **insurance**. For instance, the committee suggested using 'differentiated contributions', making the individual contributions depend on the risk of unemployment in the given profession or industry. Employees in jobs with a low risk of unemployment paid lower fees than those with in jobs with high levels of unemployment. The solution nourished a pre-existing debate on whether some industries were (ab)using the unemployment insurance system more than others. Employers in the financial sector had complained that industries with jobs on short-notice terms were 'tapping more into the unemployment insurance system than we do' and hence called for differentiated contributions according to the length of the terms of notice.

The idea of differentiated contributions, however, was exposed to **redistribution** critique, pointing to the fact that membership of the Danish scheme was voluntary. Even the centre-right newspaper *Berlingske* noted that the outcome of differentiated contributions would be that 'all those with low risk within the existing unemployment funds will try to move to funds with low risk', thereby pulling them together in different 'risk pools', which would 'probably have unacceptable distributional consequences'. Similarly, but in stronger language, the Social Democrats stated that differentiated contributions were 'antisocial. Those, who are exposed the most to unemployment shouldn't pay the most'.

The Zeuthen Committee also rebooted the aforementioned recurring **insurance** test of employers' abuse of insurance to lay off workers in 'quiet' periods. The metal workers' union claimed that around 170,000 lay-offs a year simply functioned as 'relief' for employers. This justified the committee's proposal to let employers pay for the second day of unemployment, which was strongly opposed by the employers themselves. For instance, employers in the construction industry argued that short-term lay-offs were simply due to weather conditions and criticised how the committees' 'distinguished economists can believe that master builder Hansen[11] can control God and the weather. Expectations of this kind ought to belong to the faculty of theology.' Another **insurance** proposal of differentiated contributions came from the DA, which called for an 'actual insurance system' by allowing high earners to pay a larger fee in order to get a compensation closer to the wage level of their industry.

While all these **insurance** solutions were shelved, the idea that there was a need to make unemployment more 'visible' for the two sides of industry by letting them contribute more survived. The final finance reform of the unemployment insurance system, which officially became part of a tax reform and not ALMPA, is noteworthy because it provided an instrument that would requalify the role of **insurance** in the system. I will return to this after the following section.

Requalifying the purpose of job offers

During discussions on financing, the job offers scheme was crucially put to the test by various critiques. First, from the perspective of the city of **redistribution**, employers' motivation for offering these jobs was seen as exploitation, and had the effect of making different groups of workers compete against each other.[12] A number of stories in the media showed how both private and public employers were using unemployed people enrolled in the job offer scheme as regular labour. In the private sector, the phenomenon was especially widespread in the restaurant business, which used what were known as 'cheap girls' as permanent staff. One worker who had been employed through the job-offer scheme reported having 'applied for work down here and [being] told that I could get a subsidy from my municipality'. According to the restaurant business workers' union, it was 'unfortunately the exception if an employer hires an unemployed person with wage subsidies as extraordinary labour. They are hired as cheap labour for tasks that are absolutely necessary. And by constantly renewing [the contract of] the unemployed who are temporarily employed, a part of the regular labour force is in reality replaced by the unemployed'. An economist from the Zeuthen Committee labelled the job offers 'badly disguised state subsidies to businesses' where the 'long-term unemployed in job offers were stealing jobs from the permanently employed'. The job offers seemed to serve a similar function in the public sector. Social Democrats called it 'grotesque when the municipality of Copenhagen lays off 2,000 of the permanent staff in order to make room for 1,500 long-term unemployed'. According to a union representing low-skilled local authority employees, 'it often happens that local authority employees are fired, and then two years later are back in the same job as long-term unemployed'. As a way of addressing this critique, the then Conservative minister of labour suggested tying the job-offer scheme to the job-rotation scheme, thereby avoiding a situation where 'others are pushed aside, once the unemployed move in'.

The second critique of the job-offer scheme concerned its function for unemployed people. As seen earlier, when the scheme was created in 1978, its main legitimating function was to enable unemployed people to retain their right to compensation. Such **insurance**-based justification was now criticised, which allowed for a complete repositioning of the job-offer scheme. Qualified according to the **paternal** city, *Venstre* denounced the rationale of job offers for having 'the underlying purpose of bringing people back on passive relief'. Terms like 'incubator youth' and the 'put-away-factory' flourished. The chair of *Radikale Venstre*, Marianne Jelved, joined in and found it 'plainly offensive … when young people are "sneaked" into the unemployment insurance system through artificial municipal employment projects. Hereafter, everyone thinks that everything in the garden is lovely.… It is an easy solution, but, to me, at the same time, an indecent solution'. Likewise, the Social Commission called for putting an end to 'riding on the eternal merry-go-round of unemployment' and suggested removing the right to regain entitlement for compensation by employment in the job offers.

The right to regain entitlement was also criticised from the perspective of the city of **investment**. The argument here was that the job offers should serve the purpose of improving the qualifications of unemployed people and thus increasing their prospects of finding a regular job. According to two economists from the committee, the right to regain entitlement was 'making it difficult to advance and "tailor" the activation offers'. It implied 'the danger of, in practice, limiting the aim of activation [and] securing for the unemployed another round in the unemployment insurance system', with the result that the unemployed person 'gradually loses qualifications, job training and self-confidence'. Apart from removing the right to regain entitlement, one solution was to 'expedite the time for the activation offers for particularly vulnerable groups'. The city of **investment** now not only addressed the needs of insiders on the labour market, but also those of the unemployed. Although the term 'activation' would henceforth stick to job offers and other schemes targeting unemployed people, the strengthening of educational **investment** would problematise the singular **activity** aim of 'activating' the unemployed.

The tension between **investment** and **activity**, between activation as enhancing qualifications and as work, was put to the test in 1993 when the Social Democrats formed a new coalition government with *Radikale Venstre* and two other small centre-right parties. It was hence up to the new government to shape the reform that would replace the temporary laws adopted less than a year before. As a result of the criticism, it was clear that the job-offer scheme had to be addressed in the reform. However, although the new Social Democrat minister of labour, Jytte Andersen, considered job offers an 'evil on the labour market', she did not intend to abolish the scheme 'because, you see, if we did that, the unemployed would be kicked out of the unemployment insurance system after two-and-a-half years. Today, the job offers are a condition for keeping unemployment benefits'. The job offers thus served a legitimate insurance purpose.

Meanwhile, the minister repositioned the job-offer scheme as the solution to another problem residing in the city of **demand**. Andersen wanted 'to find better ways of making use of' the unemployment funds and, here, job offers could be a way of creating jobs. At the same time she distanced herself from **activity** solutions of reducing unemployment by making unemployed people more active and mobile. 'We must not activate the unemployed. We must activate the funds so they can be used for generating employment.' The minister hence wanted to abolish the requirement (that was based on **insurance**) of preventing the unemployed person from making use of a job offer before their entitlement to compensation was about to expire. Andersen also intended to relax the **activity** requirements of 'being at the disposal of the labour market', that is, having to apply for a number of jobs every week:

> In a situation with such high unemployment, we could turn a blind eye to the ones who have already received 50 rejections. For instance, today there are 200 shoe factory workers but only 12 jobs remain. Today the shoe factory workers must, alternately, apply for the same jobs. It's utter nonsense.

Demand was further used as a justification for the responsibility of the government to create jobs. The reform thus presupposed 'that the wheels start turning as well as the creation of activity in society, otherwise it won't function as intended'. By the same logic, the metal workers' union had urged the previous government to 'spend time on creating jobs rather than simply "stirring the pot"'.

The **demand** rationale of the situation also provided scope for the city of **redistribution**. At least in this period of recession, the unemployed person should be allowed to do things that are first and foremost worthy tasks related to being a citizen – activities, according to the minister, in areas such as 'culture or in the housing association'. Education could also be qualified in this way. According to SiD, the largest union representing unskilled workers, 'people should have the right to choose an education that provides them joy for the rest of their lives. It's better to educate people to become whole persons than qualify them narrowly for jobs which don't exist anyway'. The technicians' union went further and wanted to 'free the unemployed from being at the disposal of the labour market', abolish the job offers and offer all unemployed people an unconditional 'citizen's income'.

However, the response to the latter proposal revealed that there were limits to the minister's critique of **activity**. To Andersen, the proposal entailed enabling the unemployed person to 'withdraw from being available' and essentially introducing a guaranteed basic income, which was perceived as 'dangerous to our responsibility towards the unemployed'. The requirement to be available to the labour market was in fact, according to the minister, a legitimate way of responsibilising the governing authorities. Adjusting the balance within the city of **activity**, Andersen wanted public authorities to 'attach greater importance to the quality of the jobseeking rather than the quantity'.

The government's solution was, in something that was reminiscent of the ideas of the 'third labour market', to establish 'flexible employment areas' by 'activating unemployment benefits … in employment projects on the condition that some of the unemployed, without optimal labour power, are hired'. In justifying this solution, the minister would oscillate between **activity** and **paternal** cities. The fact that these projects would not 'create export trade' was also relevant:

> We must live up to the obligation that people must have a reason to get out of bed. One can be annoyed about the people sitting on the benches with their big dogs and drinking beers. They've had some opportunities, but perhaps no demands were made on them. Yes, of course, we too have a responsibility here, but I believe that the reorientation to quid pro quo is a timely arrival.

The lack of responsible behaviour was thus rooted in a lack of conditions and requirements (**paternal**). Not only would the 'new' job offers 'mobilise' unemployed people by giving them 'a reason to get out of bed', they would also increase flexibility among the working population by enabling them to act as 'service personnel at train stations' or carry out tasks such as '"fever patrols", nursing sick children for parents with a job outside the home' (**activity**).

It was not only the **activity** and **paternal** cities that provided justification for the further use of coercion. Echoing previous

investment-based calls for more 'tailored' activation, the minister argued for measures to take effect 'much earlier'. Moreover:

> [T]he offers must be targeted at the labour market-related needs of the unemployed individual. Not all have the same needs. In my opinion it must be a right for the unemployed individual, but also a duty to ensure that the individual receives the targeted offer.

Rights thus not only had to be less 'categorical' but also become 'duties'. The fusion of rights and duties would thus answer the **investment** challenge of how to ensure that unemployed people in fact invested in themselves and make use of their (equalising) opportunities.

The plurality of these justifications took the job-offer scheme far from its initial function of enabling unemployed people to regain entitlement to compensation. Although the government still justified the 'non-abolishment' of the scheme with the city of **insurance**, it was a matter of protecting unemployed people; the new arrangements would gradually sediment and turn the job offers into something else. The final ALMPA is the first proof of this dynamic and thus marks a 'tipping point' towards activation.

The ambiguous worth of job rotation

As mentioned earlier, the temporary law of 1992 had introduced various leave schemes, named 'job rotation', to provide unemployed people with entry points into work. A year later, the ambitious scheme appeared to have failed. Only a fraction of the expected participants had made use of the scheme. Unions, however, still saw a great potential in job rotation as a means labour redistribution: 'If only 5% of the labour force is permanently in job rotation, we can create 100,000 new jobs'. Earlier a Social Democrat mayor had also argued for the use of job rotation as a way of 'better distributing the remaining labour'. In addition, it would 'reduce the number of people who ought to have a job offer'.

According to the government, the barrier preventing widespread use of the scheme was the employers' requirement to replace the employee who was on leave with an unemployed person. Although it was still justified for **redistribution** purposes, the abandonment of the requirement would displace the scope of the scheme. Its purpose was no longer necessarily to tackle unemployment, but to 'prevent lay-offs'. In this way the new job-rotation scheme was decoupled from unemployment, while the leave element could be used for **investment** in further training for employees, or possibly for unconditional 'sabbatical leave'. The latter would function as a kind of **activity** reward that was only granted to those with at least three years of employment. **Activity** was also evident in the overall justification of job rotation, since it was a way to 'make the labour market more supple, thus getting more rotation and increasing dynamism in society'.

Sabbatical leave, however, was seen as unattractive to those imbued with a strong work ethic of **activity**. One employment consultant explained that 'for better or for worse, work is at the centre of an adult life. Outside of it – weekends and holidays – are short periods in which one, pure and simple, is 'off duty'. If you have the same conception of leave, it is understandable that a leave of 13 weeks instead of three is no longer that attractive'. This consultant hence suggested establishing 'leave counselling', where unemployed people would be advising others on 'how to set up goals and plan how to create growth and development in a period of leave'. This proposal, however, was not adopted in the final ALMPA legislation.

Sedimentation and subsequent changes

It probably comes as no surprise that, having addressed all the arguments advanced by these tests, the final reform adopted by the parliament consisted of a composite and rather complex set of instruments and laws.[13]

With regard to financing, the idea of strengthening the **insurance** elements was abandoned in favour of tax reform. Whereas the state's contributions to the insurance funds had been part of its core budget, they were now separated into three funds dealing with unemployment benefits, activation and sick pay respectively. The contributions would be collected by a special 'labour market contribution' from gross earnings that would be adjusted every two years.[14] This would accommodate the wish of LO for an 'economic connection between unemployment benefits and activation'. In this way, the costs of unemployment were made visible, but at the same time the reform would, from the perspective of the taxpaying working population, justify further scrutiny and tests concerning the costs and effects of activation.

The pivotal elements of the reform, however, concerned leave, activation and job offers. With regard to the former, the modification of the scheme downplayed the aim of distributing labour between people in work and the unemployed (**redistribution**), in favour of increasing 'dynamism' (**activity**), qualifications (**investment**) and labour distribution, with the aim of *preventing* people in work from becoming unemployed. Now, only the sabbatical leave obliged the employer to replace the employee with an unemployed person.[15]

However, educational and childcare leave schemes were extended to unemployed people as part of the final reforms. Educational leave granted unemployed people the right to up to a year's participation in an educational programme (**investment**). During such time they would still receive unemployment benefits, but the period would not count within the overall period of entitlement.[16]

The activation and job-offer elements were integrated into a system where, much like the French PARE, enrolment begins with the formulation of an 'individual action plan'. The plan describes the 'employment goals of the unemployed', outlining 'activities to achieve the goals', which are informed by 'the wishes and qualifications of the unemployed, considering the needs of the labour market'.[17] Benefits are retained if the unemployed person 'without satisfactory reason refuses to participate in the preparation of the action plan, or refuses an offer with reference to the action plan'.[18] Next to **insurance**-based tests that look backwards to test whether unemployment is self-inflicted[19] the ALMPA introduces instruments that are 'continuously revised', with the ever-present possibility of putting the unemployed person's present and future actions to the test. The pre-existing **activity** obligation to be 'at the disposal of the labour market' (§62) also did this, but the action plan allows for a greater variety of instruments related to both **paternal** and **investment** cities. Further, the plan normalises the possibility of sanctions in case of refusal. Figure 5.2 illustrates the requalification of the job offers into the new 'job offer' scheme.

There are basically three possible 'activities' within the action plan. The first activity is 'job training', which is similar to the job-offer scheme, but with the significant difference that it can be introduced from day one and not only once the right to compensation is about to expire. Another notable change is that while subsidised work previously requalified the unemployed person for compensation, job training is part of the entitlement period.[20] Job training accommodates the city of **activity**, but in response to **redistribution** criticism, the salary must be set 'according to collective agreements' and not be 'anti-competitive'.[21] The second activity accommodating **investment** is education, which can be either 'ordinary educational activities' or a 'specifically arranged educational programme' (§16). The third activity is a 'specifically arranged job-training course', which is only

Figure 5.2: Requalification of the 'job-offer' scheme

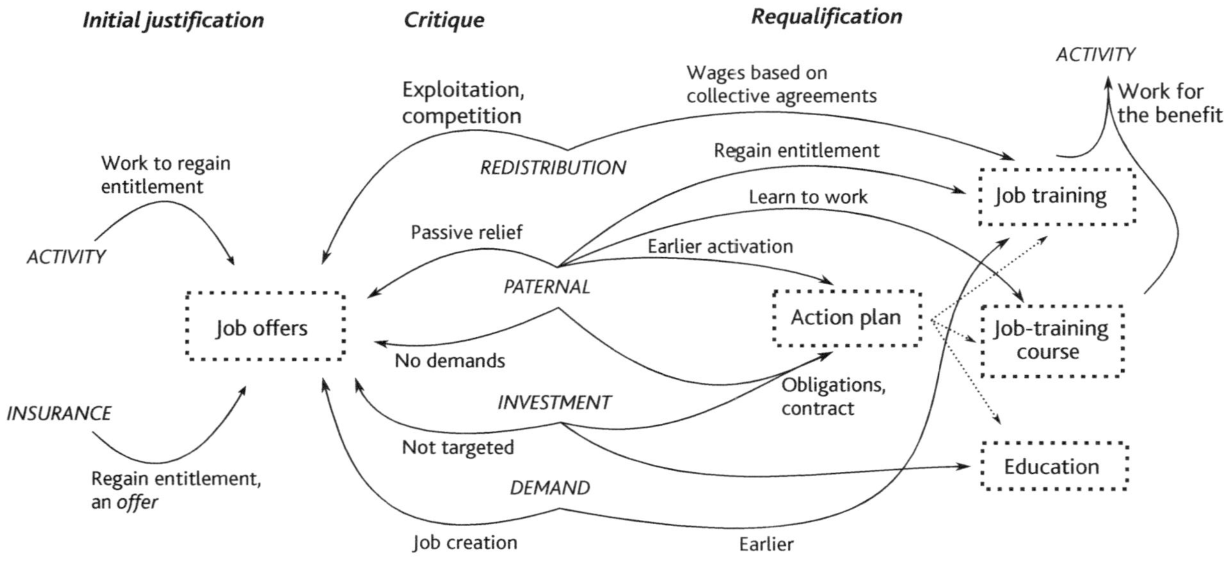

for unemployed people 'with difficulties obtaining employment under normal wage and working conditions' (§22). In other words, these are jobs for the 'incompetent' of the **paternal** city in need of training in order to work, consisting of activities 'which would otherwise not be carried out by ordinary paid labour' (§22).

ALMPA also changed the periods of benefit entitlement. At first sight, the change from a total period of around nine years to seven appears modest in quantitative terms. However, the qualitative changes relating to what takes place *within* the period are radical. First, the distinction between periods of compensation and periods of work (such as job offers) that requalify unemployed people for compensation no longer exists. Instead, the entitlement period is split into two 'part periods' of four and three years. The first period consists of at least one year of activities based on the action plan, mentioned earlier. In the second period, efforts must be targeted towards 'full-time activities' (§33). If this is not possible, the unemployed person 'receives an offer of employment of an average of 20 hours' (§34). This univocal objective of working in the second period removes the qualification of the unemployed as in of compensation (insurance). The unemployed person is no longer compensated, but exclusively rewarded for their 'active' behaviour, which is evaluated according to how they are qualified. Do they have potential for acquiring qualifications (**investment**)? Are they simply having difficulties putting themselves at the disposal of the labour market (**activity**)? Or are they basically unemployable with little potential (**paternal**)? In this way, unemployed people are continually put to the test, a test that, as the law states, is based on 'discretion' as opposed to facts (§3). If one instrument fails, the unemployed person is requalified, action plans are revised, and another instrument, or 'combination' of instruments (§25), is tested. The experimental character of the new arrangement is underlined by the fact that the unemployed person may be offered other 'trial and development initiatives' apart from the activities listed earlier (§26).

Thus, by requalifying a few instruments with relatively minor adjustments, ALMPA tipped the whole unemployment insurance system towards activation. This is not to say that the unemployment insurance system from one day to the next was 'active' or 'activated', but rather that it was now *prepared* for consecutive tests and transformations that would only strengthen activation aims. Further, the activation of ALMPA cannot be placed in the 'good' against 'bad' activation dichotomy presented in Chapter 1. Unlike Torfing (1999, 2004) who sees ALMPA as an example of 'good' activation, containing 'empowerment' and enhancing 'human capital', as opposed to 'bad' 'quid pro quo' and use of 'motivation, control and punishment', this chapter has shown that 'good' and 'bad' elements are completely intertwined in the justifications as well as the instruments of ALMPA.

This has certainly been the case in Denmark since ALMPA. Since 1993, all serious talk about job sharing and a guaranteed citizen's income have died away (Kolstrup, 2014, p 228). Rather, consecutive reforms have aimed to increase unemployed people's motivation by shortening the entitlement period to four year in 1998 and to two years in 2010 (**incentives**), strengthening obligations to be available and geographically mobile (**activity**), and speeding up and intensifying activation measures (Christensen and Petersen, 2014). Reforms since 2003 have toned down the educational possibilities in favour of **incentives**, by lowering benefits (justified by criticism from several commissions of the 'generosity' of the system) (Christensen, 2017),[22] and **activity** measures, by intensifying jobseeking requirements and control and raising employment requirements in order to qualify for benefit entitlement (Christensen and Petersen, 2014, pp 644, 662).

The reduction of the entitlement period (and hence the city of **incentives**) was seriously put to the test in the aftermath of the North Atlantic financial crisis when a large and unforeseen number of unemployed people were in danger of losing their right to entitlement. However, the test and criticism process only resulted in minor changes in favour of **insurance** and **demand** measures, such as temporarily extending the entitlement period and encouraging the creation of 'emergency jobs' through state subsidies (Mailand, 2015), and intensifying other activation instruments. Although a reform in 2012 temporarily increased the entitlement period by six months, its main 'solution' was more intense and personalised instruments (from the city of **activity**), such as the so-called 'job alert', giving unemployed people a right to fast and extraordinary support to find a job (Kolstrup, 2014, pp 705–7).

The final outcome of the handling of the crisis was the establishment of an unemployment insurance commission in 2014 that was to deliver recommendations for reforming the system within a year. The commission's recommendations were almost literally translated into a reform the same year (effective from 2017). The most remarkable innovation was the introduction of insights from behavioural economics to help adjust the system. The commission used behavioural economics to question the assumption (in the city of **incentives**) that people always do what is 'rational and give them the biggest utility in the long perspective' (Dagpengekommissionen, 2015, p 19). Instead, behavioural economics [rather: instead, the commission relied] relied on a distinct **paternal** qualification of the unemployed subject. According to this rationale, since unemployed people think in the short term, have 'weak self-control' and are 'overoptimistic', they often make irrational decisions (Dagpengekommissionen, 2015, p 19). In a compromise with **incentives** and **activity**, the commission used these 'insights' to introduce measures such as a 'one-day waiting period' every four months and 'flexible' means to regain entitlement. Such instruments would spell out the long-term (monetary) interests for the 'incompetent' (**incentives**) and make sure unemployed people are always 'in search of all possible types of jobs, including the very short-term and those with a low wage' (**activity**) (Dagpengekommissionen, 2015, p 26).

Recently, unions have criticised the lowering benefit levels for no longer providing proper compensation and income security (**insurance**). To compensate, the unions have threatened to demand more job security (such as longer terms of notice), thus breaking the compromise of the 'Danish model' of the flexicurity of trading high compensation rates for low job protection. Future collective bargaining will tell whether this new dynamic will manifest in policy changes.

Notes

[1] A note on methods. Since the Infomedia database had not registered *Jyllandsposten* electronically for the period of the first Danish case described, this section only refers to articles from two newspapers, *Politiken* and *Berlingske*. However, since the reform was heavily debated over a long period of time, the database nonetheless has the biggest sample of articles overall. Since *Jyllandsposten* does not differ radically in its political position on welfare matters from *Berlingske*, its inclusion would most likely not lead to any new qualifications or critiques.

[2] Exact references to quotations can be found in Hansen (2017).

[3] Folk high schools are private school (subsidised by the state) providing non-formal education for adults, independent of the normal educational system.

[4] Today, *Venstre* presents itself as a liberal centre-right party.

[5] DA is the umbrella organisation that represents most private employers' industry associations.

[6] The use of 'activation' as a collective designation for the instruments aiming at moving unemployed people off benefits and into employment gained a footing in relation to the introduction of the so-called 'youth allowance' in 1990 (Kolstrup, 2013, p 214 onwards; Torfing, 2004, p 171). See also Chapter 7, pp 147–50.

[7] The numbers relate to national Danish statistics. Looking at the Organisation for Economic Co-operation and Development's harmonised unemployment rates, the Danish unemployment rate in fact dropped to below 5% in 1986.

[8] Modigliani and Papademos' theory was a refinement of Edmun Phelps and Milton Friedman's theories of a 'natural rate of unemployment' that radically questioned the Phillips curve's alleged inverse relation between the rate of inflation and unemployment (Friedman, 1968; Phelps, 1968).

[9] Traditionally placed in the very centre of Danish politics, *Radikale Venstre* has participated in several centre-right as well as centre-left governments. The party was thus both part of the centre-right government led by the conservatives from 1988–90 as well as the government led by the social democrats from 1993–2000.

[10] LO, representing skilled and unskilled workers as well as workers with short-term further education in both the public and private sector, was, and still is, the largest confederation of trade unions.

[11] Common Danish surname.

[12] The term was not yet part of Danish lingua at the time, but the critique resembled a dynamic of 'social dumping'.

[13] The reason why *Venstre* and the conservatives rejected the reform, despite the fact that it contained an array of their own proposals, was primarily because they were never invited to the negotiations, which only took place between the four parties in government (Torfing, 2004, p 206).

[14] Folketinget, *Lov om arbejdsmarkedsfonde*, 1993. København: Skatteministeriet.

[15] Folketinget, *Lov om orlov*, 1993. København: Beskæftigelsesministeriet. §9.

[16] Folketinget, *Lov om ændring af lov om arbejdsformidling og arbejdsløshedsforsikring m.v. (Arbejdskravet, dagpengeperioden m.v.)*, 1993. København: Beskæftigelsesministeriet. §55.

[17] Folketinget, *Lov om en aktiv arbejdsmarkedspolitik*, 1993. København: Beskæftigelsesministeriet.

[18] Folketinget, *Lov om ændring af lov om arbejdsformidling og arbejdsløshedsforsikring m.v. (Arbejdskravet, dagpengeperioden m.v.)*, 1993. København: Beskæftigelsesministeriet. §16.

[19] Folketinget, *Bekendtgørelse af lov om arbejdsformidling og arbejdsløshedsforsikring m.v.*, 1992. København: Beskæftigelsesministeriet.

[20] Folketinget, *Lov om ændring af lov om arbejdsformidling og arbejdsløshedsforsikring m.v. (Arbejdskravet, dagpengeperioden m.v.)*, 1993. København: Beskæftigelsesministeriet. §12, 21.

[21] Folketinget, *Lov om en aktiv arbejdsmarkedspolitik*, 1993. København: Beskæftigelsesministeriet. §13, 14.

[22] The average compensation rate dropped from 63% in 1980 to 47% in 2018.

6

Testing thresholds:
social assistance, France, 2007–08

The process of reforming the active solidarity income (henceforth RSA) was launched at the end of 2007, which was at the beginning of Nicolas Sarkozy's presidency. RSA replaced the minimum insertion income (RMI), which had been in place since 1988. RMI had introduced both a guaranteed minimum income and measures that would aim to reintegrate the recipient into society and/or the labour market, and was organised in a contract between the recipient and the state. RSA entailed a negative tax scheme to increase incentives for recipients to take low-paid, part-time work, while also introducing a number of instruments and obligations with the aim of increasing the activity of the unemployed person. The reform also introduced intensified control of the financial behaviour of the recipient's household. Figure 6.1 provides an overview of the key events during the debate up to the passing of RSA.

The chapter is structured as follows. The first section analyses the creation of RMI with a view to presenting how the scheme was the result of compromises between certain cities of unemployment, as well as looking into subsequent modifications of the scheme. The next section addresses how the justification of RSA was closely linked to a specific critique of RMI where certain cities of unemployment were mobilised while others were denounced. The third section presents how RSA qualified and aimed to increase the worth of unemployed subjects belonging to a number of cities. The following three sections present three test situations involving, first, the behaviour of the recipient; second, the threshold between part-time and full-time work; and third, the financing of RSA. Finally, the chapter concludes with an analysis of the sedimentation of tests in the adopted law and a brief look at reforms of succeeding governments.[1]

The rise of the will to include the excluded

As mentioned in Chapter 4, the French postwar unemployment system was mainly composed of corporatist, contribution-based schemes and a tax-financed system of 'assistance' for the most needy. The 1970s

Figure 6.1: Timeline of the RSA reform process

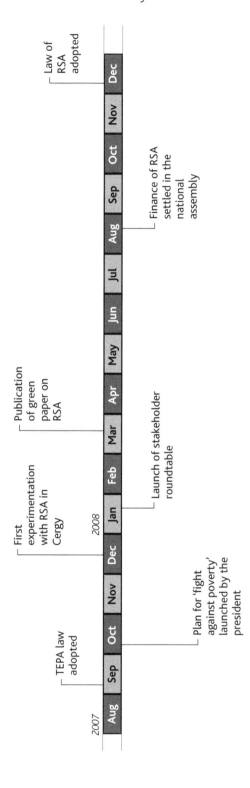

and 1980s state-led schemes of 'solidarity' were established to target the increasing number of unemployed people who had exhausted their rights and hence fell between the unemployment insurance and assistance systems. Despite the introduction of solidarity schemes in the 1980s, there were still groups without any rights to support (Béraud and Eydoux, 2011, p 132). For instance, the most important solidarity scheme, ASS, required the unemployed to have completed five years of work during the preceding ten years, thus leaving a large number of unemployed without entitlement (Daniel and Tuchszirer, 1999, p 325). This created a longstanding test situation in which the 'usual' instruments, especially those based on the **insurance** logics of contribution and compensation, were deemed inappropriate, causing substantial uncertainty as to how to qualify and handle these groups politically. The major substantial political response, a result of a compromise between several cities of unemployment, only came in 1988 with the establishment of the RMI.

In the 1970s, this hitherto marginal group of long-term unemployed people were labelled 'the new poor', subject to the equally new phenomenon of 'social exclusion'. The term had already been introduced in 1965 by the sociologist Jules Klanfer (Béland, 2007b, p 126) whose book, *Social exclusion* (Klanfer, 1965), provided a rather **paternal** explanation as to why a large number of French citizens were decoupled from the prosperous effects of the economy. Klanfer, for instance, spoke of 'personal traits' that characterised unemployed people, such as 'indecisiveness', 'lack of maturity' and an 'absence of the notion of social and personal responsibility' (Klanfer, 1965, p 69).

In the late 1970s, social exclusion entered the political debate and was coupled with policies of 'insertion'. Here social exclusion involved other qualifications. In accordance with the city **redistribution**, the problem of social exclusion was a problem of citizenship (Barbier and Fargion, 2004, p 442). In the French context, this involved social, economic and political participation, from which unemployed people were excluded and where poverty was seen as the main barrier (Béland and Hansen, 2000, p 56). This policy test was not new as such, but had been debated at least since the economist and businessman, Jacques Duboin, introduced the notion of a 'distributive economy' in the 1930s, calling for a state-guaranteed basic income. In the 1980s, increasingly popular Christian associative movements, such as Emmaüs and ATD Quart Monde, were influential in revitalising these ideas as means to tackle social exclusion.

In 1985, ATD Quart Monde, an organisation established by the Catholic priest Joseph Wresinski in the 1950s, initiated a local experiment in Rennes with an additional minimum income. Later, Wresinski chaired an influential government commission on poverty and social and economic precariousness, which in 1987 proposed a programme very similar to what became the RMI (Palier, 2002, p 306), which clearly mobilised the repertoire of **redistribution**. The report estimated that around 400,000 people were without social protection coverage, but by visiting, and documenting the accounts of, people living in extreme poverty, the work of the commission went beyond statistical descriptions of poverty. Wresinski thus challenged the traditional division between the 'unworthy' and 'worthy' poor embedded in the existing system of assistance. Rather, the poor were represented as 'partners' and citizens with right to a minimum income beyond the most basic needs because of the additional costs of a 'physical' urban life as well as of 'social participation' (Wresinski, 1987, p 64).

Concurrent with the **redistribution** qualification, the dynamics causing exclusion in the 1970s and 1980s were represented as inherently complex and related to the **investment** problem of unequal opportunities. It was a book by René Lenoir, a civil servant, from 1974 entitled *The excluded: One Frenchman out of ten* that managed to reposition social exclusion (Lenoir, 1974; see Béland, 2007b, p 126). Although Lenoir recognised material inequality as an element of social exclusion, he did not see it as the main driver. According to Lenoir, social exclusion rather derived from a complex array of factors related to urbanisation and industrialisation, aggravating and concentrating processes of mental, physical and social 'unsuitability'. Put to the test, policies were worthy if they 'prevent, rather than cure' and were able to address the complexity of the phenomenon of social exclusion, by engaging various 'craftsmen of social action' such as teachers, psychologists, social workers, associations and so on (p 84). The **investment** ideas also informed the Wresinski commission, whose report recognised that besides having at one's disposal the 'means of existence allowing to prepare the future for oneself and one's children', one should be able reap 'the fruit of one's human capital in order for the social and cultural exclusion to deteriorate' (Wresinski, 1987, p 64).

It was in this context that the non-contributory scheme of RMI was finally created in 1988.

Although the specific content of RMI was widely debated, it was unanimously adopted by the national assembly. The debate concerned how to assuage the tension between the aforementioned **redistribution** and **investment** tests as well as **activity** elements. The Socialist minister of solidarity, health and social protection, Claude Évin, had justified RMI in the national assembly in distinct **redistribution** terms as the 'prolongation of great republican principles' in which 'the right to insertion was naturally first the assurance of minimal resources' (Assemblée nationale, 1988b, p 633). He also referenced president François Mitterrand's famous 'Letter to all Frenchmen' from earlier in the same year, calling for a tax-financed minimum income to ensure that 'a means of living, or rather surviving, is guaranteed to those who have nothing, who can do nothing, who is nobody. This is the precondition for their social reinsertion'. The scheme was hence meant for those with little to no income and incapable of working (Palier, 2002, p 323). However, the incapacity was not only related to the age and the mental and physical condition of the unemployed but, importantly, also to the situation of the economy and employment. It thus disregarded the **paternal** distinction between those who can (and should) work and those who cannot (compare Castel, 1995, p 695).

However, in order to receive the minimum income, the RMI introduced an 'insertion contract' between the recipient and 'society' in which the recipient committed to engaging in an 'insertion project', with activities encompassing health, housing and counselling, and activities that targeted employment, such as professional or educational internships (**investment**) (Barbier and Théret, 2001, pp 161–2; Palier, 2002, p 324). On the one hand, mobilising arguments of **investment**, the government justified the contract as an instrument to ensure a project 'adapted to the social situation, adapted to the capacities of the persons, and in particular discussed with them' (Assemblée nationale, 1988b, p 633). On the other hand, the Socialist rapporteur, mobilising arguments of **redistribution**, argued that the minimum income ought to be a 'right' and hence non-negotiable and detached from a contract (Assemblée nationale, 1988b, p 641). The RMI did introduce conditionality, but only the possibility of sanctions, in cases where the recipient was not committed to the contract, a possibility that was offset in periods and places with low levels of job creation (Barbier, 2011, p 52). The benefit was hence positioned 'somewhere in between a totally non-conditional benefit and a benefit that was conditional on compliance' (Barbier, 2013, p 163), leaving it to local authorities to decide on the balance between unconditional **redistribution** and conditional **investment** instruments. In practice, however, RMI mainly came to serve the **redistribution** aim. The aim of upskilling was challenged by the problem of a lack of resources and overloaded institutions. Only half of recipients signed a contract and very few of those were sanctioned (Barbier and Théret, 2001, p 162).

When the scheme was evaluated three years after its initiation, it was judged effective in improving recipients' living conditions, while the **investment** effects of inclusion in the labour market were limited (Barbier and Théret, 2001, pp 168–9).

However, although marginal in the composition of the RMI, there was a third city that characterised the problem of social exclusion, namely that of **incentives**. In 1974, the same year Lenoir's book appeared, the economist Lionel Stoleru, in the book *Defeating poverty in rich countries*, claimed that the problem of poverty is not alleviated by developed welfare states but correlated with them (Stoleru, 1974). The book introduced the idea of a 'negative tax', that is, a benefit that gradually decreases until a certain income has been reached. According to its first proponent, Milton Friedman, it thus 'makes explicit the cost borne by society'.

> It operates outside the market. Like any other measure to alleviate poverty, it reduces the incentives of those helped to help themselves, but it does not eliminate incentive entirely, as a system of supplementing incomes up to some fixed minimum would. An extra dollar earned always means more money available for expenditure. (Friedman, 1962, p 162)

The negative tax was a way to test and ensure that 'everyone always has an interest in working, and in working more, in order to improve his final income, which is the sum of his earnings and the benefit he receives' (Stoleru, 1974, p 206). The negative tax accepted a lower threshold, a 'vital minimum' (Stoleru, 1974, p 23), but at the same time it inherently questioned whether the encouragement to work was sufficient. Further, it denounced the city of **investment**'s characterisation of the complexity of the origins of poverty. Rather, it was about 'coming to the assistance of those who are poor without seeking to know where the fault lies, that is to say based upon the situation and not on the origin' (Stoleru, 1974, p 206).

The 'founding father' of RMI, the Socialist prime minister and adherent of the 'second left' Michel Rocard, appointed Stoleru to prepare the law. **Incentives**-based arguments were used to justify certain delimitations, especially to the *redistributive* aims, of the scheme that would continue, in the decades to come, to function as a qualified target of critique. Importantly, this concerned the threshold between the guaranteed minimum income and the minimum wage, the so-called SMIC, as a potential factor of discouragement to work. In justifying the RMI, the minister of solidarity, health and social protection Claude Évin thus gave an assurance that the RMI would not 'lead to effects of disincentives to work or disorganisation of the labour market' since the government would 'take into account the level of SMIC in order to set the level of RMI' (Assemblée nationale, 1988a, p 720). Incentivising elements were also integrated, though in a rather marginal scale, in a 'differential' component that made the size of the benefit dependent on whether the recipient received other benefits (Vlandas, 2013).

The target population of RMI was estimated to be around 400,000 people, yet more than one million people have received RMI since the 1990s (1.1 million in 1992; 1.2 million in 2008). If one includes spouses and children of recipients, then the total number reaches 3.5 million (Palier 2010a: 84). However, the 'success' of the scheme, according to the test of **redistribution**, was increasingly problematised during the 1990s and 2000s. The evaluations were often orchestrated by the state itself as RMI marked an experimental phase with permanent evaluations of the effects of social policy instruments (Castel, 1995, p 697; Barbier, 2012; Palier, 2002, p 235).

RMI's interference with work

The criticisms of RMI arose mainly from the **incentives**, **activity** and **paternal** cities, all of which questioned the **redistribution** element of the scheme in some way. The criticisms all agreed that the problems of exclusion, and even poverty, could not be resolved by **redistribution**. It was within this setting that RSA would later arrive.

At the end of the 1990s, RMI was intensely scrutinised and criticised with reference to a problem of **incentives**. Analyses showed that recipients of RMI were losing income if they took up low-paid, part-time jobs (Palier, 2005, p 139). To take one example of a problem raised by the analyses, the RMI reform was connected to a number of 'secondary social benefits', such as the 'Christmas premium' and housing assistance, which further disincentivised the unemployed from taking low-paid jobs (Vlandas, 2013, p 120). The most important reform following in the footsteps of the critique of disincentives was the introduction of a premium for employment (PPE) in 2001. Based on the logic of the negative tax, PPE offered a (minor) tax credit to encourage low-paid jobs in order to counter 'inactivity traps' (Palier, 2005, p 139).

The PPE reform, however, did not radically change the belief that RMI performed poorly (Palier, 2010c, p 85). Thus, ideas surrounding the model of negative tax still occupied governments at the beginning of the new millennium. In 2005, the government proposed an active solidarity income (RSA), which aimed to strengthen incentives to work with in-work benefits for low-paid and often part-time employees. (In 2005, the government commission on 'Families, vulnerability and poverty' proposed an 'active solidarity income' scheme based on the idea of the negative tax that aimed to strengthen incentives to work with in-work benefits for low-paid and often part-time employees [Hirsch, 2005]. The commission was chaired by Martin Hirsch, again a representative from the Christian associative movements, the then president of Emmaüs, an influential non-governmental organisation [NGO] working against the exclusion of homeless people and created in 1949 by the Catholic priest Abbé Pierre, one of the most popular public figures in France.)

RSA was supported by all centrist parties. The fact that the Socialist candidate Ségolène Royal had included RSA in her campaign in the run-up to the 2007 presidential election did not discourage the Republican conservative UMP candidate Nicolas Sarkozy from adopting it when he was elected president in 2007. Soon after his inauguration in May, Sarkozy initiated the experimentation with the RSA scheme in 17 departments.[2] In order to carry through the experimentation with RSA and prepare the scheme for nationwide implementation, the government created a High Commission for Active Solidarity Against Poverty in October 2007 headed by Martin Hirsch, the inventor of the scheme and former chair of the 2005 commission. The appointment was somewhat controversial, since Hirsch was considered a figure of the left and had criticised Sarkozy's TEPA law.

The RSA seemed to fit with Sarkozy's electoral campaign of 'rehabilitating work', as it valued the work ethic of the city of **activity** while, with a **paternal** qualification, promising policies for 'the France that gets up early'.[3] The campaign entailed a criticism of the 35-hour week introduced with the 'Aubry Act' in 1998, and in particular of the redistribution ambition of distributing the total work load.[4] France was a 'country drugged on 35 hours' and one of the slogans of the campaign was 'work more to gain more' (Linhart, 2009). In line with this critique, the 'law in favour of work, employment and purchasing power' (TEPA) initiated the experimentation with RSA and introduced a 'fiscal shield' that reduced the income share that could be taken by direct taxes from 60% to 50% as well as a complete tax exemption for overtime work. Besides inducing **activity**, the overtime (de)regulation in particular had the aim of stimulating **demand** by increasing people's purchasing power through increased working hours (Lizé, 2013).

The tension between the **redistribution** and the government stance [the denunciation of the worth redistribution was also clear in the government's criticism of the existing RMI scheme] was also clear in the criticism of the existing RMI scheme. Sarkozy denounced the 'sledgehammer argument' of increasing social expenses and taxes to combat poverty, which had done nothing but 'serve to buy the silence of those that live on the fringes of society. Our social expenses have never been this high…. If this was a strategy that worked we would know about it'. The minimum allowances should again serve as a 'safety net and not as a settlement of all outstanding accounts'. This kind of **paternal** criticism was widespread on the right. A commentator from *Le Figaro* spoke of the 'generous allocations of the nourishing state' where 'the suicidal social minima policy had brought about a phenomenon of a descending social elevator', while a deputy from the UMP argued for a break with this 'French preference for unemployment and exclusion', which, 'with the help of some billions of social benefits, [means that] several millions of our co-citizens [are] far away from the labour market, that is, away from society full stop'. RMI was thus often criticised as being too caring. From this perspective, the social system was seen as an 'assistantship', a term denouncing the allocation of benefits as a means of 'assisting' recipients in a state of dependency. The paternal diagnostic of RMI also entailed a critique of the **investment** aim of insertion. According to Hirsch, the system of RMI had 'stiffened', leaving people in a 'permanent pseudo-insertion'. Since two thirds of RMI recipients were capable of working, 'the system had wrapped and shut up a population that it was not created for. These people are not in need of social care'. In other words, they were not in need of further **investment**. At the same time, the RMI was an exemplary case of a general problem caused by 'mechanisms of compensation' (**insurance**), in which 'society has functioned as a centrifuge throwing the least efficient outside of the system'.

The denunciation of both **investment** and **insurance** was also evident in Lionel Stoleru's diagnosis of the scheme he himself had contributed to [20 years ago]. To Stoleru, however, the main problem with RMI was still that it did not live up to the **incentives** test. While Stoleru had suggested that 'the richer a citizen is, the more positive tax he pays; the poorer he is, the more negative tax he receives', RMI 'did not have this quality', since it was 'given to the one who has nothing and completely removed from the one who finds a job and a revenue again. From the moment one gains 100 euro by working, one loses 100 euro of RMI. This is obviously not very motivating for working'. Not surprisingly, Stoleru supported the RSA project. The main challenge with regard to RSA, however, was its 'complexity'. In order to be 'efficient', the (incentives structures of the) scheme had to be 'comprehensible and comprehended'. Contrary to the PPE, which 'not one beneficiary [had] ever understood; not why, how or when he reaches it', the recipient ought to 'appropriate' the logic of the RSA in order to respond to it as an economic man.

Requalifying poverty

It was Hirsch who, together with Sarkozy, launched the RSA experimentation process in 16 departments in October 2007.[5] The process entailed a consultative stakeholder roundtable that unions, professionals, recipients of RMI and civil society associations were invited to join by initially signing a letter committing themselves to the government's objective of reducing the poverty rate by one third within five years. Most NGOs, however, were sceptical. According to *The Warning Collective*, many of the government's actions during the first five months had 'been in contradiction with the goal of reducing poverty'. Even Hirsch's former employer Emmaüs refused to 'sign a blank check to the government'. Despite the scepticism, Hirsh defended RSA with great dedication throughout the reform process.

Hirsch's 'fight against poverty' was first of all a fight against 'poverty traps' in encouraging an experimental inquiry into the variety of behavioural responses to monetary stimuli within the targeted population of two million people:

> How many children? How many working poor? How many single-parent families? It is all this data, the chosen measures, the analyses of their effects, judged in the light of this accepted objective. Setting an objective makes you follow it.… The social issue hereby becomes a political issue. Setting an objective makes it possible to see in plain sight where poverty hits the most, within which age groups and within which categories, thereby making the mechanisms that create it come into the open in order to set up the ones to combat it. This is what we have done. With special attention towards the working poor. Why? Because it is a transitional population. Accepting poverty in work is the same as making all voluntarism in favour of returning to

employment illusory, and it implies letting the organised cleavages around the more and more fragile protections expand. It is to these cleavages that the RSA must contribute with a response. It was conceived to remove poverty traps and ensure that, for those who are at an active age, work constitutes the pedestal of income which the national solidarity must not replace, but complement.

The problem of poverty was no longer a lack of **redistribution**, but one related to the allegedly problematic convergence of work and poverty. Poverty was thus repositioned, in Sarkozy's words, from a 'consequence' of 'repair' to a phenomenon with 'causes'. It became a dependent variable that, for that very same reason, could only be addressed through independent variables, and not directly.

Governing the economic, consuming, working, responsible un(der)employed

The recipient of RMI was thus 'trapped' and the RSA scheme became the liberating solution. The various instruments of RSA claimed to govern unemployed subjects from four cities: the economic men of **incentives**, the consumers of **demand**, the (un)willing to work of **activity**, and, finally, the unemployed subjects of the **paternal** city.

The **incentives** element was evidently part of the government's justification for introducing RSA. The RSA, according to Hirsch, was 'essential' because it involved 'the win–win principle' that 'if you start working again, you won't lose money', which eventually would 'motivate people to exit unemployment'. An unemployed person who participated in the experiment responded as an economic man: 'It's motivating because I know that if I do more hours, my RSA will increase'. Although the actual rate of the negative tax was not settled, the overall logic of the instrument in the RSA scheme was clear. The principle was integrated by adding a supplementary benefit on top of the existing RMI that would reward the hours worked by the un(der) employed, a reward that gradually decreased with each additional hour until it reached a threshold of between 1.1 to 1.2 times SMIC (see Figure 6.2).

However, there was more to both the justification for, and the instruments of, RSA than Stoleru's 'pure' incentives perspective. Although the core instrument rested on the economic man, the RSA as a whole responded to, and sought to govern, other unemployed subjects. First, the negative tax scheme increased the worth of

demand subjects, namely the consumer: 'Every time an unemployed person finds a job, he improves his purchasing power'. The goal of the government was hence both to 'decrease unemployment and maintain consumption'.

Second, the negative tax scheme did not solely strengthen **incentives** to change the behaviour of the economic man; regardless of the behavioural effects, it satisfied the work ethic of the city of **activity** and removed a potential excuse for its antithesis, the lazy unemployed. In Sarkozy's words, the scheme thus aimed to 'rehabilitate work' and ensure that 'not a single person can say: "If I get up this morning, I will earn as much as if I did nothing"'. Unlike **activity**, the city of **incentives** has no problem with the lazy. Rather, it assumes that everyone is lazy, in the sense of making rational, calculated, self-interested choices, and adjusts the environment accordingly. Stoleru, for instance, had no problem with artists choosing to live on benefits. 'Had RMI existed', Stoleru imagined, 'perhaps Van Gogh and Verlaine would have suffered a little less'. Prime minister François Fillon provided a similar perspective when he stated that it was not the recipients of RMI 'who should be condemned; it's the system that derails'.

However, abstaining from work was not a legitimate option in the RSA scheme. When the president visited one of the departments in which RSA had been piloted, a father told him that 'because of RSA, I was able to buy a bicycle for 15 euros for my son'. Sarkozy

Figure 6.2: The negative tax of RSA as illustrated in the Green Paper

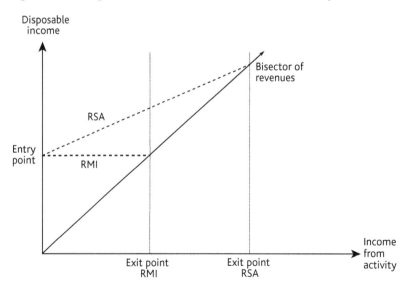

allegedly responded: 'You are out of the assistantship, you have moved from survival to life: the exit road is work, again work, always work'. RSA therefore addressed neither the poverty nor the purchasing power of *non*-working unemployed people. RSA transformed the unemployed individual from being a stigmatised 'assisted' person into an underemployed worker who strove to work more, turning an 'employee benefitting from RSA [into] an employee like anyone else'.

In a compromise between **incentives** and **activity**, RSA thus on the one hand functions as a kind of reward system to motivate (**incentives**) by, in Hirsch' words eliminating 'the absurd moment where you regret working because it makes you lose other revenues'. But on the other hand, RSA is seen as a 'signalling' system to reinstall justice for all those who 'get up early' to work (**activity**). In a televised interview, Sarkozy gave the following assurance: 'Frenchmen, it's you who pay for RMI, but with RMI you don't live, you survive. What I will do is give these people a chance to rehabilitate through work and not through assistantship'.

Activity was intensified by other justifications testing those without a proper work ethic. Sarkozy noticed that 'with 2.2 million unemployed, it is absurd to have around 500,000 vacant jobs without any takers'. Thus, while 'the vast majority of the unemployed try to find a job. There are some who don't want to set out for work. It's a minority, but it's a minority that shocks'. Hence, Sarkozy argued for a 'sanctioning process for an unemployed person who refuses two jobs that correspond to his qualifications and his salary aspirations'. In Hirsch's words, the 'rule of active search for employment' would contribute to 'putting an end to the imbalance between rights and obligations'. The 'assistantship' would thus be 'replaced by a logic of rights and obligations applicable to beneficiaries, public authorities and to companies'. Why? 'Because there are no rights without recompense.' Thus, the RSA would naturally both reinforce the quality of personalised support and ensure the effective application of sanctions towards those who do not play the game. 'RSA must be the decisive little push towards work, not a new form of lifetime revenue.' In this way, the sanctions and obligations served as a way of providing discipline ('the decisive little push') to responsibilise the hitherto assisted and hence incompetent **paternal** unemployed individual as well as a potential punishment for a resilient lazy minority from the city of **activity**.

Despite the radical denunciation of the **redistribution** elements that had been pivotal to legitimising the RMI, the RSA received very little criticism that radically questioned its general justification or instruments. Since RSA had been part of the Socialists' electoral programme, they were overall in support of Sarkozy's initiative. Most criticism came from sociologists and unemployed people who argued that RSA strengthened the idea that unemployment is the fault of the unemployed. The 'responsibilisation of the individual', one sociologist noted, turned the unemployed into 'culprits' in 'failure'. A collective of unemployed people criticised RSA for suspecting them of 'fraud'. The criticism was a response to a draft of the legislator's proposal that had been leaked to the public and stated that RSA would include control of recipients' 'way of life' in order to track potential 'pronounced disproportions'. One commentator, mobilising the **redistribution** argument, claimed that 'the fight against poverty necessitates questioning the foundation of our economic logic and entails terminating the shaming and tracking of those who cannot manage to make ends meet'. Similarly, a social worker denounced 'the complete harassment' involved, while an unemployed person denounced the 'systematic surveillance' of RMI recipients. A criticism of a young woman and long-term recipient of RMI, Gwenn Rosière, is quite symptomatic of how this rather radical critique could be absorbed and turned into a justification for RSA. As part of the consultative stakeholder roundtable, Rosière responded to a local call for opinions on the RSA scheme that was about to be launched in her department. Her highly critical letter somehow reached Hirsch, who responded and initiated a correspondence that would later be published in a book (Hirsch, 2008). Rosière initially posed a critique in line with the one presented in this paragraph, addressing inequalities in wealth and excessive use of control towards RMI recipients, but her letters, as well as the whole book, ended up in support of the project and served as an 'open letter to those who think you can do nothing about it'. According to Hirsch, Rosière, 'seemed, in the most natural way, to have understood our approach'. The absence of a substantial critique of the moral economy underpinning the justification of RSA meant that the criticism either missed its target by only denouncing coercive and controlling measures, or was absorbed into the pragmatic experimental quest of how *exactly* to govern.

Putting recipients' behaviour to the test

The lack of a radical critique of RSA coincided with the extensive evaluation of the experiments taking place throughout the country (Okbani, 2013). In the same experimental spirit, the high commissioner produced a Green Paper inviting stakeholders and citizens to contribute to solving a number of *specific* challenges relating to RSA (Hirsch, 2008). Thus, alongside the ongoing debates to substantiate RSA, a series of tests was introduced to identify who the unemployed were and what motivated their behaviour.

First of all the experiments led to tests *within* the city of **incentives**. Although simple in theory, the negative tax element of RSA gave rise to a number of questions about how in practice to handle the thresholds between benefits and work ('bisectors' as well as the gradient of the gradual decrease of benefits; see Figure 6.2). For instance, the Socialist president of one department complained that the government's rate of decrease of RSA would be higher than the one his own department had experimented with, which would make 'the incentive to return to employment a lot smaller'. The economist Thomas Piketty questioned whether the rise in 'profits' from around 150 euros in the PPE to 200 euros for taking a part-time job, as well as the abandonment of the maximum duration of one year, would really 'boost the rate of exit from RMI to part-time work'.[6]

However, the tests did not simply confirm the existence of the universality of the economic man. A local social worker, for instance, divided recipients into two groups. On the one hand were the economic men for whom the 'RSA would supplement their meagre resources' and would therefore be 'a strong encouragement'. On the other hand, there was a group of recipients who were 'really helpless facing employment. And when a contract appears they need a considerable support, sometimes a mediation with the employer, simply because they no longer dare ask if they can join their colleagues in the coffee breaks'. The social worker thus pointed to barriers to **activity** that, for some, remained regardless of **incentives**. Another social worker believed that unemployed people were more concerned with acquiring worth in the city of **activity** than behaving economically rationally: 'Work is predominantly seen as a way to insure the future and acquire a social status. Often the beneficiaries accept a job, even if they have no financial interest in doing so'. Similarly, a recipient, working 12 hours a week despite any change in income, justified her behaviour according to city of **activity** credo of being active: 'I like it. It gets me moving'.

Alongside the experiments, a number of surveys of unemployed were conducted in order to trace the barriers to returning to employment. The surveys put cities of unemployment to the test vis-à-vis each other. For instance, an opinion poll showed that 32% considered the absence of job offers to be the biggest obstacle to employment (**demand**), while 8% mentioned health issues and 6% age (**insurance**).

Twenty-seven percent emphasised that the main obstacle was the fact that the offers were 'not suitable'. 'Not suitable' was kind of a black box that could be interpreted according to different cities; to 39% of respondents, offers were unsuitable since they did not correspond to their qualifications (**investment**), whereas for 19% the offers were either too short-term (**insurance**) or it was uncertain whether they would gain financially by taking the offer (**incentives**). Similarly, 62% of unemployed people in another survey pointed to their inadequate skills for the profiles that employers were seeking. This could be taken as a problem of inadequate upskilling (**investment**), but could also be interpreted as an example of the unadaptable, inflexible unemployed person (**activity**).

While beneficiaries thus did not really seem to put great emphasis on *their own* inner economic man, 86% of them estimated that the incentives of RSA in general would encourage them to become professionally active. Another survey conducted by the evaluation committee of the high commission confirmed that 42% of the beneficiaries in the 'zones' of experimentation 'would, thanks to RSA, accept a job that they would have refused before'. Although this confirmed that many recipients *would* like to respond to the economic stimuli, the committee concluded that the only 'certainty' with regards to the effects of RSA was that 'tailor-made support helps with mobility or childcare removes some of the barriers to employment' (**activity**). Similarly, another survey conducted by the ministry of work and specifically targeting parents showed that jobseeking was mainly limited by an 'absence of means of transport, the price of transport and childcare'. Yet another survey, this time of recipients of PPE, confirmed the mobility problem: six out often recipients evoked the 'cost of jobseeking (transport, correspondence)'. The evaluations thus led to a number of proposals aimed at improving the means of mobility to enable unemployed people to access **activity**. One of Hirsch's advisers proposed the financing of driving licences, and a politician from the UMP suggested offering an 'option' that would temporarily cover displacement expenses and childcare. The Socialists went even further and called for the establishment of a 'genuine public service of early childhood, whose absence limits the access of women to work'.

The evaluations thus came to underpin the need for intensifying **incentives** and **activity** in the instruments RSA as well as the need for treating unemployed people as a diverse group with different needs and values.

The problematic thresholds in and out of part-time work

An important justificatory context to understanding why the RSA was primarily concerned with poor part-time workers was the SMIC, the guaranteed minimum wage and the main instrument in France to prevent the phenomenon of the working poor. An influential report (Cahuc et al, 2008) by a group of economists for the government's council of economic analysis argued that with the increasing amount of part-time work, the SMIC was 'not an effective instrument to reduce poverty'. The report was in fact commissioned to argue for fixing the rate of SMIC, which the government considered too high, but it also served as a justification for RSA. The economists on the one hand wanted to transfer the question of minimum wages to the negotiations of the two sides of industry, and on the other hand let RSA become the main instrument to fight poverty.

Although the negative tax scheme of RSA strengthened **incentives** for the unemployed to take part-time jobs in particular, it was uncertain whether it would have any significant effect. However, the consequences for the threshold from part-time to full-time work were potentially disincentivising. One economist spoke of the 'risk of perpetual part-time work'. To Piketty, RSA would lead to a 'strong reduction in the difference between working 20 and 35 hours a week'. UMP members had similar concerns. The difference between part-time and full-time work of around 200 euros was 'too weak' and 'not consistent with "work more to gain more"'. Another influential economist, Michel Godet, was even harsher in his critique of the 'perverse effects' of incentivising part-time work. According to Godet:

> A person working at 60% [of a full working week] on an RSA contract can have the same resources available as a wage earner working full time and paid SMIC, and even more if one considers the connected advantages of RMI that beneficiaries of RMI continue to benefit from.

How, then, asked Godet, was it 'possible to transform the good intentions of the active solidarities into unjust, useless, and perverse transfers? By enriching the working poor, one risks in fact maintaining them in the trap of part-time work and discourage full-time wage earners. The latter will be rebellious from not gaining more while they work more'. Not only did RSA lead to 'perverse' **incentives**, it also infringed the work ethic of the full-time workers paid close to the SMIC rate (**activity**). RSA was thus criticised by mobilising the same cities that had been used to justify it. Accordingly, RSA also faced criticism of the same **paternal** kind that had been directed at RMI. To a conservative debater, the RSA 'remained the most complete form of the assistantship' and simply consisted of 'playing good Samaritans'.

Hirsch responded directly to Godet's 'falsehoods'. RSA ensured that 'a person that passes from inactivity to activity will not end up with revenues superior to a low-wage-earner. The latter will therefore also receive an additional income of active solidarity'. Regarding the 'connected advantages' of RMI, they would no longer be 'attached to a status, but be proportional to the revenue'. Finally, Hirsch warned against this kind of criticism:

> Before the presidential election everyone, or almost, was favourable to the RSA. During the past year, it has had few detractors.… Today, when [the president] makes it in strict respect of its initial principles, one sees the temptation of denigration, the fear of acting out, the apology of the status quo.… It is however remarkable to note that those who created the RMI … are in favour of transforming it into the RSA. I find it more comfortable to be loyal to their convictions rather than changing positions … or not having one!

Critiques of RSA were thus both wrong and afraid of progress, or even worse, simply cynical or indifferent. There were thus limits to the criticism that the process of the consultative stakeholder roundtable had encouraged.

Nonetheless, the perverse effects *were* also qualified and criticised from the **insurance** and **redistribution** cities. From the **insurance** perspective, part-time work was a symptom of increasing insecurity on the labour market. According to one sociologist, RSA would 'multiply bad odd jobs by institutionalising a second labour market based on the precariat'. This was mainly due to 'perverse' incentives, not for recipients, but for employers, who would be 'content with hiring part-time workers knowing that the employees benefit from assistance'. Also, the Socialists warned against an 'increase in precariousness'. Concurrently, the problem was qualified according to the city of **redistribution** as a consequence of exploitative employers. An economist argued for 'sanctioning employers who profit from RSA in order to multiply unworthy jobs', and also called for measures that 'oblige the industries to open negotiations on minimum wages and the reduction of part-time work'. Moreover, the FO, one of the largest unions, wanted the government to ensure that 'capital would genuinely be harnessed'. Rather than putting the RSA to the test, these criticisms pointed towards solutions outside of the scheme and current reform process (minimum wages and regulation of part-time work). The debate regarding the financing of RSA became symptomatic of this **marginalisation** of more radical critiques.

Financing put to the test

Despite the fact that the majority of political actors supported the content of RSA, the adoption of the law was nonetheless contested. The controversy surrounded the question of how to finance the RSA. Initially, Sarkozy wanted to finance the RSA partly by abolishing the PPE. The proposal led to substantial criticism, legitimised by the city of **redistribution**, from both the left and the right. For instance, the social liberal, and then third-largest party, MoDem, argued that the 'RSA was perfectly well-founded but the solidarity cannot rest on the most poor without calling on the most rich'. The Socialists complained that 'RSA in reality is an arrangement that undresses the poor full-time workers in order to dress the poor part-time workers!'.

The government accommodated the criticism, but without endorsing the **redistribution**-based critique. Rather it requalified it in **demand** terms. The financing of PPE would not be redeployed to RSA, 'because we are going through a period of weak growth. It does not seem optimal to amputate purchasing power at a time where economic activity must be supported'.[7] The government thus proposed to finance RSA by raising a tax on property. The proposal, however, did not stop the criticism. Because of the 'fiscal shield', the richest part of the population would not be paying the additional tax. The government's final proposal, which was adopted by the national assembly, accommodated the critique and installed a 'global ceiling' on tax breaks that would work outside of the fiscal shield.

Somewhat paradoxically, the criticism resulted in both substantial changes in the financing of RSA while also legitimising its content, which, as shown earlier, was justified by a rather radical denunciation of the effects of **redistribution**. It may have become financed in a less unequal manner, but RSA itself strengthened instruments that would fundamentally contradict the aim of more income equality, at least between non-working recipients and the rest of society.

Sedimentation and subsequent changes

The adoption of RSA in the national assembly and in the senate was run through quickly in a process of 'urgency'. After a few debates it was adopted by the two chambers at the end of November 2008 and signed by the president on 1 December, exactly 20 years after the adoption of RMI. RSA would come into force as of June 2009, but the law did not bring the experiment to a halt – it merely normalised it. At the same time as the law became applicable, the findings from the initial experiments were presented to the government.[8] Furthermore, during the coming five years, the policies were evaluated by an 'evaluation committee' in relation to progress towards the objective of reducing poverty as well as incentivising work (art. 1). The findings were discussed at an annual 'national conference' attended by the relevant stakeholders (art. 32).

Besides the law generalising RSA, a decree specified the details regarding the conditionality attached to recipients' financial situation, modes of administration, sanctioning measures and the negative tax.[9] The negative tax was set at a rate of accumulation of 62%, meaning that each time recipients gains 100 euros, for instance, they will lose 38 euros of their RSA, since only 62% of the work-related income will be deduced from the RSA income (art.D. 262-4). The RSA takes into account 'all resources of the household', including other social services such as the 'Christmas premium' and housing assistance.[10] **Incentives** are thus ensured from the first to the last hour of work. This therefore 'incites the exercise of professional activity and fights against the poverty of certain workers, regardless of whether they are wage-earning or not' (art.L. 262-1).

Once recipients are deemed eligible, following the fulfilment of a vast number of test criteria (over 25 years old, thresholds regarding household income and savings and so on), they are subject to certain 'rights and obligations' (art.L. 262-27 to 37). The recipient has the 'right to social and professional support adapted to his needs and organised by one dedicated referent' (art.L. 262-27). The support is always up for revision, thereby installing a permanent test situation, since if 'the examination of the situation of the beneficiary brings out that, due to difficulties, another organisation would be better to directly conduct the necessary support actions ... the referent proposes a new orientation to the president of the general council' (art.L. 262-30).

The support actions are described in the 'personalised project for the access to employment', which is developed 'together with the referent' (art.L. 262-34). This 'contract', which is 'freely debated … specifies the positive and repeated actions of job searches that the beneficiary commits to carry out' (art.L. 262-35).[11] The elaboration of the contract takes into account a number of factors relevant to the mobility of the beneficiary (**activity**). Some factors (potentially) set limits to the scope of **activity**, such as 'training' and 'qualifications', as well as the 'personal and family situation', while others work to encourage more **activity** such as taking into account the 'situation of the local labour market' and reconsidering 'the nature and characteristics of the applied jobs' and 'the expected wage level' (art.L. 262-35). All this information defines a 'reasonable job offer', which the beneficiary only has the right to refuse twice (art.L. 262-35). In such cases, beneficiaries are 'erased from the list of jobseekers' and the allocation is suspended (art.L. 262-37). In general, sanctions are valid once 'the beneficiary does not respect a stipulation of the contract' (art.L. 262-35). The contract (and its potential revision) is thus a permanent test of the availability (refusals, search effort and so on) and adaptability (willingness to be geographically mobile, to adjust demands for skills and wages, and so on).

The requirement for improving one's employability also opens up rights for the recipient. The 'personalised help for the return to employment' has the 'aim of taking charge of all or parts of the reported costs on the occasion of the resumption of a professional activity, whether it is a job, taking a training course, or creating a company' (Premier ministre, 2009, art.R. 5133-10). The costs comprise 'transport, dressing, accommodation, hosting young children, obtaining a diploma, license, certification or authorisation that entails a professional activity' (art.R. 5133-11).

RSA did allow some **investment**, but, as in the justification of the scheme, it was clearly a marginal city. The beneficiary is encouraged to engage in 'contracts of employment support', that is, employment contracts (the recipient is termed the 'wage earner'), but with special 'insertion companies' and 'insertion workshops'.[12] The contract of the recipient may have the aim of 'professional education', but the main goal of the contracts is to "develop the experience and competences of the wage earner" (art.L. 5132).

Finally, all recipients are subject to 'control' to counter the risk of 'fraud'. Control of fraud relates to the city of **insurance**, and concerns the question of whether the recipient has actually been exposed to the risk that entitles him to compensation. Meanwhile, there is something else at stake here. The city of **insurance** is primarily interested in the *event* of unemployment and in 'speculative' behaviour, such as continuing to receive compensation even when the recipient is no longer unemployed. However, the problem here seems not to be entitlement to compensation, but rather entitlement to charity in the **paternal** sense. The control of the recipient, or rather the recipient's household, encompasses an 'evaluation' of whether there is a 'clear disproportion' between a 'way of life' and the 'resources declared' (L'Assemblée nationale et le Sénat, 2008, art.L. 262-4). The evaluation takes into account a list of 'elements' connected to the household , including constructed and non-constructed property, maintenance of buildings and means of transport, as well as more intimate elements such as appliances, objects of art, jewellery, and spending on holidays, restaurants, cultural goods and services, and sports and recreational clubs.[13] It is thus in fact not the actual resources of the household that determines whether the household deserves the allocation, but its *behaviour*, including the most intimate behaviour. The test of entitlement is thus permanent and implies, for instance, that it is forbidden for relatives to support the recipient financially in any way (Helfter, 2015).

Nonetheless, the test does qualify the recipient in terms that fit well with the justifications of RSA, for instance that the recipient should always be motivated to work, and thus the 'way of life' should always be less pleasurable than someone on the labour market. It also fits the **activity** justification that it is only through work that one gains worthiness and freedom to live without showing moderation. Finally, it ensures a **paternal** relation of subordination in which recipients, through their behaviour, show the breadwinner humility and respect. In this way, the control of the 'way of life' of the recipient('s household) can be seen as the sedimentation of concurrent dynamics in the public debate. The governing of unemployed people concerns the behaviour of unemployed people, that is, it has the ability to *transform* things from the way they are, as well as to ensure that the current state of affairs, regardless of whether they change anything, do *not* put the hierarchies and moralities of society to the test.

In terms of the promised effects of reducing poverty, RSA was close to a complete failure. In 2011, two years after its adoption, the national RSA evaluation committee estimated the reduction of poverty to be close to zero (Eydoux and Gomel, 2014, p 15). They arrived at a similar conclusion with regard to the effect on employment (p 19). However, the subsequent response to the lack of effects appears to be increasing the dose rather than reconsidering the treatment.

In 2015, the Socialist government under the presidency of François Hollande merged the RSA and PPE to create a single 'activity premium', which was also extended to include 18- to 25-year-olds. The understanding, aligned with the city of **incentives**, was that the RSA was too 'complex', thus blurring the motivational structures for taking up (part-time) work. Again, the justification was that it was valuable to 'incite to resumption of activity as well as to work', thus consolidating the worth of **activity**. In September 2018, President Emmanuel Macron launched yet another reform, the poverty plan, of the system that strengthened the logics legitimised by RSA. The reform addresses the 'precariousness' of the labour market but without mobilising **insurance**-based solutions. Instead, precariousness is to be 'prevented' by **investment**, such as creating an obligation for 16- to 18-year-olds to continue education and increasing 'social support' schemes while strengthening sanctions in cases of non–compliance. Resembling the slogan of the reform presented in the forthcoming chapter, 'Everyone can be useful', the justification of these measures is to ensure that 'no one can say that there is no place for them'. And, similar to the Danish reform, the 'can' is really an 'ought to'. However, the reform mobilises the full repertoire of the moral economy of activation. To strengthen **incentives** further, Macron has promised to increase the 'activity premium' by 50% and to reduce complexity further by merging all benefits into a 'universal activity income'. However, it is **activity** and **paternal** tests that are of main concern. Inspired by local initiatives, the reform proposes to make RSA conditional on doing 'voluntary work', in this way qualifying not only the premium but the basic RSA as a reward for **activity**. Further, the aim of the RSA ought to permit recipients to 'return to dignity in and through work', since 'emancipation is built up by work' (Cortes, 2018). There is a **paternal** dimension here: the 'support goes with control, a responsibilisation', since there are people who 'have settled in a form of exclusion and built their existence in it'. It is no surprise, as Chapter 7 shows, that Macron finds the case of Denmark inspiring. In other words, Macron does not seem to be dreaming of the universal, decommodifying, social democratic model of Esping-Andersen, but rather the contemporary, recommodifying version completely in tune with the moral economy of activation.

Notes

[1]   Exact references to quotations can be found in Hansen (2017).

[2]   In the administrative divisions of France, the department is one of three levels of government, below the national level, situated between the regional and the municipal level.

[3] 'Getting up early' refers to the French proverb '*Le monde appartient à ceux qui se lèvent tôt*', corresponding to the English, 'The early bird catches the worm'. Initiative and responsibility hence ought to be (further) rewarded.

[4] See Chapter 4, p 70.

[5] In the end, 41 out of around 100 departments took part in the pilot.

[6] The testing also led to a lot of debate concerning the motivation to take on part-time work, which will be presented in the next section.

[7] The lower expectation for growth and increasing public deficit in spring 2008 were the first signs of the impact of the financial crisis on the French economy.

[8] Assemblée nationale et le Sénat (2008) 'Loi no 2008-1249 du 1er décembre 2008 généralisant le revenu de solidarité active et réformant les politiques d'insertion', *Journal Officiel de la République Française 0281*, www.legifrance.gouv.fr.

[9] Premier ministre (2009) 'Décret n° 2009-404 du 15 avril 2009 relatif au revenu de solidarité active', *Journal Officiel de la République Française 0089*, www.legifrance.gouv.fr.

[10] Assemblée nationale et le Sénat (2008) 'Loi no 2008-1249 du 1er décembre 2008 généralisant le revenu de solidarité active et réformant les politiques d'insertion', *Journal Officiel de la République Française 0281*, www.legifrance.gouv.fr.

[11] The form of the 'project' was inspired by the personalised action project (PAP), which was introduced earlier in in the system of unemployment insurance (see Chapter 4).

[12] Assemblée nationale et le Sénat (2008) 'Loi no 2008-1249 du 1er décembre 2008 généralisant le revenu de solidarité active et réformant les politiques d'insertion', *Journal Officiel de la République Française 0281*, www.legifrance.gouv.fr.

[13] Premier ministre (2009) 'Décret no 22009-404 du 15 avril 2009 relatif au revenu de solidarité active', *Journal Officiel de la République Française 0089*, www.legifrance.gouv.fr.

7

Intimate scandals:
social assistance, Denmark, 2011–13

This final chapter of Part II presents the final and most recent case of a reform process – in several ways a spectacular process intensifying governance that was already comprehensive and had been progressively moving towards a system of activation for 25 years. The reform process 'Everyone can be useful' (henceforth ECU) was initiated in May 2011 when the future Social Democrat prime minister Helle Thorning-Schmidt gave a speech on Labour Day. ECU, which was adopted around two years later, transformed the benefits system for uninsured unemployed people – the so-called 'cash benefits system'– in a highly composite way.[1] It reduced benefits and installed an 'education injunction' for young recipients, required all 'able' recipients to work for their benefit, strengthened sanctions, introduced new instruments aimed at 'vulnerable' recipients and young single parents, and created a complex system of profiling in order to categorise the recipients according to a variety of instruments.[2]

Like the vast majority of past reforms, ECU was supported by the major parties, in this case all parties except the Red-Green Alliance (a coalition of movements and former parties on the left). Just as in the past, there was very little involvement from the unions, which traditionally put their efforts into the unemployment insurance system. During the period from the first reform proposal to the adoption of ECU, the process was 'interrupted' by two public scandals in which two individual recipients of cash benefits (the benefit for uninsured unemployed people) exemplified its dysfunctions.[3] In different ways, the scandals put to the test the question of whether the system was in fact underpinning the 'active society'. Figure 7.1 provides an overview of the most significant events.

The chapter is structured as follows. The first section looks into the state's involvement in the governing of uninsured unemployed people since the first 'social' reform in 1933. It highlights key changes with a focus on the youth and previous workfare measures. The next five sections present the key qualifications and tests during the reform process, starting with the diagnosis of rising unemployment and in particular youth unemployment in the aftermath of the North Atlantic

Figure 7.1: Timeline of the ECU reform process

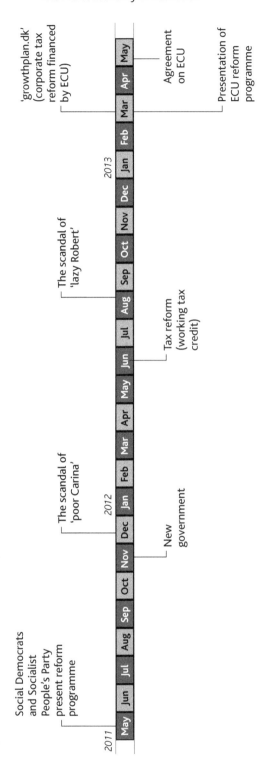

financial crisis. The second and third sections present the two scandals concerning individual long-term unemployed people, known as 'poor Carina' and 'lazy Robert'. The fourth section analyses the problem of institutionalising the categorisation of recipients with a system of 'preliminary assessment'. The fifth section presents how so-called 'utility jobs' became a panacea for all able recipients. The final section analyses the legal and institutional content of the final reform with a particular focus on the system of preliminary assessment and briefly outlines subsequent reforms of the cash benefit system.

The uninsured unemployed and the rise of the welfare state

In 1933, the first comprehensive reform of the poor relief system dating back to the 19th century marked the unfolding of the welfare state for decades to come. However, the ideas shaping this and consecutive reforms were far from the mobilisation of the city of **redistribution** that Esping-Andersen would later attribute to the development and essence of the Danish welfare state (Esping-Andersen, 1985, 1990). Neither did they radically break with the former system.

The chief architect of the reform was the Social Democrat minister of social affairs K.K. Steincke. On the one hand, the reform expanded social rights extensively; on the other hand, the rights deliberately excluded certain marginal groups of the population. Uninsured unemployed people were predominantly part of these excluded groups, for whom the old poor relief instruments remained in place. This implied that the recipients of help could be deprived of their right to vote (a clear sign of **paternal** disqualification) and 'recalcitrants' were sent to workhouses (Kolstrup, 2011, p 199). The law distinguished between those whose needs were deserved and another undeserving group with sub-categories of 'workshy, grossly negligent breadwinners, habitual drunkards' and 'tramps, destitutes and prostitutes' (Kolstrup, 2011, p 199), in other words, a composite group of unworthy **paternal** and **activity** subjects. Although the former group was treated with less stigma, the help was not a compensation in the city of **insurance** sense, but a loan to be repaid (Kolstrup, 2011, p 202).

Another group excluded from the expansion of rights that also sidelined uninsured unemployed people was the so-called 'antisocial'. Inspired by eugenic thought, Steincke believed that the 'unhampered reproduction' of this group of mentally deficient people, psychopaths, alcoholics and prostitutes constituted a 'threat of degeneration' that would undermine the welfare state financially, socially and morally

(Koch, 1996, p 55; see also 2006). Extensive programmes of compulsory sterilisation thus provided a means to reduce the use of internment, which was considered both costly and inhuman (Koch, 1996, p 58).

While the 'antisocial' group was considered incorrigible, unemployed young people were qualified differently in the reform of 1933, although still within the **paternal** and **activity** cities. The recession and rising unemployment of the 1930s spurred a fear of a 'radicalisation' of young people towards Nazism and Communism among the established parties (Christensen, 2012b, p 460). One response was the establishment of a number of so-called 'work colonies' where unemployed people would be exposed to physical work and educational programmes. In the beginning, subscription to the colonies was voluntary, but it soon became conditional on receiving any financial support and was extended to young people up to 24 years old as well as long-term unemployed people who had lost their right to unemployment insurance (Christensen, 2012b, p 462). Mandatory placement was justified as the **paternal** responsibilisation of the 'incompetent', whose irrational emotions could lead them down the wrong track. A Social Democrat member of parliament argued that the 'young one suffers from restlessness and depression, nervousness and discontent to everything and everyone, easily loses the sense of responsibility and self-control, and gives into feelings, varying from complete despondency to wild desperation' (Sode-Madsen 1985, p 36). Everyone would thus benefit from going to the colonies whether they volunteered or not.

> The youth, whose core is still fresh, will volunteer, and those left are the few who are victims of the unemployment psychosis. Those who need a stay with work and education the most are perhaps so passive that they cannot pull themselves together to do anything. (Sode-Madsen 1985, p 75)

It was not only the work colonies that would prevent 'radicalisation'; the economic boom of the postwar period would also avoid the creation of a youth proletariat whose members never acquired the necessary work discipline to hold a job (Christensen, 2012b, p 460). The economic boom of the postwar period rendered the work colonies superfluous (Sode-Madsen, 1985), but the instrument was the first of many targeting unemployed young people.

Although the work colonies and the programmes of sterilisation persisted up until the 1960s, other ideas from other cities of unemployment contributed to the characterisation of uninsured unemployed people. In **redistribution** terms, unemployed people were increasingly considered as 'fellow citizens' whose poverty was the result of events beyond their control (Kolstrup, 2012, p 188). In the logic of **investment**, unemployed people had 'potential' and could be 'resocialised' or 'rehabilitated' by the new profession of social work (Kolstrup, 2012, p 172). The culmination of these ideas was the Social Assistance Act of 1974. The Act combined elements from three cities: individualised needs-oriented assistance from a social worker would release the potential of the unemployed person (**investment**), while the financial support (without sanctions) should help to maintain previous living conditions, thereby providing security (**insurance**) and the necessary means to exert citizenship (**redistribution**) (Kolstrup, 2012, p 213; 2013, p 139).

However, in the 1980s, shortly after it was implemented (1976) and in the midst of the aftermath of the oil crisis, the Act was questioned from a variety of perspectives. First, the strengthening of the logic of **investment** through social work was criticised from the city of **redistribution** for relying too much on 'professional judgement', leading to illegality and no guaranteed minimum income (Kolstrup, 2014, pp 142–5). Second, its benefit levels were criticised from the city of **insurance** for discouraging people from enrolling in the unemployment insurance system, which led to the introduction of a 'ceiling' to ensure that benefits did not exceed unemployment benefits (p 162). Third, the Act was criticised for disincentivising the recipient to work (**incentives**) among others by the then minister of social affairs, Aase Olesen, who would later chair the influential Social Commission mentioned in Chapter 5 (see p 98).

These criticisms gained serious impetus in the late 1980s and 1990s, leading to far-reaching changes. The spotlight, once again, turned on young people. In emphasising 'no work, no money', the centre-right government in 1989 introduced special instruments targeting young people. Young unemployed people (18- to 19-year-olds) were entitled to a lower benefit to increase their incentive to work (**incentives**) or educate themselves (**investment**), and were required to participate in 'activation' projects that combined work and training after 14 days of unemployment (**activity**, **investment**) (Torfing, 2004, p 174; Kolstrup, 2014, p 218). In the same period, the Social Commission published its work (such as Socialkommissionen, 1992), which described unemployed people as having a lack of educational skills, problems of social inheritance and a lack of incentives to work. During the 1990s, the low 'youth allowance' was gradually extended to everyone under 25 (Kolstrup, 2013, pp 222–6). Under the social democrat-led government, reduced benefits were increasingly arranged to underpin **investment** by pushing young unemployed people towards education (Kolstrup, 2014, pp 197–9). The Active Social Policy Act of 1997 universalised many of the measures targeting young people. Instruments of 'activation' henceforth applied to everyone and were to be mobilised as soon as possible, with non-compliance to be met with sanctions (Kolstrup, 2014, pp 205–6). The Act emphasised recipients' 'rights and duties' as well as their 'responsibility' (Kolstrup, 2014, p 200). Furthermore, the goal of making the recipient return to the labour market overshadowed all other aspects (Kolstrup, 2014, p 201).

In the 2000s, the entrance of a centre-right government led to certain displacements, but also a general intensification in the sense of increasing sanctions and control over the behaviour of uninsured unemployed people. The **incentives** to work, especially for families, and especially immigrant and ethnic minority families, were consistently scrutinised (Kvist and Harsløf, 2014). Families had access to additional support that lowered the financial 'carrot' for working and thus constituted 'problems of interaction'. A number of instruments were introduced and intensified: a general 'cash benefits ceiling'; the 'integration benefit', a targeted low benefit for people living in Denmark for less than seven out of the previous eight years (labelled 'start help'); and the so-called '225 hours rule' requiring married recipients to work a number of hours in a given period in order to prove that they were available for the labour market (Kolstrup, 2014). Concurrently, the upskilling dimension of activation was increasingly toned down; rather, it should be 'job-orientated' (Kolstrup, 2014, p 264). The displacement from **investment** towards **activity** and **incentives**, as well as the intensified use of sanctions and incentives, were justified by an influential evaluation of Danish activation measures that fundamentally questioned whether the upskilling instruments had any positive effect on employment (Larsen, 2013, pp 139–43). Economists concluded that the participation in 'active labour market programmes' had extremely little effect, if not a negative one, on the unemployed person's chance of becoming employed. However, this was not a critique of the idea of 'activation' as such, since the programmes had another, much more efficient, an effect that, inspired by earlier studies in the US, was labelled the 'threat effect':

> For some unemployed, participation in ALMPs [active labour market programmes] might not be very attractive, perhaps because it is stigmatizing, it is like a tax on leisure time (you receive your unemployment benefits, but you have to turn up at 'work' each day), and the payoffs are clearly not very promising. It is therefore argued that to avoid participation [the] unemployed will increase their job seeking effort and lower their reservation wages, and as a consequence they will leave unemployment faster when faced with a threat of programme participation than without the threat. (Rosholm and Svarer, 2004, p 3)

The 'threat effect', in other words, made unemployed people less lazy and more mobile. Rosholm and Svarer thus came to the conclusion that:

> [I]f policy makers wanted explicitly to achieve a maximal threat effect, there would be several ways of doing that, including the introduction of strict search requirements and severe sanctions for non-compliance, lowering the [unemployment insurance] benefits, introducing programmes that are truly cold, wet, hard and have no skill-enhancing components (e.g., cleaning beaches) and so on. (Rosholm and Svarer, 2004, p 35)

Another important and contested policy instrument was the categorisation of recipients of cash benefits. In 2000, the first national system of profiling, or 'preliminary assessment', divided unemployed people into five categories corresponding to specific targeted instruments. This, and subsequent systems, responded to both a need for a more precise system of governance and a critique of the judgement of case workers (Nielsen, 2015). In 2004, these categories were replaced by five new 'match categories' that estimated the proximity of the unemployed to the labour market, and insisted on focusing on 'the resources and opportunities of the unemployed' rather than problems (**investment**) (Nielsen, 2015, pp 51, 54). In 2010, the five categories were merged into three categories: the 'job-ready', the 'action-ready' and the 'temporarily passive' (p 52). Although the main aim of this categorisation was to align governance with the end goal of employment (**activity**), the latter category also provided some scope for the type of social work envisioned in the 1974 Act. By distinguishing between different needs and behavioural traits, the categorisation institutionalised and separated the different subjects of the **paternal**, **investment**, **incentives** and **activity** cities that had been used to justify the changes. I will return to this point later in the chapter.

Crisis diagnosis and the 'third way' out

In November 2011, a new government was formed, comprising the Social Democrats, the Socialist People's Party (SF) and the Social Liberal Party *Radikale Venstre*. Before the election, the three parties, which together formed the Red–Green Alliance, had already announced changes to the cash benefit system (the system of social assistance for uninsured unemployed people). One of the core elements of the changes was to abandon what was the alliance termed 'poverty benefits' (the 'cash benefit ceiling' and the other reduced benefits that the previous government had introduced). These reduced benefits had been supported by the Social Democrats when they were first introduced, but in the post-financial crisis climate in which rising material inequalities and the austerity agenda were put to the test, new winds seemed to blow. Echoing the joint election programme of the Social Democrats and SF (Socialdemokraterne og SF, 2010), and in line with classic **demand** thinking, the new government initiated a so-called 'kickstart', with public investments contributing to 'job creation' to address the crisis.

However, in accordance with the city of **investment**, the crisis was also perceived as a problem of competitiveness. According to the prime minister Helle Thorning-Schmidt, the Keynesian stimulation of the economy was insufficient and could only be a short-term instrument to deflect the most immediate effects. Competitiveness was 'not just a matter of taxes and wages [but] also about our educational level, our infrastructure and about the way our society functions in general.… We all know quite well that we must live by being skilful and productive'. The government thus asked for further 'investment in people' to be 'be ready to ride on the wave, once we get new growth'.

The **investment** diagnosis became an issue of urgency in relation to uneducated young people. Similarly to the work of the Social Commission around 20 years earlier, the union-sponsored think tank the Economic Council of the Labour Movement estimated the risk of being on cash benefits to be more than ten times higher for young people without post-secondary education.

Meanwhile, youth unemployment remained high (around 15% compared with around 7% in 2007) after the new government entered office. The minister of employment, the social democrat Mette Frederiksen, was 'deeply worried' and called for a change of course since 'nine out of ten under-30s on cash benefits haven't completed an education' and thus risked 'becoming the losers of the future'. The **investment** diagnosis implied that if young people were to have equal or better opportunities, there was only one redeeming path: more skills. Thus, according to the minister, 'without the will to obtain an education, [there will be] no cash benefits'. Also, the unions' think tank (Economic Council of the Labour Movement) suggested imposing an 'education obligation' on young unemployed people that would 'send a signal to the young and their parents that there is no getting away from getting an education'.[4] The emphasis on upskilling cash benefit recipients was further justified by a critique of existing extensive use of jobseeking courses as 'meaningless', that is, not living up to the **activity** test of bringing them closer to employment. The critique was nourished by accounts from unemployed participants of such courses, in particular a popular blog[5] that criticised the **paternal** elements of the many associated personality and self-development tests for treating them as if they were pupils in elementary school. The courses were thus labelled 'dickybird courses', referring to the common use of DOPE (dove, owl, peacock, eagle) personality tests.

The scandal of 'poor Carina'

While the government had announced its intention to reform the cash benefit system, the process was 'interrupted' by two public scandals that concerned two long-term recipients of cash benefits and brought other cities of unemployment into the debate. The scandal of 'poor Carina' turned the intimate life of recipients of cash benefits into a public spectacle. It also turned the debate on poverty into a question of the cash benefit system's effect on the lifestyle of recipients in which the **paternal**, **incentives** and **activity** cities came to play a dominant role.

One of the first actions of the centre-left government in office was to abandon the so-called 'poverty benefits' it had criticised during the election as being incompatible with the poverty threshold. Just a few weeks after parliament's vote, the scandal of 'poor Carina' unfolded, a scandal that later fed back into the debate concerning the reform of the cash benefit system. Even today, five years later, 'poor Carina' is still part of the public memory. The controversy began when Özlem Cekic, a politician from SF, the socialist centre-left party in government with the Social Democrats and *Radikale Venstre*, suggested that the state should offer Christmas aid for poor people. In response to this, Joachim B. Olsen, a sceptical politician from the new Liberal Alliance Party, with an unequivocal free-market ethos, stated that it was 'scornful of the millions of starving people around the world to speak of poor people in Denmark'. Cekic felt confident enough to invite her critic to debate the question of poverty in Denmark, as well as the legitimacy of abandoning low benefits. With media attention, she organised a visit to an allegedly poor family to put the disagreement to an exemplary reality test – but within which city? The test was first and foremost aligned with the **paternal** city. It was a question of the need for charity, and while other cities later entered the scandal, it never became a matter of compensation (**insurance**), lack of jobs (**demand**) or equality (**redistribution**).

The visit was at the home of a 36-year-old, single mother (who remained anonymous, but was referred to as 'Carina') of two children, who agreed to have her household budget scrutinised. Carina had a total income of 15,728 DKK (€2,000) per month, with 5,000 DKK (€700) available for food, clothes and leisure activities. Her budget was outlined in detail (see Table 7.1).

According to Olsen, Carina's situation did not stand the **paternal** test, and thus failed to qualify for charity assistance. Rather he concluded that 'material poverty' did not exist in Denmark and that the '25% of the population on public benefits' could be attributed to 'the lack of a responsible social policy in Denmark when it comes to including people in the labour market' (J.B. Olsen, cited in Petersen, 2014, p 47).

Soon, Carina's household budget was the object of fierce debate on social media and among most political actors. Was it irresponsible of her to spend money on cigarettes in her situation? Was her telephone

Table 7.1: 'Poor Carina's' budget (in DKK)

Income		Expenses	
Cash benefit	9,800	Rent	7,400
Housing benefit	3,019	Electricity	700
Child allowance	2,908	Telephone	500
		TV license	196
		Internet	148
		Debt	600
		Medicine	70
		Dog food	283
		Football	300
		Cigarettes	500
	15,729		10,697

bill too high? Should she get rid of her dog? And so on. In this sense, the scandal is a radical example of how the testing and control of a household, previously seen in the French RSA (see Chapter 6), goes beyond the question of formal entitlement, or more precisely, as in the French case, of how the question of entitlement is subject to continual testing of the competence and behaviour of the recipient.

Throughout the scandal that followed, Carina became an exemplar of a plurality of subjects from other cities of unemployment. SF tried, unsuccessfully, to turn the attention towards the lack of jobs and the government's responsibility to create more employment opportunities (**demand**). Instead, **paternal** testing continued. Here, Carina was proof of a certain loss of self-control and 'childish' behaviour among recipients of cash benefits. In response, the minister of social affairs Karen Hækkerup criticised the 'norm slide' towards an 'entitlement mentality' in society (Petersen, 2014, pp 51–3). The influential economist Nina Smith (who had earlier participated in the Social Commission) denounced the lack of 'moderation', the result of people who had 'become spoiled' and took 'many welfare services for granted'. An ex-recipient of benefits claimed to know that 'in the underclass, all they think about is getting money from the municipality'. Here, the 'victimhood mentality' thrived, causing people to 'disclaim their responsibility for their own life'. Recipients, thus, could take no refuge in the city of **insurance**. According to the head of a jobcentre, 'many [recipients] develop a lifestyle where they get used to the life on benefits'.

The explanation, according to Smith, was a lack of self-governing virtues such as 'upbringing' and 'respect' (paternal). Similarly, the minister of employment Mette Frederiksen saw 'passive benefits' as doing unemployed people a 'disservice', since 'You don't get more freedom, you don't get more responsibility, you don't get the basis for uprooting your own life in order to move on'. The 'disservice' manifested itself a 'far too large a propensity' among local caseworkers to 'indirectly maintain people on cash benefits because the caseworkers, with all their heart, wish to secure people's income'. Frederiksen herself had an alternative attitude towards the unemployed:

> To me, making demands on people is a consequence of respecting them. The day we don't make demands, we don't respect people. And what is the alternative? That some of them get stuck and then we can meet again in 20 years and, once again, find a young woman near her 40s who has been sitting 18 years on cash benefits? That simply won't do.

Paternal measures were not only necessary to responsibilise recipients. As Carina's case illustrated, there was the danger of the mentality of unemployed parents transferring to their children. Thus the problem with Carina was 'that this woman has been on cash benefits all her adult life', meaning that 'the child grows up in a family where it never sees anything else'. A think tank, Kraka, supported this reasoning, estimating that around 40% of young recipients of cash benefits have parents have also been on cash benefits within the past ten years, thereby concluding that the 'social inheritance' of young people with 'cash benefits parents' resulted in them having a 3.6 times higher chance of themselves becoming recipients of cash benefits.

In parallel with the **paternal** test, Carina's case exemplified the lack of monetary **incentives** to work. The question of whether Carina's situation was simply a result of rational economic behaviour was put to the test in a number of evaluations of the single parent recipient. A liberal think tank, Cepos, estimated that this group would only gain 1,000 DKK (130 euros) a month by taking a job. 'It is so little that for some it will be outweighed by the effort of taking the bus to and from work', asked the think tank, before concluding that 'appeals do not deliver more hands on the labour market. Incentives do'.

Another analysis, this time from the ministry of finance, revealed that 14,250 people would gain no more than 1,350 DKK a month from taking an unskilled job. The social democratic minister of finance Bjarne Corydon recognised that this was '14,250 too many'. Some of the **incentives** problems were created by the removal of 'poverty benefits'. The minister of employment, Mette Frederiksen, 'fully acknowledge[d] that there [were] problems of interaction between cash benefits and the labour market', but gave the assurance that 'it was never the idea that the abolition of [poverty benefits] would stand alone', thus heralding a tax reform to increase low-paid employees' rewards for going to work.

However, according to Frederiksen, the tax reform's increase of the working tax credit 'only gave an answer to *some* of the problems with Carina' (emphasis added). Carina also exemplified a problem of the city of **activity**, for which incentives were only secondary, since, regardless of the difference between wages and benefits, it should 'never be voluntary whether you go to work'. Hence the minister, 'as a Social Democrat', supported 'a tougher assessment of work availability than the one that stands today'. The coming reform of the cash benefit system would therefore 'accentuate the right and duty to work'.

The scandal of 'lazy Robert'

The tax reform, as well other reforms such as the early retirement pension, had delayed more detailed preparations for the coming reform of the cash benefit system. Meanwhile, the debate about the system exploded once again in September 2012 after long-term benefit recipient Robert Nielsen, who branded himself as 'lazy Robert', participated in a discussion programme on public television. In the programme, Nielsen put the city of **activity** to the test by simply disagreeing with the idea that unemployed people should be at the unconditional disposal of the labour market. He had thus often refused job offers and refused to attend appointments at the jobcentre, even though he was subsequently sanctioned. Referring to a janitor's job at a McDonald's fast-food outlet that he had left after a half a year because of falling out with the manager, Robert justified his right to cash benefits:

> 'As a human being I am faced with a choice in the job centre; shall I take a shitty job in McDonald's for 100 kroner an hour, or do I want to continue on cash benefits? And here I say that the job is so poor that I would rather be on cash benefits; if not, society must provide an offer that corresponds to my competences and strengths.'

There were elements of both **redistribution** and **investment** in his reasoning. Regarding the former, cash benefits was a means, like strikes and demonstrations, of demanding a job that 'you could be proud of' and having the 'right not to become aggrieved when you work'. Robert Nielsen thus basically echoed Esping-Andersen's principle of decommodification (supposedly a feature of the Scandinavian countries) to ensure that 'citizens can freely, and without potential loss of job, income, or general welfare, opt out of work when they themselves consider it necessary' (Esping-Andersen, 1990, p 23). Regarding the latter, Nielsen demanded a job that corresponded to his competences (although he had not completed an education) and a job that 'was developing for oneself and the surroundings'. However, in the following months, the city of **activity** was not impaired but reinforced. The ironic self-naming of 'lazy Robert' was rather taken very seriously. While in Carina's case the object of scrutiny was mainly her *budget*, in Nielsen's it was his *availability*. How was it possible, as he had proclaimed, to 'fly under the radar' of the jobcentre? What exactly happened when he quit the job at McDonald's? Why did the sanctions not seem to affect him? And so on.

The Liberal Party *Venstre* wanted to 'make the sanctions so tough all over the country that specimens of recipients of cash benefits resembling lazy Robert, who tried to avoid ending up doing something, will be punished so severely that they die out.' According to one newspaper report, Nielsen illustrated that 'workshy non-Western immigrant women are … far from the only problem…. Far into all classes of society … it has become completely natural that one can say no to work that does not fit oneself and let diligent Eastern Europeans do the job'. Robert Nielsen thus became another symptom of coinciding ills in the city of **activity**, namely inflexible, picky unemployed people and employers with vacant jobs. According to *Venstre*, it was 'absurd' that despite 'thousands on unemployment benefits and cash benefits … we have nonetheless put ourselves in the situation where there are jobs that unemployed Danes do not take'. It was therefore necessary to 'break with the attitude that it is better being on passive support than picking strawberries. We must re-establish that there is more prestige in getting out of bed than in sleeping late'.

The criticism also turned towards the governing of recipients in the local jobcentres, thus putting the city of **investment** to the test. A conservative newspaper claimed that the jobcentres were too focused on upskilling unemployed people, resulting in a tendency for society to despise 'Danes and foreigners who go to work every day to clean and help in the kitchens, in the stables or in the greenhouses'. The chair of the Social Services Directors' Union recognised that it was 'paradoxical that we import a labour force when we have unemployment' and that 'perhaps we should be even stricter with sanctions'. The municipalities' confederation, KL, insisted that it *did* sanction recipients extensively (30% of them during the previous year), and that 'we have some tough rules which means that the jobless must make a dedicated effort to find a job if they want to receive the benefit'. However, 'unfortunately there is a smaller group of jobless who can, but do not want to, make a sufficient effort to get a job. This group should feel the financial effects rapidly if they do not live up to the obligation to be available for work'. The confederation suggested an 'intensified obligation to be available for work' for this group, whereby it was no longer up to the jobcentre to prove insufficient availability, but up to unemployed people themselves to prove the opposite.

The government largely acknowledged the criticisms of Robert Nielsen and the systemic failures that facilitated cases such as his. The prime minister Thorning-Schmidt insisted that the government would 'inspect the employment initiatives closely and if there are people out there like 'lazy Robert', tightened demands will be placed upon them'. Like the municipalities, she also separated recipients into two groups who would need different instruments. Next to the 'Roberts' there were 'all the many people who would like to have a job' who 'should not suffer from the few who resist taking a job' and thus would be subject to less control.

However, adding the parallel **investment** analysis of the situation relating to unemployed young people, questions surrounding the **incentives** and (ir)responsibility (**paternal**) of 'poor Carina' and the (in)**activity** of 'lazy Robert' suggested a need for a more detailed categorisation of recipients to distinguish between the disparate groups of unemployed subjects.

Categorising between and within cities

As mentioned earlier, the existing system of preliminary assessment for benefits recipients operated on the basis three categories of uninsured unemployed people: the 'job-ready', the 'action-ready' and the 'temporarily passive'. The use of the latter category, 'match category 3, came to be seen as contributing to the problem of long-term claimants such as Carina and Robert Nielson. One think tank argued that the category facilitated a 'kind of 'citizens's income' in which 'rights and duties' were suspended', and that municipalities had an economic incentive to place people in this category. The minister of employment, Mette Frederiksen, regretted that 'so many are put in match category 3 because, other things being equal, it's harder [from] there to get back to the labour market', implicitly criticising the judgement of case workers responsible for allocating claimants into the different categories. Thus, the minister reasoned, all persons in match category 3 should instead participate in active measures. Her reasoning echoed the 'disservice' discourse used to describe Carina's situation.

In itself, the 'temporarily passive' match category was considered dangerous, since it superimposed on unemployed people 'a classification which could have a self-reinforcing effect' and hence put them at 'imminent risk of becoming trapped in cash benefits', with the result that 'if you don't get out and about among other people [you] may fare worse'. Rather, the classification ought to be in the positive language of opportunities, entailing 'another philosophy of man'. According to Frederiksen, changing the category was the first step towards 'confronting the passive culture in the cash benefit system. We shall no longer simply look at people, but give them an active initiative'. Although those in this group needed 'extra help', the 'objective' was now 'work for everyone'. The minister had 'from personal experience seen how some recipients of cash benefits, whom the system had given up on, suddenly begin to flourish when they are put in an environment that believes in them'. Governing unemployed people necessitated 'a belief that people can do more than we get to see just now', that is, 'Everyone can be useful'. The message to long-term unemployed or young mentally ill people would no longer be that they 'do not have to get up in the morning', which was simply a 'too tough a message' to send. The principle of compensation (**insurance**) was thus seen as constraining people rather than emancipating them. The true 'solidary' message was that 'yes it is tough, and the road will be rocky, but we will invest some money, some time and some energy in order for you to become part of the community'.

The goal of for group was thus the same as for all other unemployed people, but the instruments differed. A report ordered by the ministry of employment showed that the most vulnerable recipients were 'thrown backwards and forwards' between the different divisions of the municipalities. Frederiksen argued for a 'cross-disciplinary', 'coordinated' and 'holistic' initiative with supportive 'mentors'. Immigrant women were also qualified as a group that had (wrongly) been categorised in the passive match 3 category. The cash benefits system was 'de facto a parallel early retirement pension for women with minority backgrounds'. In future, with the introduction of an 'integration injunction', 'we will make demands, have expectations and count on the immigrants'. The future system of preliminary assessment would thus no longer care about 'where people come from, but what opportunities they have for succeeding in society'. While 'vulnerable' recipients were in need of 'care and patience', non-vulnerable groups needed more uncompromising instruments. The threshold thus defined the two types of subject *within* the city of **investment**: those with and those without a capacity to fulfil their potential.

The former group, however, comprised various subjects. First, the designation 'non-vulnerable' evoked the case of 'lazy Robert' and the city of **activity**, whereby 'people who can work must work' and hence the 'rules of availability [had to be] tightened so that one cannot choose to do without work, that is, do without the community'. While sanctions were a 'natural consequence of rights and duties', they should 'primarily be used towards the resourceful recipients of cash benefits'. Second, the message and instruments were a response to the perceived crisis, embodied by both Carina and Robert Nielsen, of long-term unemployment experienced by those without an education. The solution was that unemployed young people would be faced with an 'education injunction' and a new benefit that would no longer comprise cash benefits but 'education help'. Financial support was henceforth conditional on engaging in educational activities. According to Frederiksen, this was *not* to be considered 'financial whipping':

> No, because the greatest gift we can give those who can obtain an education is to press them to do it. To some it is necessary that we add a financial pressure because otherwise they think that it is easier to refrain from doing it.

Young people were hence characterised in **paternal** terms as being easily tempted down the wrong path, as economic men in need of **incentives**, and finally as people who, for the benefit of themselves and society, ought to accumulate human capital (**investment**). In relation to the latter, the minister argued that young people were not taking advantage of the opportunities they were offered. The reasons for this resided both in unemployed people themselves – 'There are too many who don't make an effort and don't take obtaining an education seriously' – and in inconsistent governing: 'My position is that we should be tough against the young ones who can, but who don't take the trouble. One should have the courage to say: "Now your benefit is removed"'.

'Education help' replaced the 'youth benefit' and was reduced to the equivalent of the universal state-sponsored study grant. Importantly, the category of 'youth' was widened to include 25- to 29-year-olds, who as a consequence had their benefits halved. The move was supported by a think tank whose analyses had shown that 25- to 29-year-olds were, on average, on cash benefits 25% longer than the 18- to 24-year-olds, allegedly because of the disincentivising financial support. Furthermore, the think tank claimed to have shown that young unemployed people close to becoming 25 tended to 'stick around in the system'. Although some unions criticised it for treating 'adults' as youths, the widening of the category was widely supported. Frederiksen called it a 'system error' that it 'is more profitable [for young people] to remain idle than educate themselves'. Even the chair of the social workers' union agreed that 'completely well-performing young people who could begin an education and who really do nothing but scratch their backsides because they don't really want to begin' should have a benefit corresponding to the universal state-sponsored study grant.

The prospect of getting more recipients of cash benefits into education led to criticism of the government's proposal. The technical and vocational schools questioned whether the use of coercion, forcing young people into education, was really compatible with the city of **investment**. The schools warned against enrolling students 'without motivation'. The confederation of employers in the construction industry (The Danish Construction Association) noted that 'it is impossible to cram motivation and skills down the throats of students'. There was a danger that schools would become 'depositories for social problems'. The problem was not simply that these young people performed poorly, but that they affected the ones that *were* motivated. According to the chair of the technical and vocational schools, institutions were 'struggling to avoid an image [of providing] a garbage-can education' and 'worried that the smart young ones will leave the technical and vocational schools if they have to team up with 27-year-olds who are forced there by the jobcentre'.

The **investment** problem of how to distribute investments according to potential and talent was thus put to the test. In other words, does such a system ensure equal opportunities, or rather restrict the opportunities for the (most) talented to realise their potential? The inclusion of the 'weak' entailed a risk of 'pushing the gifted pupils aside', one director of education argued. Moreover, it was uncertain whether the 'weak' were in fact weak, or had simply, in accordance with the **paternal** test, received too much comfort and security. This director wanted to divide 'pupils' into two categories that would be separated in school: first, a group of 'decent, correct and well-behaved' young people who did well, and second, a group who 'drop out or drift around in the system … and don't see any reason to get ready. If you ask them why, they say "it is cosy to attend school and I receive the universal state-sponsored study grant". Many feel they don't have to make an effort. They have a firm belief that no matter what bad choices they may make, society will ensure that they are well off'.

The government by and large acknowledged this critique. To Frederiksen, it was no use for schools 'to carry such a big social responsibility that it lowers the educational standards, or makes the young people who are eager to obtain an education get an inferior one'. The solution was a 'preliminary assessment and a very precise assessment ensuring that the ones getting the education injunction are education-prepared'. Further, the 'prepared-for-education' group was a 'composite group' in need of different instruments. The group with many drop-outs, for instance, needed a 'flex-education', the group of young people who 'would like to obtain an education but [have] weak academic premises' needed 'reading and spelling courses', while others needed 'mentoring' or 'apprenticeships'.

Justification of 'utility jobs'

Although the reform would transfer young recipients to educational programmes, there was a residual group of non-vulnerable 'adult' recipients as well as young recipients who were either not 'education-prepared' or waiting to enrol in a programme. According to the government, all such recipients were to be considered 'job-prepared'. In the earliest reform proposal, this entailed a 'right and duty' to work for cash benefits. Then the prime minister argued that 'if you are capable of working it is only good for society and the individual that you are offered a job and must show up every day and perform a task of public utility' and therefore it was 'perfectly logical that you must work for your cash benefits, if you have the slightest capacity for work'. The government wished to create special 'utility jobs' for all 'job-prepared' recipients of cash benefits, such as cleaning beaches, cities and forests. The utility jobs came to function as a kind of compromising device accommodating the critique of both the preliminary assessment system as well as of 'poor Carina' and 'lazy Robert'.

The utility jobs were inspired by existing practices in some municipalities, in particular the so-called 'immediate activation' scheme in the municipality of Aalborg, where since 2009 the jobcentre's 'project garden service' had obliged young recipients to work 34-37 hours a week in 'utility-creating projects' in order to receive benefits (Nielsen, 2014). The utility jobs first of all had a 'threat effect' similar to the one identified earlier. A Conservative member of Aalborg city council explained that there was 'a scare effect which works. So even if this is a garden project which doesn't qualify for much else than gardening, it gets some people quickly in ordinary jobs and keeps others going'. The manager of a jobcentre in Aarhus used a similar approach and claimed that 'when we confront [jobless people] with the conditions for receiving benefits, 40% immediately prefer to search for jobs by themselves'. Similarly, the Danish National Centre for Social Research recognised a 'motivational effect that makes some of the stronger jobless recipients of cash benefits find a job instead of entering the system'. There was thus an underlying idea that the 'unpleasantness' of these jobs would work in a similar way to financial **incentives**. Rather than monetary carrots, it would be freedom from the subordination of utility jobs that would make, in **paternal** terms, competent unemployed people find an ordinary job. The minister of employment Mette Frederiksen thus estimated that there would be many 'who after a short while will think that it's probably better to find paid work when one has to work to get cash benefits anyway'. A local politician from *Radikale Venstre* argued that the utility jobs would ensure better control of an unadaptable and hitherto ungovernable group of unemployed people differing from the 'majority' who 'want to work'.

> There is of course another group that does not want to apply for all jobs and that we have difficulties controlling [in terms of] whether they are really at the market's disposal. You know, we can't force them to send an application to a cleaning company. Here, the cash benefits reform will help since now their alternative will be utility jobs.

The lazy individual may not be the economic man responding to sanctions and **incentives** (like lazy Robert), but now he would be forced to work anyway.

Besides coercing recipients to find work, utility jobs also underpinned **investment** by encouraging recipients to educate themselves. The largest trade union, LO, thus had 'no problems with the municipalities getting tough in order to make the youth understand that an education and a lasting job is also best for themselves'. In this way, utility jobs eased the tension between the cities of **investment** and **activity**.

While utility jobs coerced recipients into finding work or getting an education, they also had some value in themselves. Recipients engaged in utility jobs would first of all 'be useful' and live according to the work ethic of the city of **activity**. This would also have the effect of detaching the recipient from the critique of cash benefits as a 'passive' benefit. From now on, it would have little to do with either **redistribution** or **insurance**, but would first and foremost represent a quid pro quo for labour. The recipient would neither be lazy (**activity**) nor live on other people's money (**paternal**). Utility jobs would therefore replace previous activities of job training with a 'univocal focus on work' because 'doing a piece of work has greater value than being in activation'.

Recipients working in utility jobs would also be more closely aligned with the competent subjects of the **paternal** city. They would 'get a sense of what sort of thing working time is' and 'learn to get up in the morning every day', while the jobs would have 'an educational effect that made it clear that the municipality is not a gift shop'.

The Red-Green Alliance, however, denounced the governing of unemployed people through utility jobs, describing it as 'throwing suspicion on the unemployed'. Likewise, one unemployed person participating in a scheme similar to the utility jobs programme noted that it was 'unpleasant to feel audited and be ticked off for attending or not. It is like going to elementary school again'. Mistrust is inevitable towards the irresponsible or potentially lazy, however, and evident in the difference in measures between young people and those over the age of 30: whereas young people would be met with an instant requirement to work for the benefit, the latter group would initially be 'met with trust and given six months to find a job themselves. After this, they must work for their cash benefits' (see also Regeringen, 2013, p 21).

Just as with the job-offer scheme in the Danish unemployment insurance system (see Chapter 5), utility jobs were criticised from the perspective of the city of **redistribution** for being a 'sweatshop arrangement', 'crowding out wage earners employed on completely ordinary conditions'. The government responded to the critique (which remained marginal) by ensuring a limited duration of 13 weeks for utility jobs and insisting that they would not replace ordinary work. Finally, as with the RSA reform in France (see Chapter 6), there were criticisms of the financing of ECU. Even before the reform was adopted, a large majority of the members of parliament had reserved savings deriving from the reform (reduction in benefits) to finance cuts in corporate taxes. Both Social Democrats and members of SF denounced the financing as 'socially unjust' and a 'reverse Robin Hood' arrangement. However, unlike in the case of RSA, the criticism led to no significant changes. Despite the multiple perspectives of influential political actors qualifying the recipients of cash benefits during the reform process, none considered the recipient as being in need of further **redistribution**.

Sedimentation and subsequent changes

Before going into the actual reform of the cash benefit system, it should be noted that the Carina scandal, as mentioned earlier, already played a role in the tax reform that was adopted in June 2012. Importantly, this reform entailed an increase in the tax credit on work for all 'engaged in active employment', and another tax credit on work targeting single parents in particular, thereby increasing the **incentives** for recipients such as Carina.[6]

The core of ECU came in the shape of a new and highly composite system of preliminary assessment that tested and categorised the uninsured recipient. Figure 7.2 presents an overview of the tests and categorisation.[7] While the previous system operated with one benefit, cash benefits, the reform instantly divided all recipients into two categories, each with their own benefit. On the one hand, there are 'adults' (aged 30 and over) as well as young recipients who have obtained an 'education providing a formal qualification', all of whom receive cash benefits. On the other hand, there are young recipients without an education who are entitled to 'education help', a lower benefit corresponding to SU. Recipients are thus divided into those who can stay in the city of **investment** and those who are excluded because they are either too old or have already benefitted from an investment.

The latter group of recipients of cash benefits is tested further and split up into two categories according to factors that are less clear-cut than age and formal education. From then on, the categorisation is based on probabilities. In the preliminary assessment, the recipient is 'job-prepared' or 'activity-prepared' (Beskæftigelsesministeren, 2013, p 1). The 'job-prepared' are recipients who 'are assessed to be able to get a job within a brief period … and must be available for the labour market' (Beskæftigelsesministeren, 2013, p 17). The 'activity-prepared typically have complex problems and therefore ought to receive a cross-disciplinary and holistic initiative' (Beskæftigelsesministeren, 2013, p 17). The 'activity-prepared' are not economic men. On top of cash benefits, they receive an 'activity bonus' if they commit to engaging in the suggested activities (Beskæftigelsesministeren, 2013, p 56). This entails working with a 'coordinating case worker' and mentors, and engaging with an 'early' and 'work-targeted initiative' (Regeringen et al, 2013, p 10). Although this sounds like **investment**, the activities do not seem to be fully aimed at helping recipients achieve their potential. The goal is not education or skills, but simply some kind of (protected) work, such as a job in a 'social enterprise' (Regeringen et al, 2013, p 10). Moreover, in terms of sanctions, from the perspective of the **paternal** city, these recipients are seen as people who cannot fully control themselves; thus, the 'system of sanctions must take into account that activity-prepared recipients of cash benefits do not always have the possibility of meeting the demands that are made of them' (Regeringen et al, 2013, p 9).

Figure 7.2: Categorisation in the new 'preliminary assessment' system

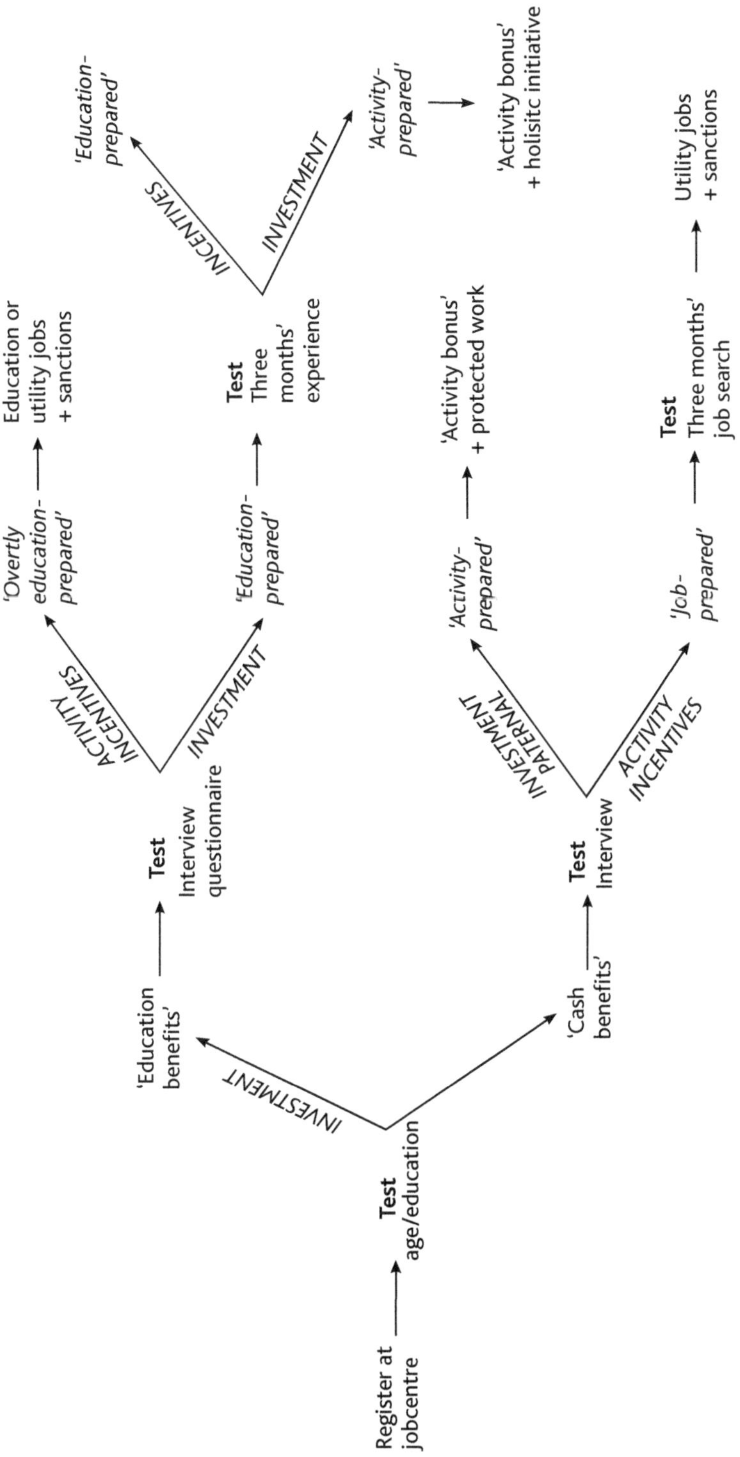

This is not at all the case with the 'job-prepared'. First of all, people in this group get a lower benefit to ensure **incentives** to work. Second, they are put to the test in the city of **activity**. In the first three months, they are met with 'unambiguous demands to search for jobs', while the municipality must 'support and council the citizen in his/her job seeking through an intensive interview course' (Styrelsen for Arbejdsmarked og Rekruttering, 2013, p 2), thus reducing the period of 'trust' by three months from the original six. If the recipient fails the test, they are treated with more suspicion, and henceforth they 'must work for their cash benefits' in utility jobs (Styrelsen for Arbejdsmarked og Rekruttering, 2013, p 2). Unlike employee trainee positions that aim to improve the skills of jobless people, to increase their opportunities of getting an 'ordinary job' or to 'clarify employment goals', utility jobs are not about upskilling but simply a means to 'keep the jobless active until the person can begin in a job or an education' (Styrelsen for Arbejdsmarked og Rekruttering, 2013, p 1). Recalling the scandal of lazy Robert, further scope for sanctions towards the 'job-prepared' are introduced to counter recalcitrant behaviour. For instance, the reform introduces the possibility of 'enhanced availability' to make sure that recipients 'cannot hang on to the benefit systems by systematically circumventing the demands that are made of them' (Regeringen et al, 2013, p 9). This lack of will 'to make oneself available for work' can result in the loss of cash benefits for up to three months.[8] Another instrument to counter the lack of availability is the so-called 'paradox alert', which is a regional 'telephone hotline that companies can call if they experience paradox problems' (Regeringen et al, 2013, p 13).

Another overlapping system of preliminary assessment is directed towards those entitled to 'education help', that is, young people without a formal education, who, as mentioned earlier, are included in the city of **investment** and are thus subject to an 'education injunction' (Folketinget, 2013c, § 1(44)). Education here is both a right and a duty. Recipients are divided into three categories: the 'activity-prepared', the 'education-prepared' and the 'overtly education-prepared'. The latter group, those that are 'assessed [as having] no barriers … for beginning and obtaining an education', are initially not deemed to be 'in need of help and support' (Styrelsen for Arbejdsmarked og Rekruttering, 2014, p 2). Rather, they are potentially lazy, which is why they are immediately required to work in 'utility jobs' and are subject to the same sanctions as the 'job-prepared'. They are sanctioned if they 'reject a job' that they are 'referred to' and must 'exploit [their] employment opportunities until they begin the ordinary education'

(Folketinget, 2013b, § 1(21, 25)). Furthermore, recipients in this group are **incentivised** not only to work, but also to educate themselves.

After initial screening based on an interview, the process of preliminary assessment is different from that for recipients of cash benefits. Here, a series of tests is initiated over three months. The preliminary assessment emphasises the fulfilment of the recipient's potential, and insists that case workers also make this the priority. It is only a question of how long it will take. The 'education-prepared' are assessed as being able to begin and complete an education 'with the right help and support' within a year (Styrelsen for Arbejdsmarked og Rekruttering, 2014, p 2). The 'activity-prepared', on the other hand, 'need extra support and help for more than a year before they can begin an education' (Styrelsen for Arbejdsmarked og Rekruttering, 2014, p 2). However, during the initial screening, 'all young people are met as education-prepared' (Styrelsen for Arbejdsmarked og Rekruttering, 2014, p 2) and it is only in 'exceptional circumstances' that the recipient can be categorised initially as 'active-prepared' (Styrelsen for Arbejdsmarked og Rekruttering, 2014, p 3). In this way, the idea 'that people can do more than we get to see just now' is institutionalised.

The first step of the 'thorough preliminary assessment' is that young people are 'forced to consider relevant educational opportunities' (Styrelsen for Arbejdsmarked og Rekruttering, 2014, p 2). Hereafter a number of activities can be initiated, such as a trainee position in a company, or counselling, interviews, upskilling and reading, writing and arithmetic tests to help the recipient 'overcome barriers on the path towards education' (Styrelsen for Arbejdsmarked og Rekruttering, 2014, pp 3–4). In the continuous assessment, case workers are encouraged to take into account a number factors that 'can be important for the likelihood of a recipient to complete an education' (Styrelsen for Arbejdsmarked og Rekruttering, 2014, p 2). There are factors of 'motivation in relation to education', such as 'well-being', 'self-confidence', 'self-esteem' and future 'expectations'; factors of educational competences such as 'dropping out' and 'performances and attitudes in elementary school'; and factors of health such as 'mental health problems', 'exercise' and 'sleep'. Finally, the 'social background' of the recipient should be considered. Including elements from the city of **insurance**, 'negative life events' can put off the 'right and duty' to education. Similarly, factors from the city of **redistribution** ('financial situation') and from the city of **activity** ('distance to education') set limits on the opportunities for the recipient. There are also factors of social inheritance relating to the city of **investment**, such as 'parents' educational background' and 'acquaintances' educational backgrounds and attitudes to education'. Finally, there are factors of social inheritance that derive from **paternal** work relating to the (lack of) upbringing of the recipient and a transfer of a 'passive culture', echoing the 'risk' to which Carina's children were allegedly exposed. These include 'parents' commitment to the young' recipient and their 'attachment to the labour market during childhood'.

However, if the recipient is categorised as 'activity-prepared' after three months, he, like the 'activity-prepared' recipients of cash benefits, is qualified as less of an economic man (he also receives the 'activity bonus') and less responsive to sanctions. He is entitled to the same intensified support, but unlike the recipients of cash benefits, he is still subject to the 'education injunction', which means that all activities must have education as their final objective and that the 'municipality is required to estimate if a person who has applied for or receives education help … continuously meets the requirements for the help by actively participating in the individually orchestrated education-targeted initiative'.[9]

In this way, the plurality of cities ensuring the active society is distributed into the highly complex institution of this system of profiling – a system that establishes more or less worthy subjects within and between cities. ECU is, on the one hand, a displacement towards the city of **investment** that insists on the potential of (almost) all young uninsured unemployed people. At the same time, it is an intensification that removes some of the last loopholes of the cities of **redistribution** and **insurance**. In the new system, benefits do not disappear, but neither are they a way to redistribute or compensate. Rather, they are qualified as quid pro quo, adjusted to incentivise work and education, and conditional on obedience towards the worthiness that corresponds to the particular categorisation of the recipient.

In 2016, just two years after the reform of ECU, the new centre-right government led by *Venstre* launched another major reform of the cash benefits system. Justified by **incentives** tests predicting increasing employment and the slogan of 'make work pay', the reform reintroduced the 'cash benefits ceiling', the 'integration benefit', and the '225-hour rule', resulting in substantial income reductions for around 50,000 recipients. However, according to the then minister of employment of *Venstre*, and former chief executive officer of the Confederation of Danish Employers (DA) Jørn Neergaard Larsen, 'poverty is not a word we focus on'. Instead, he emphasised that the purpose of the reform was to 'make people come out of the cash benefit system faster' and noted (echoing his predecessor) that the system had turned into a 'disaster with passivity and rapid growth in the number of recipients'. Finally, it worth noting how the latter measure, the 225-hour rule, entails a quite radical **activity** test. The rule requires all cash benefit and integration benefit recipients, and even some receiving the activity bonus, to have worked at least 225 hours in the previous 12 months. If they do not comply, they are sanctioned. If recipients fail the test, the law states, the person is 'considered to take advantage of his work opportunities' (Beskæftigelsesministeriet, 2016). Work itself, and not, for instance, jobseeking requirements, is thus the proof of adequate availability. In other words, for the recipient there is no longer such a thing as lacking **demand**.

Notes

[1] Exact references to quotations can be found in Hansen (2017).

[2] It also entailed a controversial extension of the 'support obligation' of married couples to all couples 'resembling' married couples. Since the extension had little to do with unemployment and was only sparsely debated, it is disregarded in the following presentation. The support obligation was removed in 2016.

[3] For an analysis of the role of media as well as the impact of the scandals on public 'attitudes', see Hedegaard (2014).

[4] This need for coercion in order to make sure young people invested in themselves took a particular form that is addressed later in the chapter.

[5] In Chapter 8, I return to the notion of the blog as a novel and powerful type of critique.

[6] Folketinget, 'Lov om ændring af ligningsloven, lov om en børne- og ungeydelse og personskatteloven', *LOV nr 920.* 2013. København: Skatteministeriet. §1.

[7] The figure does not include the various tests that prove that the claimant is unable to provide for him/herself. These includes a measure of personal wealth (no more than 1,400 euros) and proof that no one else can provide for that person.

[8] Folketinget, 'Lov om ændring af lov om aktiv socialpolitik, SU-loven, lov om børnetilskud og forskudsvis udbetaling af børnebidrag og forskellige andre love', *LOV nr 894 af 04/07/2013.* København: Beskæftigelsesministeriet. §1, 21.

[9] Folketinget, 'Lov om ændring af lov om aktiv socialpolitik, SU-loven, lov om børnetilskud og forskudsvis udbetaling af børnebidrag og forskellige andre love', *LOV nr 894 af 04/07/2013.* København: Beskæftigelsesministeriet. §1, 21.

PART III

Patterns

8

Chemotherapy: the content of the moral economy of activation

By looking into the public debates surrounding four major activation reforms, the four preceding chapters have exposed the ideas, politics and policies at stake in the 'active turn'. This chapter and the following one discuss key patterns that cut across the four cases and argue for their relevance beyond the selected cases and countries. This chapter discusses the *content* of the moral economy of activation, while Chapter 9 points to the key *dynamics*. The first section of the current chapter addresses content by discussing the role of the seven cities of unemployment in the four reforms. The following section compares findings relating to the theories of 'good' and 'bad' activation presented earlier in Chapter 1. The main argument is that non-coercive activation approaches posited by the social investment literature are contradicted by the internal morality of **investment** as well as by the way it is used to justify and make compromises in practice. The final section discusses whether and how neoliberalism differs from or taps into the moral economy of activation. I argue that although moral activation has clear neoliberal traits, labelling it simply as 'neoliberal' loses sight both of important variations in neoliberal thought within the activation debate and what the term 'neoliberal' can credibly encapsulate.

Each country has its own particular history of governing unemployment, embodying different test situations and compromises; even within clusters of welfare regimes, divergence is substantial. The great variety of instruments in the four reforms (individual contracts, interviews, monetary sanctions, jobseeking, control, training, education, subsidies to employers, job offers, job-rotation schemes, work-for-benefit schemes, benefit level and entitlement period adjustment, entitlement criteria adjustment, categorisation tools, mobility requirements, protected work, social work and income taxation) exemplifies the point. Furthermore, each reform has its own particularity that is not necessarily illustrative of the relevant country's long-term transformation. The four cases illustrate that context, or existing historical and institutional paths, does not simply predetermine the direction of policy change. However, the changes matter because existing policies and institutions constitute the reality that is put to the test and adjusted accordingly, and to which new instruments are added.

However, by tracing similar patterns in two different countries and in two different systems of governing (of insured and uninsured unemployed people), it is likely that similar patterns of activation are occurring in other countries. This also has analytical implications. It implies that in order to understand the content and consequences of activation in a given country, it is not sufficient simply to rely on past institutional trajectories, or on the 'heroic' discourses of elections and party programmes, or expert and intellectual governmentalities. It is the merit of French pragmatic sociology to draw attention to the situations of justification and critique of concrete 'grey' policy changes where pragmatics intersect with morality. It is also in this grey politics where the mobilisation of ideas, understood as repertoires of evaluation, are essential to understand how policy changes unfold. Without ideas to qualify the complexity and composite character of instruments and institutions, political actors would be paralysed and without means to legitimate debates and make compromises. The book thus provides an analytical toolkit that can be used to understand such processes in other countries. The model of cities of unemployment and the moral economy of activation could thus be enriched and modified by studies of reforms predating the active turn, and by studies of how the moral economy of activation is mobilised in Anglo-Saxon countries without an extensive unemployment insurance system such as that found in both France and Denmark as well as in post-Communist countries and developing countries with very different policy and institutional backgrounds than those of Western 'golden age' welfare state capitalism.

A moral economy of aid and coercion

The mapping of the way in which actors in our four examples have mobilised the seven cities of unemployment exposes the politics and morality at stake in the transformations. The reforms are driven in particular by justifications from the **paternal**, **mobility**, **investment** and **incentives** cities that are tied together in multiple and distinct ways, but often resembling compromises. These are the legitimate cities, whose morality is rarely radically challenged in the active turn. Four concurrent lines of explanation of unemployment thus inform policy changes, namely: unemployment as an outcome of inadequate monetary difference between benefit and wage levels (**incentives**); unemployment as a problem of lack of adaptability and mobility of the labour force (**activity**); unemployment as a matter of insufficient employability caused by inadequate **investment** in human capital; and, finally, unemployment as the result of forms of governing that deprive people from being responsible by keeping them in a state of dependency (**paternal**). All four explanations are supported by a variety of evidence – from scientific inquiries to public scandals that are used to put policies to the test. The tests thus ask how we can increase **incentives** to cross the threshold to work. How can we make sure unemployed people are mobile and engaged in **activity** that targets, resembles or actually *is* work? How can we prevent people from becoming unemployable and how can we increase the skills of the unemployed by means of **investment** so that they become employable?

It may be tempting to approach these cities or explanations as illusory 'smokescreens'. Indeed, our four cases show that activation measures never quite seem to work as intended. However, this misses how the cities of unemployment are used to evaluate rather than to 'manipulate' the mass public by masking the reality of unemployment. Cities of unemployment qualify the reality of unemployment and prepares it for tests. Failure and critique is thus what nourishes the moral economy of activation. In this way, the active turn, despite its ambiguous success in terms of eradicating poverty and unemployment, is very real. In fact, various *immanent* critiques of the discrepancy between ideology and reality may only strengthen the moral underpinnings of the active turn. Critiques such as 'it doesn't work as intended', 'in fact unemployed do have incentives to work' and 'proper upskilling requires more resources' may have the adverse effect of encouraging policy makers to intensify activation. The rest of the chapter points to a number of moral effects of making the active turn even more real; these should at least encourage the reader to consider its attractiveness.

The first 'moral effect' is the creation of a clear, hierarchical distinction between those who work and those who do not work, as well as the 'in-betweens' of the latter category. Those who work are the employable realising their potentials (**investment**), those who are imbued with a proper work ethic and are part of (working) society (**activity**), those pursuing their rational self-interests to earn more (**incentives**) and competent persons able to provide for themselves (**paternal**). Working equals worthy. A very simple test. Accordingly, on the other side of the threshold, not working equals not worthy, but this is not a simple test. It induces infinite and intimate tests to settle what kind of worthiness is deficient and how to enhance it. I return to this in Chapter 9. The point for now is simply that the moral economy of activation, and the activation instruments it justifies, creates and enforces a community of working people in constant moral tension with non-working people. Those working are *gifted* by working (hard), using their talents, striving to earn more and being self-supporting, but they are also *burdened* by carrying the incompetent, namely those who do not exploit their opportunities and those who refuse to work. The community of working people is thus both the ideal place to live and a place that is constantly threatened by forms of living that contradict its moralities. The tension between political community and worthiness derived from participation in the labour market is 'resolved' by equalising the two.

Part of the moral economy of activation is the denunciation of 'passive' governing. The remaining three cities are, unwillingly, attached to this antithesis. The moralities of both the cities of **redistribution** and **insurance** were fiercely criticised in all of our country reforms, mainly **insurance** in the cases of the unemployment insurance systems and **redistribution** in the cases of the systems of social assistance. To name a few examples from the previous chapters, passive governing is 'cold', a 'disservice' that 'invalidates', makes unemployed people 'survive' rather than 'live', leaves them 'alone with their difficulties', and, by making no demands, fails to 'respect' them. The cities that are mobilised to justify the active turn thus keep finding and disqualifying elements of **insurance**, **redistribution** and **demand** in governing that enhance unemployment and inhibit the activation of unemployed people. The city of **investment** questions short-sighted, passive spending; in the city of **activity**, such spending breeds the scandalous attitude that money is not solely a reward for (burdensome) work; the **paternal** city warns against making unemployed people irresponsible by nursing them too much; and, according to the city of **incentives**, passive spending may always risk demotivating the economic man. According to all four cities, the focus on conjunctural unemployment neglects an array of causes of unemployment that have nothing to do with a lack of available jobs. The moral economy of activation is thus thinking *on behalf* of the unemployed. It is 'emancipatory' and 'caring'; it 'integrates', 'includes', 'brings up', removes 'traps', sets up 'trampolines', makes people 'flourish', makes them 'useful', and gives them 'opportunities' and a reason 'to get up in the morning'. In other words, it 'activates'. From the perspective of the moral economy of activation, the cities of **redistribution**, **insurance** and **demand** are not only completely useless in countering the main problem of unemployment – namely, passivity – but are the root causes. They are not completely delegitimised, however; rather, they are increasingly marginalised in the test of activation policies. **redistribution** was thus used to justify the financing of activation schemes, **insurance** justified widening the group entitled to compensation as well as activation, and **demand** justified redistribution towards the *working* poor.

The second 'moral effect' is the justification of the use of authoritative coercion that accompanies activation instruments in all four cases. By 'coercion', I mean governing that in one way or another is recognised as being unpleasant and thus something that acts against the (immediate) will of the person being coerced. The use of coercive measures is not exclusive to activation. All cities of unemployment hold arguments for coercion aimed at those who are somehow breaching the basic morality of the city. In the city of **insurance**, control measures are legitimate when aimed at the (potential) speculative or fraud-committing person claiming rights without entitlement. In the city of **redistribution**, the egoistic, or greedy person, who, for instance, is causing social dumping by taking up low-wage jobs, should be denied access to rights. In the city of **demand**, it is legitimate to somehow require people to consume and businesses to create jobs rather than save money. However, the logic of coercion is different in the moral economy of activation. In the three aforementioned cities, coercion is used to ensure that the individual is not inhibiting the general preconditions for the city to govern unemployment and uphold its moral standard. Fraud undermines the relationship between compensation and victims (**insurance**). Exploitation and competition inhibits equality and citizenship (**redistribution**). Excessive saving at the expense of consumption prevents growth (**demand**). To the four cities of activation, coercion plays a more ambiguous role. For instance, although coercion in the city of **activity** can take the role of an act of punishment to signal that lazy behaviour breaches its work ethic, coercion (for example, the obligation to search for jobs or work for benefits) has the effect of facilitating a state of worthiness, that of the unemployed person being more active. In other words, coercion is for the sake of the unemployed people who are being coerced. Similar patterns can be seen in the city of **investment**, where coercive measures to ensure that unemployed people invest in themselves are justifiable; in the city of **incentives**, where increasing the relative undesirability of being unemployed sets free the enterprise of the economic man; and in the **paternal** world, where coercion is integral to bringing up the unemployed to take responsibility for their own lives. In all cases, coercion thus functions as different forms of 'chemotherapy' – governing must be 'cruel to be kind' (Boland and Griffin, 2016).

The city of **activity** is particularly important to the moral justification of coercion. The coercive measures justified by the **investment**, **incentives** and **paternal** cities *can* be put to test. In other words, they fail if the 'chemotherapy' does not have the intended effect. However, **activity** is not always subject to the same type of test. Certainly, jobseeking and mobility requirements as well as work-for-benefit schemes can be tested as to whether they bring unemployed people closer to (ordinary) work. However, there is an additional *ceremonial* qualification in the way these measures are justified that escapes conventional testing.[1] In this qualification, a work-for-benefit scheme simply ensures that people who refuse to work are not rewarded. Regardless of the effect, the scheme lives up to the ceremonial test of **activity**. It is, in other words, a tautological test. As Peck (2001) pointed out in his diagnosis of *Workfare states*, these measures thus resembles a *spectacle* echoing the function of the workhouse (Wacquant, 2009, pp 292–8; Hansen, 2015, pp 301–4):

> Just like workhouses and prisons, workfare regimes are intended to throw a long shadow, shaping the norms, values, and behaviors of the wider populations, and *maintaining a form of order*. Sticking with the penal analogy what matters in these situations is not just the activities and immediate fate of the inmates, nor the particularities of prison architecture, but the broader social, political and economic effects of the criminal justice system. (Peck, 2001, p 23, emphasis in original)

These ceremonial **activity** tests are thus not cruel to be kind but rather send signals to the rest of society to guarantee that unemployed people who deliberately refuse to be active are not tolerated and to 'symbolize the price that has to be paid for breaking the rules' (Peck, 2001, p 349). Here, tests such as statistics documenting the scope of the problem matter less. Those who deliberately refuse may be a minority, 'but it's a minority that shocks', to paraphrase a former French president, Nicolas Sarkozy. Nourished by public indignation, as indicated by the case of 'lazy Robert' in the Chapter 7, it takes no more than a single example to trigger a call for more stringent governing of unemployed people and to initiate ceremonial tests that are seen to underpin the difference in worthiness between active and (deliberately) inactive people.

'Good' activation? A critique of social investment

As Chapter 1 shows, an influential perspective in the comparative literature on activation transforms Esping-Andersern's worlds of welfare capitalism (Esping-Andersen, 1990) into 'worlds of activation' (Barbier and Ludwig-Mayerhofer, 2004), distinguishing between two main activation policy approaches: a 'good', non-coercive, 'egalitarian' approach versus a 'bad', coercive, 'authoritarian' approach. The former 'enables', 'empowers, 'integrates' and 'supports', while the latter 'disciplines', requires 'conditional obedience' and pursues 'motivation, control and punishment'. However, in light of the reforms outlined in Chapters 4–7, this normative (as in policy approaches) as well as descriptive (as in different existing policy paths) distinction runs into two explanatory problems that both have normative implications. The first explanatory problem relates to how the analyses of the reforms contest that the justification of coercion can be confined within one 'bad' approach. As mentioned in the previous section, all four cities are mobilised to justify coercive measures. Importantly, this includes the city of **investment**, the city that correlates with the 'good' approach in its aim towards equal opportunities, prevention of unemployment and human capital investment. For instance, the obligatory contract in the French aid plan for the return to employment ensured that all 'those to whom entering a training course is not self-evident, or those who are already on the road to exclusion' would engage in the 'emancipatory' training 'adapted to the needs of each individual' and turning 'the unemployed person, by the help of professionals, into an actor in the construction of his or her own project'. In a similar way, the 'tailored' upskilling measures of the Danish Active Labour Market Policy Act entailed conferring not only 'rights' but also 'duties' 'to ensure that the individual receives the targeted offer'. Finally, in the most radical example, the so-called 'utility jobs' of the Danish reform 'Everyone can be useful', justified as a means of making young people 'understand that an education and a lasting job is also best for themselves', served the function of 'scaring' young people into education. Not only is this an explanatory problem, it also has implications for social investment as a normative policy approach. If protagonists of social investment *do* strive for a non-coercive version of activation, they need to (re)consider the question is why the justification of coercion is not only compatible with, but seen as necessary in conjunction with, **investment** instruments. Here it is worth asking what kind of relationship exists between the state and unemployed people when the former is acting as a 'social investment state' (Morel et al, 2012). To put it simply, what does it imply to *invest*? Generally speaking, investing in any kind of capital implies an expectation of accumulation that is sacrificed in the present but gained in the future – in this case the development of skills (Thévenot, 1984). The investment is thus two-fold. The investor, in this case the state, approaches from the outside, but it is up to the object of the investment to activate and ensure the return. In this sense, the investment in human capital establishes a creditor–debtor relationship in which the unemployed person is indebted, also financially and morally, to the investor and 'expected' to act accordingly (Lazzarato, 2012; Charbonneau and Hansen, 2014) interviewers Charbonneau and Hansen establish a dialogue with Maurizio Lazzarato, the author of the influential book The Making of the Indebted Man (2012).

The second explanatory problem relates to the way in which cities coexist and form compromises in the reforms. In *practice*, **investment** justifications and instruments are always added to, or combined with, tests and instruments from the remaining three cities, incentives, paternal, and activity. Composite governing calls forth tensions, but at the same time the four cities are aligned in the joint venture of activation. For instance, although **investment** tests occasionally limit the scope of **activity** tests, they do not radically question the idea that work must be the end goal. **Investment** aims towards the realisation of potentials, but in a very restrictive fashion, as illustrated by all four reforms, which exclusively regard investment as something to further a career in the labour market. The more normative implication is that in approaching social investment as a holistic policy paradigm, *a* state, the literature has neglected the way the **investment** instruments in practice do not stand alone but are mixed with a plurality of instruments that are qualified according to other moral repertoires. When the literature points to Denmark, along with the rest of the Nordic countries, as living proof of a social investment state or egalitarian activation, it overlooks how social investment instruments in practice, even in Denmark, engage in *compromises* that legitimate the use of coercion and reduce the substance of community (and thus citizenship) to being based strictly on participation in the labour market.

It's neoliberalism, stupid!

As argued in the previous section, the distinction between 'good' and 'bad' activation has a tendency to run into explanatory problems. Another term to describe (and most often denounce) current transformations in nearly all spheres of society is neoliberalism. The social investment literature, along with many other areas of scholarship (see, for example, Bourdieu, 1998; Harvey, 2005; Streeck, 2013), uses the term to designate a political project of 'deregulation', 'dismantling the welfare state' and turning it into a 'lean state' (Palier and Hay, 2017, p 335; see also Giddens, 1998; Jenson, 2010; Morel et al, 2012). However, this definition fits poorly with the experience of the four reforms in France and Denmark. None of the four cities of unemployment fits this definition. Even the city of **incentives** is not simply concerned with laisser-faire deregulation and dismantling. For instance, in the case of the French active solidarity income (RSA), **incentives** justified further spending on a negative tax to secure incentives to take on poorly paid and part-time work. In all cases, reforms do not result in deregulation, but rather further and more detailed regulation.[2]

With a few notable exceptions (Gamble, 1979; Campbell and Pedersen, 2001) it was only after the publication of Foucault's seminal lectures on neoliberalism (Foucault, 2008), that a whole field of research arose that challenged and finessed the minimal deregulatory definition of neoliberalism that is still widespread in social sciences. Scholars have begun to identify varieties of neoliberalism (Dean, 2012), from the early Geneva school (Slobodian, 2018) and the German Freiburg school of *ordo* (Biebricher and Vogelmann, 2017) to the more recent Virginia school of public choice (Triantafillou, 2017) and Chicago schools of human capital (Lemke, 2001) and law and economics (Harcourt, 2010). One of the generic insights from this literature is not that neoliberalism is against regulation and the state as such [One of the generic insights from this literature is that neoliberal ideas are not as such against state intervention and regulation of markets]; rather, so the neoliberal argument often goes, a 'strong state' is necessary to secure competition and markets (Bonefeld, 2012).

Taking these insights into account and comparing them with the moral economy of activation reveals that activation policies *do* have a number of more or less clear threads linking them with neoliberal ideas. The premise in city of **incentives** is that unemployed people are economic men deprived of playing the competitive game in the labour market. The city of **investment** qualifies unemployed people as an enterprise in need of human capital investment in order to compete on the labour market.[3] However, even after recognising the active role of the state, the moral economy of activation transgresses the scope of both the *neo* and the *liberal* of neoliberal thought. While **investment** has clear neoliberal traits, it is also informed by other streams of thought, such as the Rawlsian aim of social justice and equal opportunities, and ideas of human potential from pedagogy and social work and of social inheritance deriving from sociology (Andersson, 2009). In compromises with **incentives**, such as behavioural economics, that have been mobilised to justify recent changes in the Danish unemployment insurance system (see Chapter 5, p 115−16 the **paternal** city is justified to conjure up the rational economic man (McMahon, 2015), but mostly it is highly sceptical of the capacity of unemployed people to pursue their own interest. In addition, the aim of 'bringing up' incompetent unemployed people is not a neoliberal invention, but is as old as the Poor Laws and in its modern form has more in common with Mead's (1997b) 'new paternalism' (see Chapter 3, p 48−9. The same may be said about the work ethic of the city of **activity**; although its aim of a mobile and flexible workforce may sound neoliberal, it was also informed by the establishment of exchange services in the late 19th century. Importantly, both the **paternal** and **activity** cities do not presume the labour market to be a site of exchange and competition. They are concerned with making unemployed people active (through whatever conditions) in solidarity with the community and with making them capable of providing for themselves (and their families).

The active turn is thus a peculiar and often contradictory, composite mix of ideas to which applying the label of neoliberalism would neglect some important moral underpinnings and conflate others. 'Neoliberalism' has been invoked to describe nearly all greater societal transformations in the preceding three decades. The term is so broad that it can explain nearly everything, and thus in reality explains nothing. Attaching the neoliberal label to activation thus does little more than simply denouncing it. The recent *nuit debout* protests against the 'El Khomri Act' in France, mentioned in Chapter 4, were largely informed by this analysis, denouncing the reform as being 'in conformity with the neoliberal logic at work in the last 30 years' (Farbriaz, 2016, p 36). The cities of unemployment is an attempt to develop an analytical model that is conceptually more open and that enables an understanding that is much more precise and useful than 'it's neoliberalism, stupid!'.

The delineation of a neoliberal era often reduces the current state of affairs to a conspiracy orchestrated by elites and hidden networks such as the Mont Pelerin Society (for example, Mirowski and Plehwe, 2009; Blyth, 2013; Slobodian, 2018). This unmasking critique neglects how the *public* debates surrounding activation show that transformations, and the coercion and inequality of worth they induce, are not masked but *justified*. An example is Mouffe who advocates the need for a 'left populism' revitalising the language of 'social justice', going against the 'technocratic', 'post-political', 'neoliberal hegemony'(Mouffe, 2018). However, Mouffe neglects the fact that policy transformations are not simply the result of the evaporation of the political; rather, as Chapters 4–7 show, they are justified by their invocations of social justice. Broadening the perspective further, the findings of this book problematise the common explanation that rising income inequality throughout the countries of the Organisation for Economic Co-operation and Development (OECD) (Piketty, 2013; Cingano, 2014), including France and Denmark, is simply depoliticised, and thus legitimised, by a technocratic 'there-is-no-alternative' ideology. Rather, the legitimation of inequality is underpinned by a less holistic yet more visible and real moral economy that uses the threshold of the labour market to test and consolidate inequalities in worth (and wealth). This moral economy of activation thus functions as one of the key drivers to understanding *how* it is that, as a study by Mijs (forthcoming) suggests, the rising income inequality in most OECD countries correlates with people becoming more convinced that inequality, of which unemployment is one of the most visible manifestations, is reflective of a meritocratic process, that is, deserved. Morality matters. Intellectual critiques and protests may unmask conspiracies, such as the shady involvement of the French employers in the recent 'El Khomri Act' (see chapter 4, p 87 labour market reforms (Farbriaz, 2016), but without taking seriously (and challenging) the *politics* of the composite moral economy that continually instigates the tests to which the reforms respond. It is thus dangerous to simply denounce the moral economy of activation as false or irrational ideology. For instance, in his critique of neoliberal austerity, Blyth sees it as an 'unfair' attack on the welfare state that cannot simply stand 'the sniff test' (Blyth, 2013, p x). In his rather nostalgic call for a return to a Keynesian crisis management and welfare state that 'acted as ladders of mobility for those randomly given the skills in the genetic lottery of life to climb them', Blyth does not consider how the moral economy of activation and its policies and instruments are currently running counter to a Keynesian requalification of the labour market (Blyth, 2013, p xi). While breaking with austerity policies at the level of the European Union will provide scope for **demand**-side solutions to unemployment, national labour market policies and institutions will continue to treat unemployment as a 'structural' problem residing in the behaviour of the unemployed, including the 'lazy Greeks'.[4] Thus while Mouffe's post-politics thesis' neglect of the moral justification of activation leads her to think that unmasking politics is sufficient,

Blyth's neglect of same leads him only to address unemployment as a technical problem.

Further, unmasking critiques thus reinforce the inconvenient populist format of externalising all blame on an elite 'enemy' that conspires against the mass public. The point is not that elites and hidden networks do not play their part occasionally, but that this is only half of the story. There is a public story too, in which the mass public *partakes* rather than being ignorant bystanders. As studies of deservingness attitudes have shown (for example, Taylor-Gooby, 2013; van Oorschot and Roosma, 2017; Nielsen, 2018), after several decades of consecutive reform, the moral economy of activation has not only trickled down into the everyday governing of unemployed people, it also shapes the way people, with or without jobs, put themselves and others to the test when confronted with the risk of unemployment. Rather than denouncing changes as neoliberal, this book points to the need to understand the composite content of the moral economy of activation and the moral consequences, such as the legitimation of coercion and inequality, as well as the dynamics it instigates at both the level of public debate and at the level of everyday governing the jobcentres (discussed in Chapter 9). The object of critique thus ought not (only) to be selected elites; rather, critique entails 'refusing what we are' (Foucault, 1982, p 785), that is, questioning the ways in which the moral economy qualifies the reality of unemployment in public debate and at the jobcentres.

Notes

[1] The argument is inspired by Boltanski's distinction between 'truth tests' and 'reality tests' (Boltanski, 2011) and Agamben's work on 'spectacles' and 'glory' (Agamben, 2011; see also Dean, 2013).

[2] And more generally there is no radical downwards trend in social spending in most countries of the Organisation for Economic Co-operation and Development (Piketty, 2013, chapter 13). However, there is a substantial displacement in priorities of social spending. Elsässer and colleagues find a reprioritisation from 'income and redistributing measures, such as unemployment cash transfers, to activating services and family spending, such as day care and home-help services' (Elsässer et al, 2015, p 5).

[3] Dean was perhaps the first, after Foucault, to point to the *ordo*liberal traits within activation policies (Dean, 1998).

[4] Another example is Piketty, who, in his technical explanation of why returns on wealth exceed economic growth, fails to see how his policy

recommendations morally underpin the same, although, in his view, more 'meritocratic' inequality. Not only does he recommend 'equal access to education' modelled on the Nordic countries (Piketty, 2013, chapter 13), as shown in Chapter 6, but he also supports the principles of the negative tax used in the RSA.

9

Infinite testing: tests and critique in and below the public

Chapter 8 concluded that although the justifications for our four case-study reforms were aligned with the goal of making unemployed people active, they drew on a heterogeneous repertoire of evaluation of four cities of unemployment, each with its distinct way of understanding and putting to the test the phenomenon of unemployment as well as unemployed people themselves. This chapter explores how this multi-causal setting changes the way in which the governance of unemployed people is put to the test in the public eye as well as how unemployed people are put to the test out of public view, in jobcentres. It then shows how tests in the public arena and in jobcentres affect the voice, and potential critique, of unemployed people. Finally, it discusses the extent to which ideas of basic income and social economy/enterprise that have received growing attention in international policy debates contain credible alternatives to the moral economy of activation.

Multi-causality in the public arena

The historical contextualisations illustrating our four selected reforms in Chapters 4–7 illustrate that the reforms are not exceptional, but exemplary of ongoing policy transformations. They are links in a long chain of cumulative activation reforms that seems to have no end in the near future. This section argues that the analyses of justification and critique in the four singular reform processes provide insights into understanding why the need for more activation seems insatiable. To rephrase Crouch (2011), we may speak of the 'strange non-death of activation' (Hansen and Leschke, 2017). Activation has not only been the most consistent and expanding reform process in Europe since 2000 compared with all other labour market policies (Turrini et al, 2015, p 11), but the years following the financial crisis seem only to have consolidated the 'active turn' (Lødemel and Moreira, 2014; Smith et al, 2018).

This chapter outlines three dynamics that derive from the ways in which the moral economy of activation puts policies to the *test* and lays the foundation for consecutive reforms. The first dynamic relates to how the moral economy of activation creates tension-filled and unstable compromises. The politics of activation becomes an *experiment* with four different and sometimes competing theories and explanations for the interplay between unemployment and policies. Rather than a conflict between ready-made blueprints, they function as *tests* in public debate, suggesting various ways of *adjusting* policies incrementally. The consequence is perhaps slower, less revolutionary, changes, but also the creation of an activation path that has no logical end. There is always scope for adjustment and displacement between the four cities of unemployment.

Further, the instability created by compromise is enhanced by the complexity of the systems that makes the consequences of changes incalculable. There is always a degree of uncertainty regarding the 'whatness' of the problem of unemployment. A change in one instrument thus often has unpredicted consequences for another instrument. An example is the way the negative tax element of the French active solidarity income (RSA) prompted a series of **incentives** tests concerning interference with other allowances. Another example, within **investment**, is how the 'education injunction' of the Danish 'Everyone can be useful' reform (ECU) caused the enrolment of students 'without motivation' in technical and vocational schools, thus having a negative effect on motivated students. The normalisation of policy evaluations and experiments (as seen in both the RSA reform and the Danish Active Labour Market Policy Act, or ALMPA) can be seen as another indicator of this dynamic, whereby tests instigate more tests (see also Barbier, 2012). The format, in other words, qualifies unemployed people as a dependent variable in an experiment where a number of independent variables are tested, something that resembles the current obsession with 'evidence-based' policy making (Triantafillou, 2015). Attention is thus displaced from the question of how instruments can reduce the collective artefact of unemployment, to the question of which instruments will make the unemployed person employed, or, at least, to what extent the solution to the former problem can be said to be found in the latter.

At the same time, the composite nature of activation provides room for moral disagreement, for a *politics*, as long as it is in compliance with the imperative of somehow making unemployed people more active. Moral tensions sediment into policies and instruments that give rise to ongoing test situations. For instance, the cities of **activity** and **investment** clash over the issue of the right to refuse work that does not fit the acquired skills of the unemployed person (with reference to the French aid plan for the return to employment, or

PARE), as well over the issue of putting unemployed people to work immediately or upskilling (ALMPA, ECU). The city of **investment** and the **paternal** city contradict each other by the former insisting on the potential of unemployed people, who are thereby worthy of investment, and the latter qualifying some unemployed people as permanently incompetent, thus worthy of charity or protected work (ALMPA). Finally, the cities of **incentives** and **activity** clash over the question of freedom to choose not to work versus the obligation to work, and whether unemployed people should be motivated to work for the sake of earning (more) money, or merely for the ethical value of working (RSA).

The second dynamic relates to the way in which policy successes and failures are qualified in this experimental setting. If policy *adjustments* have the desired effect of making more unemployed people active, the tests call for more of the same. If an increase in **incentives** to work increases employment, the argument of this city goes, another increase will do the same. There are always more people to include, who can always be included faster. As long as there are vacant jobs and/or people are laid off, unemployed people can acquire more skills, be more mobile, have more motivation and be more responsible. Meanwhile, policies never quite work as intended and might even appear to fail. In this case, the moral economy interprets the situation differently, although the result is the same. When policies fail, they are evaluated as a behavioural problem fostered by passive governing that requires more active and intense measures, including sanctions. In this scenario, unemployed people, by being unemployed, remain a symptom of the dysfunctional cities of **demand**, **redistribution** and **insurance**, hence the need to increase and adjust **incentives**, **investment**, **mobility** and **paternal** governance. The same relative indifference to success and failure appears in the indifference to the state of the economy. As long as there are unemployed people to activate both, periods of recovery (for instance, in PARE) and downturns (in ALMPA) can instigate the need for more activation.

Finally, the third dynamic relates to the *ceremonial* tests, discussed in Chapter 8, that accompany the moral economy of activation, and in particular the city of **activity**. Alongside the experimental quest for more effective activation, ceremonial tests are nourished by indignation on the part of the public. The scandals concerning 'poor Carina' and 'lazy Robert' exemplify how individual cases of unemployed people characterised as unwilling and irresponsible can influence not only public opinion but actual policy change. The consequence of the three dynamics is the infinite testing of policies characterised by nostalgic, reactive critiques based on **insurance**, **demand** and **redistribution** that merely defend the past and current status quo.

The many-faced activator

In following the ways in which public opinion sediments into the policies and instruments shaping practice in jobcentres, this book has shown how multi-causality turns the state into what could be termed the many-faced activator. This comprises the facets of the educative and responsibilising pater (**paternal**), the opportunity-maximising investor (**investment**), the incentivising motivator (**incentives**), and the mobility- and flexibility-enhancing adaptor (**mobility**). But how is the multi-causal problematisation and tension between the cities mitigated in the governing of unemployed people? How to correlate which facet with which type of unemployed subject? First, tensions and uncertainties are engrained in the initial screening of unemployed people. These institutionalised tests of assessment and categorisation, often organised around interviews, basically ask what kind of moral subject the unemployed person is and thereby qualify the precise aim and content of being 'active': is it a case of gaining skills, being more flexible and mobile, finding an incentive to work, becoming responsible, and so on? This is not to say that there were no tests previously, but tests based on **insurance** and **redistribution** looked backwards, that is, they asked whether the unemployed person had done their duty in order to claim their rights. By contrast, the evaluation embodied in all four of our reforms is forward-looking, while remaining interested in the past, present and future behaviour of the unemployed person. It asks who that person is and what they have done, thereby retroactively establishing the causes of their situation, and looking forward to the necessary corrective actions. The newest policy invention, which is still in embryo, is the use of **profiling** by means of algorithms and big data, to reduce the need for human judgement in the categorisation of unemployed people, thereby ensuring 'evidence-based' and targeted rights and obligations (see Loxha and Morgandi, 2014; Eskelinen et al, 2015).

Second, in looking forward, the individual plans and contracts, contained within all the reforms to a greater or lesser extent, are central. They establish obligations and rights designed to support unemployed people according to their needs and situation. Engagement with a *plan* implies a functional and future-oriented set-up (Thévenot, 2006), whereby the activities of the authorities, as well as of unemployed people, are qualified in terms of their expected *effect* on the desired outcome. The plan radically changes the way in which unemployed people are characterised, intensifying both uncertainty as well as testing. Both the French and Danish individual plans are inherently unstable and adjusted continually according to the current situation of the unemployed person. The result is a process in which the basic moral question of who unemployed people are is continually put to the test. Experimental and continual testing in the public arena thus finds its own form in the concrete institutionalised tests used in jobcentres. Instruments of screening, interviews, categorisation and personal plans and contracts become indispensable as 'meta-tests' that set the thresholds distinguishing between the plurality of personas attached to the cities of unemployment and the instruments that underpin and define the worthiness of each of them.

The same continual testing retrospectively helps to explain the current situation. Unemployment may initially be caused by an 'accident' residing in the city of **insurance**, but once the plan begins, this is irrelevant (see, for example, Figure 4.2). Here, the unemployed individual may be assessed as someone with potential and hence worthy of **investment**, but as time goes by he or she may be deemed immobile (**activity**) or irresponsible (**paternal**). Looking forwards, the plan may be revised accordingly to result in a new end-goal, which may entail the activator adjusting their perceptions, for example from seeing the unemployed person as someone worthy of the labour market (just in need of being matched to a job), to someone who is equipped with (untapped) potential for acquiring more human capital, then in need of economic motivation, worthy of nothing but a subsidised, low-paid job, and perhaps, finally, 'worthy' only of being poor. Both the French and Danish systems of social assistance have institutionalised the latter possibility. As a consequence, the **redistribution** ideal of universality in both the French republican tradition and in the Nordic social democracies is in practice short-circuited by the many faces of the activator.

Voice and critique of unemployed people

If unemployed people are not qualified and valorised as universal citizens, it is worth asking how institutionalised and continual testing affects their voice. Within the experimental setting of continual testing, the voice of unemployed people is a means of understanding their degree of social inheritance, limits to mobility, lack of self-control, level of responsiveness to incentives and so on, and of providing the necessary engagement to fulfil the plan. The voice of the unemployed person is hence perceived as a *source* of knowledge and *sign* of engagement in the plan. The voice is a means of knowing who the person is and what the person has done (as, for instance, in the screening interviews and surveys), and a means to confirm the person's engagement in personal plan and therefore their agreement to be 'activated' and willingness to become 'active'. As in public debate, the unemployed subjects of the cities of **redistribution**, **insurance** and **demand** are not represented in this setting, and the forward-looking plans provide no scope for claiming the status of citizen, victim or crisis-hit. This is elegantly shown in Stephane Brizé's fictional but highly realistic film *The Measure of a Man* (2015), which follows the life of a French 51-year-old unemployed factory worker a year after he was dismissed along with 750 colleagues. In one of the first scenes, the main character Thierry is sitting in a café with former colleagues discussing the ongoing juridical process against their former employer. The lay-off is judged as 'unfair', since the business was not in financial distress (**demand**) and one of the colleagues thus want to continue the fight and have 'the bastards responsible for this situation condemned' (**redistribution**) and not 'leave the other 750 in the lurch' without compensation for their loss (**insurance**). Fast forward to a job-training course where Thierry's performance in a recorded, simulated job interview is being evaluated. What was presented as a non-cowardly and proud attitude in the first scene is completely turned on its head. The job coach lets Thierry's fellow participants evaluate the 'body language' and 'power of the voice'. He is described as having 'no energy', being 'cold', 'not smiling', 'sagging in the chair' and 'impolite'. The job coach adds that 'non-verbal language is 55% of the impression' and that 'the idea is to show the interviewer that you really want to be there so that you open the door for the interviewer'. It is the adaptability test of **activity** that Thierry fails. In this test, there is no room for unaccommodating, negative attitudes, for instance, towards the status of the job. At the same time, the relationship between unemployed person and job coach has **paternal** traits. We are back in the classroom, or even in the family home where children are educated to be 'polite'. Thierry's voice is thus only sought as a means of confirmation when the job coach asks (rhetorically) whether he understands and agrees with the assessment.

This example takes place below the public debate, and thus falls outside the scope of this book. However, analysis of the relevant public debate reveals that similar dynamics are at play when unemployed people raise their voice in public. The case of ECU provides some disturbing hints of this. Both the scandals concerning 'poor Carina' and 'lazy Robert' illustrate how issues of unfair governing (from the perspective of unemployed people) almost immediately result in intensified scrutiny of unemployed people reminiscent of the institutionalised tests that ask, 'Who are you, and what have you done?'. The only difference is that it takes place in the public arena in the form of intimate ceremonial tests. The following three examples exemplify how critique by unemployed people is received and qualified in public. The first two exemplify a dynamic similar to the one just mentioned, while the latter may show a way to circumvent it.

The first example comes from France. In September 2018, when the French president Emmanuel Macron passed a crowd of spectators at a 'local heritage day' at the presidential palace, a young unemployed person addressed Macron directly, saying that he had sent him a letter criticising him, in accordance with the city of **demand**, for not doing anything to provide jobs for young unemployed people. The state is put to the test (Jadot, 2018). What unfolds, however, is an **activity** test directed at the young person.

Macron (M):	But wait, I cannot see to every one of you. But I can propose solutions that you can take as your starting point to solve your problems. Are you registered at the jobcentre?
Unemployed person (U):	Yes, but there is nothing. I've sent CVs and letters of motivation but it doesn't change anything.
M:	You want to work in which industry?
U:	I am a gardener. I've sent [applications] to all the local councils but they don't hire.
M:	If you are ready and motivated…. In the hotel, restaurant, construction industries, there is not one place I go where they don't say they need people…. I cross the street and I will find them. They simply want people who are ready to work. Considered the constraint of the industry.
U:	To me, personally, it is not a problem, but when I give my CV they never call back.
M:	You take a street, you take Montparnasse [street in Paris], you do the street with all the cafés and restaurants…. Frankly, I am certain that one in two is hiring at this moment. Go!

To Macron, there is no such thing as lack of **demand**, only lack of motivation to work, and thus his recommendation to the young person resembles his current reforms of both the system of unemployment insurance and social assistance (see Chapters 4 and 6).

The second example relates to Denmark. In 2016, the 'make work pay' reform of the system of social assistance (see Chapter 7) incited the creation of a protest network called 'Fight poverty NOW', largely organised by recipients of the existing cash benefit. At a peaceful demonstration, around 3,000 people gathered in front of parliament to protest against the 'inequality' and rising poverty induced by the reform (**redistribution**). The publicly funded radio station 24/7 had teamed up with a representative from a taxi company in need of employees. While recording, they asked some of the unemployed recipients participating in the protest whether they were interested in a job 'offer'. The radio station hence staged a classic **activity** test, probing whether available jobs existed alongside (idle) unemployed people. One benefits recipient rejected the offer, and a few others hesitated. The story of the picky unemployed person who 'does not want to drive taxi' overshadowed the very protest against the reform in the news media.[1] Public and collective critique was radically transformed into individual behavioural problems. The 'solutions' suggested by Macron and Radio 24/7 were subsequently put to the test. In fact, no cafés or restaurants were hiring at Montparnasse, and only one out of 50 people at the demonstration had declined the taxi firm's job offer. However, the critics were only confirming the relevance of the *behavioral* **activity** test in these situations. As the two examples, as well as the RSA and ECU reforms, illustrate, the moral economy of activation treats the voice of the unemployed as an *object* of, rather than a(n equal) input in the democratic debate. Rather, it adopts the experimental social engineering perspective, which qualifies the unemployed person as a dependent variable, and/or the ceremonial perspective in which the will of the people is restricted to the will of the (hard-)working part of the population.

The final example is from 2010 in Denmark, where a young newly qualified academic spontaneously began to write in an online blog named 'Unemployment insurance land' (*Dagpengeland*) about his attendance at a 10-week job-training course contracted out to a private company (Aaen, 2012). At the time, the financial crisis was starting seriously to affect the labour market, so thousands of people were enrolled in similar courses, fostering a booming and lucrative industry for private job-placement companies. The blog rose in popularity on social media, where people were sharing similar experiences.

The blogger did not explicitly denounce anything, but expressed his critique in a subtle, documentarist but humourist and sarcastic style of writing, presenting a Kafkaesque world of rules and over-self-confident job coaches. The coaches relied on both the **investment** and **paternal** cities to claim worthiness and authority. With regard to **investment**, they were 'connoisseurs of the human heart', able to 'see right through people' and identify 'possibilities everywhere' for 'putting the individual first' and 'building whole persons'. To do this, they made use of a personality test capable of rendering visible the inner personality and potential of the attendees. With regard to the **paternal** city, the assumption was that the unemployed attendees are incompetent. They are told 'don't be late', 'don't be drunk' and 'don't waste time on internet surfing', and are instructed in basic skills such as hand-shaking and telephone calls. The blogger sarcastically writes that one of them 'speaks as if we were children', which makes her 'nicely easy to understand'.

Shortly before the blog attracted public attention, stories of 'meaningless' activation courses started to appear in the media. The blog matched and accelerated this critique, and provided a much more detailed account of the power relations and techniques at play in these courses. Journalists started looking for similar stories and within a very short period the activation schemes had become ridiculed, forcing politicians to somehow respond. So from starting as a humoristic account of the everyday life, the blog became part of a public debate about the activation system, to the extent where the blogger himself was asked exactly what his blog was criticising and what needed to be changed. However, much of the rather radical critique of activation – of the authority to decide who the unemployed are and what they want, and to make them into incompetent children – evaporated. Instead, the blogger's and the public's criticisms of jobseeking courses were used to justify less red tape in the unemployment insurance fund system while the future Social Democratic minister of employment used it to justify more education and upskilling in place of jobseeking (see Chapter 7). The example thus both shows how radical critiques of activation succeeded in putting policies to the test as well as how, in the end, they were absorbed in the lack of political alternatives to operationalise such critiques.

Anything new?

The most potent alternative at the moment seems to come from the nationalist and xenophobic movements and from parties tapping into the populist narrative of the neglected 'victims' of elite-driven globalisation, causing the outflow of jobs and the influx of migrants dumbing down the wages of the jobs that remain. The Danish experience, however, shows that the moral economy of activation is not necessarily irreconcilable with such movements. As described in Chapter 7, since 2001 a number of activation measures have been introduced to target immigrants. In the 'multi-causal' problematisation, immigrants have thus been treated as a group with specific behavioural traits that require targeted (and tougher) instruments. Initially a push from the far-right Danish People's Party, this is today a broader political alliance with the Social Democrats' explicit hard line towards migration, but without radically questioning the moral economy of activation. The French experience is different where the far-right National Front (now National Rally) at the elections in 2017 accused Macron of 'making the French feel guilty' when he suggested to suspend unemployment benefits in case of refusing two job offers.[2] The nostalgic and nationalist solutions to the problem of unemployment were instead to protect French companies from foreign competition and to reduce immigrants' access to jobs.

The question then is whether there are other alternatives challenging the content and dynamics of the *moral* economy of activation and do not simply point backwards in a nostalgic longing for some lost golden age. The most pertinent and debated 'alternative' idea, in particular since the 2008 financial crisis, is without doubt the instrument of basic income. The protagonists of the basic income scheme today include a variety of intellectuals and philanthropists from Joseph Stiglitz, Robert Reich and Guy Standing to Elon Musk (chief executive officer of car manufacturing and energy company Tesla) and Mark Zuckerberg (chief executive officer of social networking site Facebook) to name but a few. It was one of the key issues debated at the global political and business elite's World Economic Forum annual meeting Davos in 2017, and has started to enter party politics, as in the French Socialist Benoît Hamon's candidacy for presidency the same year. Finally, and importantly, it is currently being tested in a number of countries, such as in Finland.

At first sight, the basic income radically breaks with several of the characteristics of the moral economy activation. Importantly, it is unconditional and thus precludes the variety of obligations, sanctions and control that comes with activation policies, thereby giving unemployed people the opportunity to say no to 'bullshit jobs' (Graeber, 2018). Finally, in its common diagnosis of a labour market with diminishing jobs due to automation, it does not see unemployment as a behavioural problem but as a problem of lack of demand (that cannot, however, be solved with **demand** stimuli). In this way, some protagonists justify the basic income as a response to critiques of the moral economy of activation. It is a critique of the **paternal** qualification of unemployed people as incompetent; it challenges **activity** in distinguishing between free work and unfree labour; and it entails aims of socialising property (**redistribution**) and providing security for the precariat and working poor (**insurance**) (see, for example, Standing, 2017; van Parijs and Vanderborght, 2017).

However, basic income is an *instrument* that can be qualified, and thus shaped, in a plurality of ways, and certainly not only against the moral economy of activation. To Standing, the 'breadth of support … promises a more robust movement' (Standing, 2017, p 17), but it also reveals the many contradictory moral purposes that the instrument can serve. Basic income can be seen as an effective way of ensuring **incentives** to work, which seems to be the main justification behind the experiment in Finland (Standing, 2017, pp 260–3). It can be justified as a **paternal** charity for those excluded from the labour market due to lack of talent (Murray, 2005). By arguing for creation of better quality of jobs, through the possibility of exiting the labour market, basic income reinforces that the labour market is really *the* place to be. Unemployed people will still, and, since all unemployment traps are removed, *always* be financially as well as be morally inferior. Further, since basic income is not necessarily replacing all other social benefits and services (van Parijs and Vanderborght, 2017, p 262), it may function in conjunction with additional activation 'benefits' and instruments with obligations and control. Hence, if basic income is to provide a radical alternative, the *instrument* will need be more closely tied to *tests* that run counter to the content and dynamics of the moral economy of activation (which will probably discourage many of the current proponents).

A policy idea that may provide unemployed people with a voice that challenges the moral economy of activation is social economy or social enterprises, which put simply, are characterised by an imperative to reinvest eventual profits in social purposes.[3] Social enterprises is a composite of ideas from the cooperative movement, Third Way ideas of social entrepreneurship and social investment, and ideas from management of entrepreneurship and belief in market-based solutions (Hulgård, 2011; Teasdale, 2012). In relation to the unemployed, the so-called WISE (work integration social enterprise) is of particular interest (Defourny and Nyssens, 2010). The WISE can be seen as yet another instrument in the repertoire of activation. Such enterprises include community-based work for (vulnerable) unemployed people (**activity**) and responsibilising (**paternal**) workfare schemes similar to the utility jobs scheme described in Chapter 7. Unemployed people may also have opportunities for upskilling, and hence increase their chances of moving on to an ordinary job (**investment**). Finally, as is often the case in Denmark (Juul-Olsen, 2016), WISE schemes are used by local authorities to test the 'ability to work'. Hence, just like basic income, they can be qualified and used in accordance with the moral economy of activation.

However, following Larner's (2014) study of social enterprises, the WISE may nonetheless contain radical challenges to the moral economy of activation. First, the cooperative element of a democratic and co-creating management of social enterprises gives unemployed people a voice that the moral economy of activation is not inclined to grant. It is not simply a matter of voice in relation to the personal plan, but also in relation to the organisation and production of the enterprise as such. Hence the social enterprise may be a place for meaningful work that produces value that ordinary businesses shun in their search for profit. Social enterprises, for instance, produce social 'by-products', such as 'social cohesion' and strengthening of local communities. If work within WISE is recognised as different but proper work, unemployed people might find ways to acquire worthiness *without* mimicking the promised land of 'ordinary' work; they, in a sense, activate themselves beyond the moral economy of activation. The work undertaken in WISE could thus resemble Ulrich Beck's 'civil labour' that is clearly distinguished from the growing tendencies to activation observed in the late 1990s (Beck, 2000). To Beck, civil labour, unlike activation, first serves a 'political' purpose of allowing (unemployed) citizens to 'become at once partners and critics of the state' (p 143).

> Civil labour should by no means be confused with the pressure being put everywhere on benefit claimants to undertake work in the community. Civil labour is voluntary, self-organized labour, where what should be done, and how it should be done, are in the hands of those who actually do it. The democratic spirit that animates civil labour, and with it the society of self-active individuals, will perish if one commits the centuries-old mistake of confusing it with compulsory labour. (Beck, 2000, p 127)

If qualified and justified *tactically*, basic income and social economy *can* provide space and pathways towards new ways of putting work and unemployment to the test. In times where jobs are being automated at a hitherto unseen pace and where the economy's impact on the climate and environment remind us that growth, and hence the value of work, is no longer a self-evident good, this is perhaps more needed than ever.

Notes

[1] Hammer, J.M. (2016) '*Haydar tilbød job til demonstranter: jeg ønsker ikke at køre taxa*', 6 October, www.bt.dk/politik/haydar-tilboed-job-til-demonstranter-jeg-oensker-ikke-at-koere-taxa-0.

[2] L'Obs. '*Débat en direct: Macron conclut: "Mme Le Pen, vous n'avez pas de projet pour le pays"*', www.nouvelobs.com/presidentielle-2017/20170503. OBS8904/debat-en-direct-macron-conclut-mme-le-pen-vous-n-avez-pas-de-projet-pour-le-pays.html.

[3] The argument on social enterprises is based on an analysis previously published in Danish (Hansen, 2018).

References

Aaen, L. (2012) *Dagpengeland: En sand historie om aktivering*. København: Gyldendal.

Abrahamson, P. (2010) 'European welfare states beyond neoliberalism: toward the social investment state', *Development and Society*, 39(1), pp. 61–95.

Agamben, G. (2011) *The kingdom and the glory: For a theological genealogy of economy and government*. Stanford, CA: Stanford University Press.

Andersson, J. (2009) *The library and the workshop: Social democracy and capitalism in the knowledge age*. Stanford, CA: Stanford University Press.

Angel-Urdinola, D.F., Kuddo, A. and Semlali, A. (2013) *Building effective employment programs for unemployed youth in the Middle East and North Africa*. Washington, DC: World Bank.

Apeldoorn, B. van (2003) 'European unemployment and transnational capitalist class strategy', in Overbeek, H. (ed) *The political economy of European employment*. New York, NY: Routledge, pp. 113–134.

Assemblée nationale (1988a) 'Débats parlementaires, lundi 10 octobre 1988, No 21 [1] A. N. (C. R.)', *Journal Officiel de la République Française*, www.legifrance.gouv.fr.

Assemblée nationale (1988b) 'Débats parlementaires, mercredi 5 octobre 1988, No 19 [1] A. N. (C. R.)', *Journal Officiel de la République Française*, www.legifrance.gouv.fr.

Aubry, M. and Fabius, L. (2000) 'Lettre de Mme Martine Aubry, ministre de l'emploi et de la solidarité et M. Laurent Fabius, ministre de l'économie, des finances et de l'industrie au MEDEF, sur les observations du Gouvernement sur la convention Unédic, notamment l'amélioration de l'indemnisation chômage', www.vie-publique.fr.

Aurich, P. (2008) 'Activating the unemployed: directions and divisions in Europe', *European Journal of Social Security*, 13(Sec. 294), pp. 294–313.

Babcock, L., W.J. Congdon, L.F. Katz, and S. Mullainathan (2012) 'Notes on behavioral economics and labor market policy', *IZA Journal of Labor Policy*, 1(2), pp. 1–14.

Barbier, J.-C. (2002) 'Peut-on parler d'« activation » de la protection sociale en Europe ?', *Revue Française de Sociologie*, 43(2), pp. 307–332.

Barbier, J.-C. (2007) 'The French activation strategy in a comparative perspective', in Serrano Pascual, A. (ed) *Reshaping welfare states and activation regimes in Europe*. Brussels: Peter Lang, pp. 145–172.

Barbier, J.-C. (2011) 'Activer les pauvres et les chômeurs par l'emploi ? Leçons d'une stratégie de réforme', *Politiques Sociales et Familiales*, 104 (Les politiques de lutte contre la pauvreté), pp. 47–58.

Barbier, J.-C. (2012) 'Évaluations "expérimentales": quelque leçons de l'histoire', *Politiques Sociales et Familiales*, 110, pp. 19–31.

Barbier, J.-C. (2013) 'Changes in social citizenship in France in a comparative perspective: "activation strategies" and their traces', in Evers, A. and Guillemard, A.-M. (eds) *Social policy and citizenship: The changing landscape*. New York, NY: Oxford University Press, pp. 150–171.

Barbier, J.-C. (2014) 'Languages of "social policy" at "the EU level"', in Béland, D. and Petersen, K. (eds) *Analysing social policy concepts and language: Comparative and transnational perpectives*. 1st edn. Bristol: Bristol University Press, pp. 59–80.

Barbier, J.-C. and Fargion, V. (2004) 'Continental inconsistencies on the path to activation', *European Societies*, 6, pp. 437–460.

Barbier, J.-C. and Ludwig-Mayerhofer, W. (2004) 'Introduction: the many worlds of activation', *European Societies*, 6(4), pp. 423–436.

Barbier, J.-C. and Théret, B. (2001) 'Welfare to work or work to welfare: the French case?', in Gilbert, N. and Van Voorhis, R.A. (eds) *Activating the unemployed*. New Brunswick, NJ: Transaction.

Barthe, Y., D. de Blic, J.-P. Heurtin, É. Lagneau, C. Lemieux, D. Linhardt, C. Moreau de Bellaing, C. Rémy, and D. Trom (2013) 'Sociologie pragmatique : mode d'emploi', *Politix*, 103(3), pp. 175–204.

Baxandall, P. (2004) *Constructing unemployment: The politics of joblessness in East and West*. Aldershot: Ashgate.

Beck, U. (2000) *The brave new world of work*. Cambridge: Polity Press.

Behrent, M. C. (2010) 'Accidents happen: Francois Ewald, the "antirevolutionary" Foucault, and the intellectual politics of the French welfare state', *Journal of Modern History*, 82(September), pp. 585–624.

Béland, D. (2005) 'Ideas and social policy: An institutionalist perspective', *Social Policy and Administration*, 39(1), pp. 1–18.

Béland, D. (2007) 'The social exclusion discourse: ideas and policy change', *Policy & Politics*, 35(1), p. 123–139.

Béland, D. and Cox, R.H. (2010) *Ideas and politics in social science research*. Oxford: Oxford University Press.

Béland, D. and Hansen, R. (2000) 'Reforming the French welfare state: solidarity, social exclusion and the three crises of citizenship', *West European Politics*, 23(1), pp. 47–64.

Belgian Presidency (2010) *Active labour market policies for the Europe 2020 Strategy – Finding ways to move foreward, Antwerp 28–29 October 2010.* Brussels: Department of Work and Social Economy.

Bénatouïl, T. (1999) 'A tale of two sociologies: the critical and the pragmatic stance in contemporary French sociology', *European Journal of Social Theory*, 2(3), pp. 379–396.

Béraud, M. and Eydoux, A. (2011) 'Redefining unemployment and employment statuses: the impact of activation on social citizenship in France', in Betzelt, S. and Bothfeld, S. (eds) *Activation and Labour Market Reforms in Europe: Challenges to Social Citizenship.* London: Palgrave Macmillan UK, pp. 125–146.

Berger, P. L. and Luckmann, T. (1966) *The social construction of reality.* Middlesex: Penguin.

Beskæftigelsesministeren (2013) 'Lovforslag nr. L 223: Forslag til Lov om ændring af lov om en aktiv beskæftigelsesindsats, lov om ansvaret for og styringen af den aktive beskæftigelsesindsats og forskellige andre love'. Folketingstidende. København: Folketinget.

Beskæftigelsesministeriet (2016) *VEJ nr 10310 af 20/12/2016.* (Vejledning om 225-timersreglen for ægtepar og ugifte der modtager hjælp efter lov om aktiv socialpolitik § 11)

Betzelt, S. and Bothfeld, S. (2011) *Activation and labour market reforms in Europe: Challenges to social citizenship.* Basingstoke: Palgrave Macmillan.

Biebricher, T. (2008) 'Genealogy and governmentality', *Journal of the Philosophy of History*, 2(3), pp. 363–396.

Biebricher, T. and Vogelmann, F. (eds) (2017) *The birth of austerity: German ordoliberalism and contemporary neoliberalism.* Rowman & Littlefield International.

Blair, T. and Schroeder, G. (1998) 'Europe: The Third Way/Die Neue Mitte', Working Documents no 2. Johannesburg: Friedrich Ebert Stiftung.

Block, F. and Somers, M. (2003) 'In the shadow of Speenhamland: social policy and the old Poor Law', *Politics & Society*, 31(2), pp. 283–323.

Blok, A. and Meilvang, M. (2014) 'Picturing urban green attachments: civic activists moving between familiar and public engagements in the city', *Sociology*, 49(1), pp. 1–19.

Blokker, P. (2011) 'Pragmatic sociology: theoretical evolvement and empirical application', *European Journal of Social Theory*, 14(3), pp. 251–261.

Blyth, M. (2002) *Great transformations: Economic ideas and institutional change in the twentieth century.* Cambridge: Cambridge University Press.

Blyth, M. (2013) *Austerity: The history of a dangerous idea.* Oxford: Oxford University Press.

Boland, T. and Griffin, R. (2015) *The sociology of unemployment*. Manchester: Manchester University Press.

Boland, T. and Griffin, R. (2016) 'Making sacrifices: how ungenerous gifts constitute jobseekers as scapegoats', *Distinktion*, 17(2), pp. 174–191.

Boltanski, L. (2011) *On critique: A sociology of emancipation*. Cambridge: Polity Press.

Boltanski, L. (2012) *Love and justice as competences*. Cambridge: Polity Press.

Boltanski, L. and Chiapello, È. (2005) 'The new spirit of capitalism', *International Journal of Politics, Culture, and Society*, 18(3–4), pp. 161–188.

Boltanski, L. and Thévenot, L. (1981) 'Finding one's way in social space: a study based on games', *Social Science Information*, 22(4–5), pp. 631–680.

Boltanski, L. and Thévenot, L. (1987) *Les économies de la grandeur: Cahiers du centre d'études de l'emploi*. Paris: Presses universitaires de France.

Boltanski, L. and Thévenot, L. (1991) *De la justification: Les économies de la grandeur*. Paris: Gallimard.

Boltanski, L. and Thévenot, L. (1999) 'The sociology of critical capacity', *European Journal of Social Theory*, 2(3), pp. 359–377.

Boltanski, L. and Thévenot, L. (2000) 'The reality of moral expectations: a sociology of situated judgement', *Philosophical Explorations*, 3(3), pp. 208–231.

Boltanski, L. and Thévenot, L. (2006) *On justification: Economies of worth*. Princeton, NJ: Princeton University Press.

Bonefeld, W. (2012) 'Freedom and the strong state: on German ordoliberalism', *New Political Economy*, 17(5), pp. 633–656.

Bonoli, G. (2010) 'The political economy of active labor-market policy', *Politics and Society*, 38(4), pp. 435–457.

Bonoli, G. (2013) *The origins of active social policy*. Oxford: Oxford University Press.

Borghi, V. (2011) 'One-way Europe? Institutional guidelines, emerging regimes of justification, and paradoxical turns in European welfare capitalism', *European Journal of Social Theory*, 14(3), pp. 321–341.

Bourdieu, P. (1994) *Raisons pratiques: Sur la théorie de l'action*. Paris: Éditions du Seuil.

Bourdieu, P. (1998) 'The essence of neoliberalism: utopia of endless exploitation', *Le Monde Diplomatique*, December.

Brady, M. (2014) 'Ethnographies of neoliberal governmentalities: from the neoliberal apparatus to neoliberalism and governmental assemblages', *Foucault Studies*, (18), pp. 11–33.

Brown, A.J.G. and Koettl, J. (2012) *Active labor market programs: How, why, when, and to what extent are they effective?* Washington, DC: World Bank.

Bruno, I. (2009) 'The "indefinite discipline" of competitiveness: benchmarking as a neoliberal technology of government', *Minerva*, 47(3), p. 261.

Cahuc, P., G. Cette and A. Zylberberg (2008) *Salaire minimum et bas revenus: comment concilier justice sociale et efficacité économique ?* Paris: Conseil d'analyse économique.

Campbell, J.L. (2004) *Institutional change and globalization.* Princeton, NJ: Princeton University Press.

Campbell, J.L. and Pedersen, O.K. (2001) 'The rise of neoliberalism and institutional analysis', in Campbell, J.L. and Pedersen, O.K. (eds) *The rise of neoliberalism and institutional analysis.* Princeton, NJ: Princeton University Press, pp. 1–24.

Carstensen, M.B. and Hansen, M.P. (2018) 'Legitimation as justification', *European Journal of Political Research*, Epub.

Carstensen, M.B. and Schmidt, V. A. (2016) 'Power through, over and in ideas: conceptualizing ideational power in discursive institutionalism', *Journal of European Public Policy*, 23(3), pp. 318–337.

Castel, R. (1995) *Les métamorphoses de la question sociale: une chronique du salariat.* Paris: Fayard.

Caswell, D., Marston, G. and Larsen, J.E. (2010) 'Unemployed citizen or "at risk" client? Classification systems and employment services in Denmark and Australia', *Critical Social Policy*, 30(3), p. 384.

Celik, T.H. (2016) 'Fiscal state-citizen alignment: tracing the sociohistorical conditions of the financial crisis', *Critical Historical Studies*, 3(1), pp. 105–141.

Celikates, R. (2012) 'Systematic misrecognition and the practice of critique: Bourdieu, Boltanski and the role of critical theory', in Bankowsky, M. and Le Goff, A. (eds) *Recognition theory and contemporary French moral and political philosophy.* Manchester: Manchester University Press. pp. 160–172.

Chabanet, D. (2012) 'The long history of a new cause: the mobilization of the unemployed in France', in Chabanet, D. and Faniel, J. (eds) *The mobilization of the unemployed in Europe: From acquiescence to protest?* Basingstoke: Palgrave Macmillan, pp. 29–56.

Charbonneau, M. and Hansen, M.P. (2014) 'Debt, neoliberalism and crisis: interview with Maurizio Lazzarato on the indebted condition', *Sociology*, 48(5), pp. 1039–1047.

Cheyns, E. (2011) 'Multi-stakeholder initiatives for sustainable agriculture: limits of the "Inclusiveness" paradigm', in Ponte, S., Gibbon, P. and Vestergaard, J. (eds) *Governing through standards: Origins, drivers and limitations*. Basingstoke: Palgrave Macmillan, pp. 318–354.

Childs, M.W. (1936) *Sweden: The Middle Way*, New Haven: Yale University Press.

Christensen, A.B. (2017) 'Dagpengesystemets transformation i den danske velfærdsstat', *Tidsskrift for Velferdsforskning*, 20(3), pp. 230–245.

Christensen, J. (2011) 'Arbejdsløshedsforsikring og arbejdsanvisning', in Petersen, J.H., Petersen, K. and Christiansen, N. F. (eds) *Dansk velfærdshistorie: Mellem skøn og ret*. Odense: Syddansk Universitetsforlag, pp. 491–573.

Christensen, J. (2012a) 'Arbejdsløshedsforsikring og arbejdsanvisning', in Petersen, J.H., Petersen, K. and Christiansen, N.F. (eds) *Dansk velfærdshistorie: Velfærdsstatens storhedstid*. Odense: Syddansk Universitetsforlag, pp. 487–545.

Christensen, J. (2012b) 'Arbejdsløshedsforsikring og arbejdsanvisning', in Petersen, J.H., Petersen, K. and Christiansen, N.F. (eds) *Dansk velfærdshistorie: Velfærdsstaten i støbeskeen*. Odense: Syddansk Universitetsforlag, pp. 451–515.

Christensen, J. (2013) 'Arbejdsløshedsforsikring og aktivering', in Petersen, J.H., Petersen, K. and Christiansen, N. F. (eds) *Dansk velfærdshistorie: Velfærdsstaten i tidehverv*. Odense: Syddansk Universitetsforlag, pp. 523–610.

Christensen, J. and Petersen, J.H. (2014) 'Arbejdsløshedsforsikring og aktivering', in Petersen, J. H., Petersen, K. and Christiansen, N.F. (eds) *Dansk velfærdshistorie: Hvor glider vi hen?* Odense: Syddansk Universitetsforlag, pp. 613–716.

Chung, H., Taylor-Gooby, P. and Leruth, B. (2018) 'Political legitimacy and welfare state futures: introduction', *Social Policy & Administration*, 52(4), pp. 835–846.

Cingano, F. (2014) 'Trends in Income Inequality and its Impact on Economic Growth', OECD Social, Employment and Migration Working Papers, No. 163, OECD Publishing.

Cloutier, C. and Langley, A. (2013) 'The logic of institutional logics: insights From French pragmatist sociology', *Journal of Management Inquiry*, 22(4), pp. 360–380.

Cole, A. (2008) *Governing and governance in France*. Cambridge: Cambridge University Press.

Collier, S.J. (2012) 'Neoliberalism as big Leviathan, or … ? A response to Wacquant and Hilgers', *Social Anthropology*, 20(2), pp. 186–195.

Cortes, A. (2018) '*Travailler pour toucher le RSA? Macron fait un pas vers une vieille idée de la droite*', *Marianne*, 14 June, www.marianne.net/politique/travailler-pour-toucher-le-rsa-macron-fait-un-pas-vers-une-vieille-idee-de-la-droite.

Cox, R.H. (2001) 'The social construction of an imperative: why welfare reform happened in Denmark and the Netherlands but not in Germany', *World Politics*, 53(April), pp. 463–498.

Crouch, C. (2011) *The strange non death of neoliberalism*. Cambridge: Polity Press.

Cruikshank, B. (1993) 'The will to empower: technologies of citizenship and the war on poverty', *Socialist Review*, 23(4), pp. 29–55.

Dagpengekommissionen (2015) *Dagpengekommissionens samlede anbefalinger*. København: Beskæftigelsesministeriet.

Daguerre, A. (2007) *Active labour market policies and welfare reform: Europe and the US in comparative perspective*. Houndmillls: Palgrave Macmillan.

Daniel, C. and Tuchszirer, C. (1999) *L'état face aux chômeurs: L'indemnisation du chômage de 1884 à nos jours*. Paris: Flammarion.

Dansou, K. and Langley, A. (2012) 'Institutional work and the notion of test', *M@n@gement*, 15(5), pp. 503–527.

Dean, H. (2007) 'The ethics of welfare-to-work', *Policy & Politics*, 35(4), pp. 573–590.

Dean, M. (1995) 'Governing the unemployed self in an active society', *Economy and Society*, 24(4), pp. 559–583.

Dean, M. (1998) 'Administering asceticism: reworking the ethical life of the unemployed citizen', in Hindess, B. and Dean, M. (eds) *Governing Australia: Studies in contemporary rationalities of government*. Cambridge: Cambridge University Press, pp. 87–107.

Dean, M. (2012) 'Rethinking neoliberalism', *Journal of Sociology*, 48(3), pp. 1–14.

Dean, M. (2013) *The signature of power: Sovereignty, governmentality and biopolitics*. London: Sage.

Defert, D. (1991) '"Popular life" and insurance technology', in Burchell, G., Gordon, C. and Miller, P. (eds) *The Foucault effect: Studies in governmentality*. Chicago, IL: University of Chicago Press, pp. 211–233.

Defourny, J. and Nyssens, M. (2010) 'Conceptions of social enterprise and social entrepreneurship in Europe and the United States: convergences and divergences', *Journal of Social Entrepreneurship*, 1(1), pp. 32–53.

Delanty, G. (2011) 'Varieties of critique in sociological theory and their methodologocal implications for social research', *Irish Journal of Sociology*, 19(1), pp. 68–92.

de la Porte, C., Pochet, P. and Belgium, G.R. (2001) 'Social benchmarking, policy making and new governance in the EU', *Journal of European Social Policy*, 11(4), pp. 291–307.

Demazière, D. (2013) 'Le chômage a-t-il encore un sens ? Enseignements d'une comparaison dans trois métropoles', *Sociologie du Travail*, 2013(55), pp. 191–213.

Desrosières, A. and Thévenot, L. (1988) *Les catégories socioprofessionelles*. Paris: Éditions La Découverte.

Dingeldey, I. (2007) 'Between work and enablement – the different paths to transformation of the welfare state: a comparative analysis of activating labour market policies', *European Journal of Political Research*, 46, pp. 823–851.

Dingeldey, I. (2009) 'Activating labour market policies and the restructuring of welfare and state: a comparative view on changing forms of governance', *ZeS-Arbeitspapir*, 1, 01/2009.

Dwyer, P. (2010) *Understanding social citizenship: Themes and perspectives for policy and practice*. Bristol: Policy Press.

Edling, N. (2008) 'Regulating unemployment the Continental way: the transfer of municipal labour exchanges to Scandinavia 1890-1914', *European Review of History*, 15(1), pp. 23–40.

Eichhorst, W. and Konle-Seidl, R. (2008) *Contingent convergence: A comparative analysis of activation policies*. 3905. Bonn. Discussion Paper No. 3905, December 2008, IZA.

Eichhorst, W. and Rinne, U. (2014) *Promoting youth unemployment through activation strategies*. Employment Working Paper No. 163. Geneva: ILO.

Elsässer, L., Rademacher, I. and Schäfer, A. (2015) 'Cracks in the foundation. Retrenchment in advanced welfare states', *economic sociology_the european electronic newsletter*, 16(3), pp. 4–16.

Emmenegger, P., S. Häusermann, B. Palier, and M. Seeleib-Kaiser (eds) (2012) *The age of dualization: The changing face of inequality in deindustrializing societies*. New York, NY: Oxford University Press.

Emmenegger, P., J. Kvist, P. Marx, K. Petersen (2015) 'Three Worlds of Welfare Capitalism: The making of a classic', *Journal of European Social Policy*, 25(1), pp. 3–13.

Enjolras, B., J. L. Laville, L. Fraisse, and H. Trickey (2000) 'Between subsidiarity and social assistance: the French route to activation', in Lødemel, I. and Trickey, H. (eds) *'An offer you can't refuse': Workfare in international perspective*. Bristol: Policy Press, pp. 41–69.

Escudero, V., Mourelo, E.L. and Morano, C.P. (2016) *What works: Active labour market policies in Latin America and the Caribbean*. Geneva: ILO.

Eskelinen, L., Petersen, J.S. and Bolvig, I. (2015) *Profilering af ledige: Analyse af profileringsværktøjer i fire lande*. København: KORA.

Esmark, A. (2011) 'Europeanisation of employment polity: changing partnership inclusion in Denmark, Great Britain and France', in Torfing, J. and Triantafillou, P. (eds) *Interactive policymaking, metagovernance and democracy*. Colchester: ECPR Press, pp. 75–94.

Esmark, A. and Schoop, S.R. (2017) 'Deserving social benefits? Political framing and media framing of "deservingness" in two welfare reforms in Denmark', *Journal of European Social Policy*, 27(5), pp. 417–432.

Esping-Andersen, G. (1985) *Politics against markets: The social democratic road to power*. Princeton, NJ: Princeton University Press.

Esping-Andersen, G. (1990) *The three worlds of welfare capitalism*. Cambridge: Polity Press.

Esping-Andersen, G. (1999) *Social foundations of postindustrial economies*. Oxford: Oxford University Press.

Esping-Andersen, G. (2002) *Why we need a new welfare state*. New York, NY: Oxford University Press.

Esping-Andersen, G. (2007) 'Equal opportunities and the welfare state', *Contexts*, 6(3), pp. 23–27.

Estevao, M.M. (2003) *Do active labor market policies increase employment?*, IMF Working Paper Working Paper No. 03/234, IMF.

Etzioni, A. (ed) (1995) *New communitarian thinking: Persons, virtues, institutions, and communities*. Charlottesville, VA: University Press of Virginia.

Eulriet, I. (2008) 'Analysing political ideas and political action', *Economy and Society*, 37(1), pp. 135–150.

Ewald, F. (1986) *L'Etat providence*. Paris: Grasset.

Ewald, F. (1990) 'Norms, discipline and the law', *Representations*, 30, pp. 138–161.

Ewald, F. (1991) 'Insurance and risk', in Burchell, G., Gordon, C. and Miller, P. (eds) *The Foucault effect: Studies in governmentality*. Chicago, IL: University of Chicago Press, pp. 197–211.

Ewald, F. (2000) 'Ernest-Antoine Seillière (entretien)', *Risques: Les Cahiers de l'Assurance*, 43(Septembre).

Ewald, F. and Kessler, D. (2000) 'Les noces du risque et de la politique', *Le Débat*, 109(2), pp. 55–72.

Eydoux, A. and Béraud, M. (2011) 'Accelerating governance reforms: the French case', in van Berkel, R., de Graaf, W. and Sirovátka, T. (eds) *The governance of active welfare states in Europe*. Basingstoke: Palgrave Macmillan, pp. 38–61.

Eydoux, A. and Gomel, B. (2014) 'Introduction', in Eydoux, A. and Gomel, B. (eds) *Apprendre (de l'échec) du RSA*. Rueil-Malmaison: Wolters Kluver, pp. 15–41.

Farbriaz, P. (ed) (2016) *Nuit debout: les textes*. Paris: Les petits matins.

Fischer, F. and Gottweiss, H. (eds) (2012) *The argumentative turn revisited: Public policy as communicative practice*. Durham, NC and London: Duke University Press.

Foucault, M. (1982) 'The subject and power', *Critical Inquiry*, 8(Summer), pp. 777–795.

Foucault, M. (1984) 'Polemics, politics, and problematizations: an interview with Michel Foucault', in Rabinow, P. (ed) *The Foucault reader*. New York, NY: Pantheon, pp. 381–390.

Foucault, M. (2003) 'Polemics, politics, and problematizations: an interview with Michel Foucault', in Rabinow, P. and Rose, N. (eds) *The essential Foucault*. New York, NY: The New Press, pp. 18–24.

Foucault, M. (2007) *Security, territory, population: Lectures at the Collège de France 1977–78*. New York, NY: Palgrave Macmillan.

Foucault, M. (2008) *The birth of biopolitics: Lectures at the Collège de France 1978–79*. New York, NY: Palgrave Macmillan.

Fraser, N. and Honneth, A. (eds) (2004) *Redistribution or recognition?: A political-philosophical exchange*. London: Verso.

Friedman, M. (1962) *Capitalism and freedom*. Chicago, IL: University of Chicago Press.

Friedman, M. (1968) 'The role of monetary policy', *American Economic Review Papers and Proceedings*, 58(1), pp. 1–17.

Galbraith, J.K. (1987) *A history of economics: The past as the present*. London: Penguin.

Gamble, A. (1979) 'The free economy and the strong state', in R. Milliband and J. Saville (eds) *The Socialist Register 1979*, London: Merlin Press, pp. 1–25.

Garraty, J.A. (1978) *Unemployment in history: Economic thought and public policy*. New York, NY: Harper & Row.

Garsten, C. and Jacobsson, K. (2004) *Learning to be employable: New agendas on work, responsibility and learning in a globalizing world*. New York, NY: Pagrave Macmillan.

Gass, J.R. (1988) Towards the 'Active Society'. *OECD Observer* 152, pp. 4–8.

Giddens, A. (1994) *Beyond left and right: The future of radical politics*. Stanford: Stanford University Press.

Giddens, A. (1998) *The third way: The renewal of social democracy*. Cambridge: Polity Press.

Glynos, J. and Howarth, D. (2007) *Logics of critical explanation in social and political theory*. Abingdon: Routledge.

Goffman, E. (1974) *Frame analysis: An essay on the organization of experience*. Cambridge, MA: Harvard University Press.

Graeber, D. (2018) *Bullshit jobs: A theory*. New York: Simon & Schuster.

Haahr, J.H. (2004) 'Open co-ordination as advanced liberal government', *Journal of European Public Policy*, 11(2), p. 209.

Hacker, J. (2004) 'Privatizing risk without privatizing the welfare state: The hidden politics of social policy retrenchment in the United States', *American Political Science Review*, 98(2), pp. 243-260.

Hall, P. (1993) 'Policy paradigms, social learning, and the state: the case of economic policymaking in Britain', *Comparative Politics*, 25, pp. 275–296.

Hammer, J.M. (2016) '*Haydar tilbød job til demonstranter: jeg ønsker ikke at køre taxa*', 6 October, www.bt.dk/politik/haydar-tilboed-job-til-demonstranter-jeg-oensker-ikke-at-koere-taxa-0.

Handler, J.F. (2004) *Social citizenship and workfare in the United States and Western Europe: The paradox of inclusion*. Cambridge: Cambridge University Press.

Hansen, M.P. (2015) 'Foucault's flirt? Neoliberalism, the left and the welfare state: a commentary on *La dernière leçon de Michel Foucault* and *Critiquer Foucault*', *Foucault Studies*, 20, pp. 291–306.

Hansen, M.P. (2016) 'Non-normative critique: Foucault and pragmatic sociology as tactical re-politicization', *European Journal of Social Theory*, 19(1), pp. 127–145.

Hansen, M.P. (2017) *Trying the unemployed. Justification and critique, emancipation and coercion towards the 'active society'. A study of contemporary reforms in France and Denmark*, PhD Thesis 10.2017. Copenhagen: Copenhagen Business School.

Hansen, M.P. (2018) 'Det "sociale" og arbejdets værd(ier) i sociale virksomheder', in Sørensen, K.I. and Lund, A.B. (eds) *Komparative analyser af dansk socialøkonomi: Sorgfrit udkomme & timeligt velvære?* Frederiksberg: CBS Center for civilsamfundsstudier, pp. 111–124.

Hansen, M.P. and Leschke, J. (2017) 'The strange non-death of ALMPs', in O'Reilly, J., C. Moyart, T. Nazio, and M. Smith (eds) *Youth unemployment: STYLE handbook*. Bristol: Policy Press, pp. 235–237.

Hansen, M.P. and Triantafillou, P. (2011) 'The Lisbon strategy and the alignment of economic and social concerns', *Journal of European Social Policy*, 21(3), p. 197.

Harcourt, B.E. (2010) 'Neoliberal penalty: a brief genealogy', *Theoretical Criminology*, 14(1), pp. 74–92.

Harvey, D. (2005) *A brief history of neoliberalism*. Oxford: Oxford University Press.

Hay, C. (2008) 'Constructivist institutionalism', in Binder, S., Rhodes, R.A.W. and Rockman, B.A. (eds) *The Oxford handbook of political institutions*. Oxford: Oxford University Press, pp. 56–73.

Hedegaard, T.F. (2014) 'Stereotypes and welfare attitudes: A panel survey of how "Poor Carina" and "Lazy Robert" affected attitudes towards social assistance in Denmark', *Nordic Journal of Social Research*, 5, pp. 139-160.

Helfter, C. (2015) 'Contrepoint – pauvreté: cercles familiaux et éligibilité aux prestations', *Informations Sociales*, 2(188), p. 19.

Hernstein, R.J. and Murray, C. (1994) *The bell curve: Intelligence and class structure in American life*. New York, NY: Free Press.

Hirsch, M. (2005). *Au possible, nous sommes tenus. La nouvelle équation sociale: 15 résolutions pour combattre la pauvreté des enfants*. Paris: Ministère des solidarités, de la santé et de la famille.

Hirsch, M. (2008) *Livre vert. Vers un revenu de Solidairité active*. Paris: Le haut commissaire aux solidarités actives contre la pauvreté.

Holden, M. and Scerri, A. (2015) 'Justification, compromise and test: developing a pragmatic sociology of critique to understand the outcomes of urban redevelopment', *Planning Theory*, 14(4), pp. 360–383.

Holmlund, B. (2015) 'Notes on unemployment insurance and behavioral economics'. Bilag 10.7.B. Danish Commission on Unemployment Insurance. København: Beskæftigelsesministeriet.

Honneth, A. (2010) 'Dissolutions of the social: on the social theory of Luc Boltanski and Laurent Thévenot', *Constellations*, 17(3), pp. 376–388.

Hulgård, L. (2011) 'Social economy and social enterprise: An emerging alternative to mainstream market economy?', *China Journal of Social Work*, 4(3), pp. 201–215.

Jadot, J. (2018) '"*Je traverse la rue, je vous en trouve*" du travail: on a testé le conseil donné par Emmanuel Macron à un chômeur', Franceinfo, 17 September.

Jagd, S. (2011) 'Pragmatic sociology and competing orders of worth in organizations', *European Journal of Social Theory*, 14(3), pp. 343–359.

Jensen, B. (2008) *Hvad skrev aviserne om de arbejdsløse?* Købenahvn: Gyldendal.

Jenson, J. (2010) 'Diffusing ideas for after neoliberalism: the social investment perspective in Europe and Latin America', *Global Social Policy*, 10(1), pp. 59–84.

Jessop, B. (1993) 'Towards a Schumpeterian workfare state? Preliminary remarks on post-Fordist political economy', *Studies in Political Economy*, 40(1), pp. 7–39.

Jessop, B. (2003) 'Changes in welfare regimes and the search for flexibility and employability', in Overbeek, H. (ed) *The political economy of European employment*. Abingdon: Routledge, p. 29.

Justesen, L. and Mik-Meyer, N. (2012) *Qualitative research methods in organization studies*. Copenhagen: Hans Reitzels Forlag.

Juul-Olsen, M. (2016) 'Socialøkonomiske virksomheder og integration af sårbare borgere på arbejdsmarkedet', in Hulgård, E., Juul-Olsen, M. and Nielsen, E.N. (eds) *Samskabelse og socialt entreprenørskab*. København: Hans Reitzel, pp. 179–212.

Kasza, G.J. (2002) 'The illussion of welfare "regimes"', *Journal of Social Policy*, 31(2), pp. 271–287.

Keynes, John Maynard. (2006) *General theory of employment, interest and money*, London: Atlantic Books.

Klanfer, J. (1965) *L'exclusion sociale: Etude de la marginalité dans les sociétés occidentales*. Paris: Science et service, Bureau de recherches sociales.

Koch, L. (1996) *Racehygiejne i Danmark 1920–56*. København: Informations forlag.

Koch, L. (2006) 'Eugenics in Scandinavia', *The European Legacy*, 11(3), pp. 299–309.

Kolstrup, S. (2011) 'Fra fattiglov til forsorgslov', in Petersen, J. H., Petersen, K., and Christiansen, N. F. (eds) *Dansk velfærdshistorie: Mellem skøn og ret*. Odense: Syddansk universitetsforlag, pp. 146–232.

Kolstrup, S. (2012) 'Fra forsorgslov til bistandslov', in Petersen, J.H., Petersen, K. and Christiansen, N.F. (eds) *Dansk velfærdshistorie: Velfærdsstatens storhedstid*. Odense: Syddansk universitetsforlag, pp. 163–238.

Kolstrup, S. (2013) 'Bistandloven – idealer og praksis', in Petersen, J.H., Petersen, K. and Christiansen, N.F. (eds) *Dansk velfærdshistorie: Velfærdsstaten i tidehverv*. Odense: Syddansk Universitetsforlag, pp. 137–242.

Kolstrup, S. (2014) 'Aktiveringslinjens gennembrudsår og konsolidering', in Petersen, J.H., Petersen, K. and Christiansen, N.F. (eds) *Dansk velfærdshistorie: Hvor glider vi hen?* Odense: Syddansk Universitetsforlag, pp. 177–335.

Koopman, C. (2013) *Genealogy as critique: Foucault and the problems of modernity*. Bloomington, IN: Indiana University Press.

Korpi, W. and Palme, J. (1998) 'The paradox of redistribution and strategies of equality: welfare state institutions, inequality, and poverty in Western countries', *American Sociological Review*, 63(October), pp. 661–687.

Kristensen, P.H. (2013) 'The distinctiveness of Nordic welfare states in the transformation to the projective city and the new spirits of capitalism', in du Gay, P. and Morgan, G. (eds) *New spirits of capitalism?* Oxford: Oxford University Press, pp. 1–22.

Kvist, J. and Harsløf, I. (2014) 'Workfare with welfare revisited: instigating dual tracks for insiders and outsiders', in Lødemel, I. and Moreira, A. (eds) *Activation or workfare? Governance and the neo-liberal convergence*. Oxford: Oxford University Press, pp. 48–68.

Laclau, E. and Mouffe, C. (1985) *Hegemony and socialist strategy: Towards a radical democratic politics*. London: Verso.

Lamont, M. and Thévenot, L. (2000a) 'Introduction: toward a renewed comparative cultural sociology', in Lamont, M. and Thévenot, L. (eds) *Rethinking comparative cultural sociology: Repertoires of evaluation in France and the United States*. Cambridge: Cambridge University Press, pp 1–24.

Lamont, M. and Thévenot, L. (2000b) *Rethinking comparative cultural sociology: Repertoires of evaluation in France and the United States*. Cambridge: Cambridge University Press.

Lane, J.F. (2018) 'From "moule" to "modulation": logics of Deleuzean "control" in recent reforms to French labour law', *Modern & Contemporary France*, 26(3), pp. 245–259.

Larner, W. (2000) 'Post-welfare state governance: towards a code of social and family responsibility', *Social Politics: International Studies in Gender, State & Society*, 7(2), pp. 244–265.

Larner, W. (2014) 'The limits of post-politics: rethinking radical social enterprise', in Wilson, J. and Swyngedouw, E. (eds) *The post-political and its discontents: Spaces of depoliticisation, spectres of radical politics*. Edinburgh: Edinburgh University Press, pp. 189–207.

Larsen, C.A. (2008) 'The institutional logic of welfare attitudes: how welfare regimes influence public support', *Comparative Political Studies*, 41(2), pp. 145–168.

Larsen, C.A. and Andersen, J.G. (2009) 'How economic ideas changed the Danish welfare state: the case of neoliberal ideas and highly organized Social Democratic interests', *Governance*, 22(2), pp. 239–261.

Larsen, F., N. Abildgaard, T. Bredgaard, and L Dalsgaard (2001) *Kommunal aktivering: Mellem disciplinering og integration*. Aalborg: Aalborg universitetsforlag.

Larsen, R.E. (2013) *Fra ledighed til ledighad*. Aarhus: Dana.

Lazzarato, M. (2012) *The making of indebted man: An essay on the neoliberal condition*. Los Angeles, CA: Semiotext(e).

Lefebvre, A. and D. Méda (2006) *Faut-il brûler le modèle social français?* Paris: Le Seuil.

Lehtonen, T.-K. and Liukko, J. (2011) 'The forms and limits of insurance solidarity', *Journal of Business Ethics*, 103, pp. 33–44.

Lemke, T. (2001) '"The birth of bio-politics": Michel Foucault's lecture at the Collège de France on neo-liberal governmentality', *Economy and Society*, 30(2), pp. 190–207.

Lenoir, R. (1974) *Les exclus: Un français sur dix*. Paris: Éditions du Seuil.

Lessenich, S. (2011) 'Constructing the socialized self: mobilization and control in the "active society"', in Bröckling, U., Krasmann, S. and Lemke, T. (eds) *Governmentality: Current issues and future challenges*. New York, NY: Routledge, pp. 304–321.

Linhart, D. (2009) *Modernisation et précarisation de la vie au travail, Papeles del CEIC*, 2009(1) # 43, http://identidadcolectiva.es/pdf/43.pdf.

Lizé, L. (2013) 'Notice 9 : politiques de l'emploi et du marché du travail', *La protection sociale en France. La documentation Française*, pp. 133–146.

L'Obs. '*Débat en direct: Macron conclut: "Mme Le Pen, vous n'avez pas de projet pour le pays"*', www.nouvelobs.com/presidentielle-2017/20170503. OBS8904/debat-en-direct-macron-conclut-mme-le-pen-vous-n-avez-pas-de-projet-pour-le-pays.html.

Lødemel, I. and Moreira, A. (eds) (2014) *Activation or workfare? Governance and the neo-liberal convergence*. Oxford: Oxford University Press.

Lødemel, I. and Trickey, H. (eds) (2001) *'An offer you can't refuse': Workfare in international perspective*. Bristol: Policy Press.

Loxha, A. and Morgandi, M. (2014) *Profiling the unemployed: A review of OECD experiences and implications for emerging economies*. Social Protection and labor discussion paper; no. SP 1424. Washington, DC: World Bank Group.

Lyon-Caen, G. (2001) 'Un agrément, des désagréments...', *Droit Social*, 4(Avril), pp. 377–383.

Madsen, P.K. (2002) 'The Danish model of "flexicurity": a paradise with some snakes'. Paper presented at Interactions Between Labour Market and Social Protection. Brussels, 16 May.

Mailand, M. (2015) *Dagpengereformer og flexicurity i forandring: Delrapport 1 i projektet 'Dagpengereformer og flexicurity'*. København: FAOS.

Manow, P. (2004) '*The good, the bad, and the ugly': EspingAndersen's regime typology and the religious roots of the Western welfare state*, MPIfG Working Paper. Köln: 04/3 Max Planck Institute for the Study of Societies.

Marshall, T.H. (1992 [1964]) 'Citizenship and social class' in T.H. Marshall and T. Bottomore, *Citizenship and social class*. London: Pluto Press, pp. 1–51.

Marston, G. and McDonald, C. (2006) *Analysing social policy: A governmental approach*. Cheltenham: Edward Elgar Publishing.

Martin, J.P. (2014) *Activation and active labour market policies in OECD countries: Stylized facts and evidence on their effectiveness*. Policy Paper No. 84 Bonn: IZA.

Martin, J.P. and Grubb, D. (2001) 'What works among active labour market policies: evidence from OECD countries' experiences', *Swedish Economic Policy Review*, 8(2), pp. 9–60.

McDonald, C. and Marston, G. (2005) 'Workfare as welfare: governing unemployment in the advanced liberal state', *Critical Social Policy*, 25(3), p. 374–401.

McMahon, J. (2015) 'Behavioral economics as neoliberalism: producing and governing homo economicus', *Contemporary Political Theory*, 14(2), pp. 137–158.

Mead, L.M. (1997a) 'The new paternalism: supervisory approaches to poverty'. Washington, DC: Brookings Institution Press.

Mead, L.M. (1997b) 'The rise of paternalism', in Mead, L.M. (ed) *The new paternalism: Supervisory approaches to poverty*. Washington, DC: Brookings Institution Press.

Mehta, J. (2011) 'The varied role of ideas in politics: from "whether" to "how"', in Béland, D. and Cox, R.H. (eds) *Ideas and politics in social science research*. Oxford: Oxford University Press, pp. 23–46.

Meilvang, M.L., Carlsen, H.B. and Blok, A. (2018) 'Methods of engagement: on civic participation formats as composition devices in urban planning', *European Journal of Cultural and Political Sociology*, 5(1–2), pp. 12–41.

Meyer, N.I., Petersen, K.H. and Sørensen, V. (1978) *Oprør fra midten*. København: Gyldendal.

Mijs, J.J.B. (forthcoming) 'The paradox of inequality: income inequality and belief in meritocracy go hand in hand', *Socio-Economic Review*.

Mirowski, P. and Plehwe, D. (2009) *The road from Mont Pèlerin: The making of the neoliberal thought collective*. Cambridge, MA: Harvard University Press.

Modigliani, F. and Papademos, L. (1975) 'Targets for monetary policy in the coming year', *Brookings Papers on Economic Activity*, 1975(1), pp. 141–165.

Morel, N., Pailer, B. and Palme, J. (2012a) 'Beyond the welfare state as we knew it?', in Morel, N., Palier, B., and Palme, J. (eds) *Towards a social investment state? Ideas, policies and challenges*. Bristol: Policy Press, pp. 1–30.

Morel, N., Palier, B. and Palme, J. (eds) (2012b) *Towards a social investment state? Ideas, policies and challenges*. Bristol: Policy Press.

Mouffe, C. (2000) *The democratic paradox*. London: Verso.

Mouffe, C. (2018) *For a left populism*. New York, NY: Verso.

Murray, C. (2005) *In our hands: A plan to replace the welfare state*. Washington, DC: AEI Press.

Natali, D. and Bonoli, G. (2012) *The politics of the new welfare state*. Oxford: Oxford University Press.

Nielsen, M.H. (2014) 'Nytteaktiveringens retfærdiggørelse: et pragmatisk sociologisk perspektiv på aktivering af arbejdsløse', *Dansk Sociologi*, 25(1), pp. 9–33.

Nielsen, M.H. (2015) 'Det aktive menneskes triumf? En analyse af de omfattende forandringer af kategoriseringen af kontanthjælpsmodtageren', *Tidsskrift for Arbejdsliv*, 17(1), pp. 44–60.

Nielsen, M.H. (2018) 'Four normative languages of welfare: a pragmatic sociological investigation', *Distinktion: Journal of Social Theory*, 19(1), pp. 47–67.

Nothdurfter, U. (2016) 'The street-level delivery of activation policies: constraints and possibilities for a practice of citizenship', *European Journal of Social Work*, 19(3–4), pp. 420–440.

OECD (Organisation for Economic Co-operation and Development) (1989) *The future of social protection*. Social Policy Studies. Paris: OECD.

OECD (2015) *OECD employment outlook 2015*. OECD: Paris, doi: 10.1787/empl_outlook-2015-en.

Okbani, N. (2013) 'How a controversial minimum scheme can be legitimated by its evaluations: the case of the RSA evaluations in France', Paper presented at 1st International Conference on Public Policy, June 2013, Grenoble, France, archives-ouvertes.fr.

Oliviennes, D. (1994) 'La préférence française pour le chômage', *Le Débat*, 82(5), pp. 138–153.

Palier, B. (2000) '"Defrosting" the French welfare state', *West European Politics*, 23(2), pp. 113–136.

Palier, B. (2001) 'Beyond retrenchment: four problems in current welfares state research and one suggestion how to overcome them', in Klasen, J. (ed) *What future for social security?* The Hague: Kluwer Law International, pp. 105–120.

Palier, B. (2002) *Gouverner la securité sociale: Les réformes du système français de protection socioale depuis 1945.* Paris: Presses Universitaires de France.

Palier, B. (2005) 'Ambigious agreement, cumulative change: French social policy in the 1990s', in Streeck, W. and Thelen, K. (eds) *Beyond continuity: Institutional economies in advanced political economies.* Oxford: Oxford University Press, pp. 128–144.

Palier, B. (2010a) *A long goodbye to Bismarck?: The politics of welfare reform in continental Europe.* Amsterdam: Amsterdam University Press.

Palier, B. (2010b) 'The long conservative corporatist road to welfare reforms', in Palier, B. (ed) *A long goodbye to Bismarck? The politics of welfare reforms in continental Europe.* Amsterdam: Amsterdam University Press, pp. 333–388.

Palier, B. (2010c) 'The dualizations of the French welfare system', in Palier, B. (ed) *A long goodbye to Bismarck? The politics of welfare reforms in continental Europe.* Amsterdam: Amsterdam University Press, pp. 73-100.

Palier, B. and Hay, C. (2017) 'The reconfiguration of the welfare state in Europe', in King, D. and Le Galès, P. (eds) *Reconfiguring European states in crisis.* Oxford: Oxford University Press, pp. 331–352.

Panizza, F. and Miorelli, R. (2013) 'Taking discourse seriously: discursive institutionalism and post-structuralist discourse theory', *Political Studies*, 61(2), pp. 301–318.

Patriotta, G., Gond, J.P. and Schultz, F. (2011) 'Maintaining legitimacy: controversies, orders of worth, and public justifications', *Journal of Management Studies*, 48(8), pp. 1806–1836.

Peck, J. (2001) *Workfare states.* New York, NY: Guilford Press.

Pedersen, O.K. (2010) 'Institutional competitiveness: how nations came to compete', in Morgan, G., J. L. Campbell, C. Crouch, O. K. Pedersen, and R. Whitley (eds) *The Oxford handbook of institutional comparative analysis.* Oxford: Oxford University Press, pp. 625–658.

Petersen, J.H. (2014) *Pligt og ret, Ret og pligt.* Odense: Syddansk Universitetsforlag.

Petersen, J.H., Petersen, K. and Christiansen, N.F. (2013) 'Det socialpolitiske idelandskab', in Petersen, J.H., Petersen, K. and Christiansen, N.F. (eds) *Dansk velfærdshistorie: Velfærdsstaten i tidehverv.* Odense: Syddansk Universitetsforlag, pp. 73–136.

Phelps, E.S. (1968) 'Money-wage dynamics and labor market equilibrium', *Journal of Political Economy*, 76(4), pp. 678–711.

Pierson, P. (1994) *Dismantling the welfare state?: Reagan, Thatcher and the politics of retrenchment.* Cambridge: Cambridge University Press.

Piketty, T. (2008) 'Revenu de solidarité active: l'imposture Thomas Piketty', *Libération*, 2 September.

Piketty, T. (2013) *Le capital au XXIe siècle.* Paris: Éditions du Seuil.

Polanyi, K. (1944) *The great transformation.* Boston: Beacon Press.

Ponte, S. and Gibbon, P. (2005) 'Quality standards, conventions and the governance of global value chains', *Economy and Society*, 34(1), pp. 1–31.

Rawls, J. (1999) *A theory of justice.* Revised edn. Oxford: Oxford University Press.

Regeringen (Socialdemokraterne, Radikale Venstre and Socialistisk Folkeparti) and Venstre, Dansk Folkeparti, Det Konservative Folkeparti and Liberal Alliance (2013) 'Aftale om en reform af kontanthjælpssystemet – flere i uddannelse og job , 18 April 2013', København: Beskæftigelsesministeriet.

Regeringen (2013) *Alle kan gøre nytte: Udspil til en kontanthjælpsreform.* København: Beskæftigelsesministeriet.

Rodgers, D.T. (1998) *Atlantic crossings.* Cambridge: Harvard.

Rosanvallon, P. (1976) *L'âge de l'autogestion.* Paris: Éditions du Seuil.

Rosanvallon, P. (1981) *La crise de l'état-providence.* Paris: Éditions du Seuil.

Rosanvallon, P. (1995) *La nouvelle question sociale: Repenser l'état-providence.* Paris: Éditions du Seuil.

Rose, N. (2000) 'Government and control', *British Journal of Criminology*, 40, pp. 321–339.

Rosholm, M. and Svarer, M. (2004) *Estimating the threat effect of active labour market programmes*, IZA Discussion Paper. Bonn: Institute for the Study of Labor.

Salais, R. (2005) 'Decrire et evaluer la pluralité des modèles sociaux en Europe. Une approche en termes de dispositifs d'action publique', in Chatel, E., Kirat, T. and Salais, R. (eds) *L'action publique et ses dispositifs: Institution, économie, politique.* Paris: L'Harmattan, pp. 163–188.

Salais, R. (2006) 'Reforming the European social model and the politics of indicators: from unemployment rate to the employment rate in the European Employment Strategy', in Serrano, A. and Jepsen, M. (eds) *Unravelling the European social model.* Cambridge: Polity Press, pp. 189–212.

Salais, R. (2011) 'Labour-related conventions and configurations of meaning: France, Germany and Great Britain prior to the Second World War', *Historical Social Research/Historische Sozialforschung*, 36(4), pp. 218-247.

Salais, R., Baverez, N. and Reynaud, B. (1986) *L'invention du chômage: Histoire et transformations d'une catégorie en France des années 1890 aux années 1980*. Paris: Presses universitaires de France.

Sandmo, A. (2011) *Economics evolving*, Princeton: Princeton University Press.

Sapir, A. (2006) 'Globalization and the reform of European social models', *Journal of Common Market Studies*, 44(2), pp. 369–390.

Schmidt, V.A. (2006) *Democracy in Europe: The EU and national polities*. Oxford: Oxford University Press.

Schmidt, V.A. (2008) 'Discursive institutionalism: the explanatory power of ideas and discourse', *Annual Review of Political Science*, 11, pp. 303–326.

Schmidt, V.A. (2011) *Analyzing ideas and tracing discoursive interactions in institutional change: From historical institutionalism to discoursive institutionalism*, CES Working Paper, Open Forum CES Paper Series no. 3, Cambridge, MA: Center for European Studies at Harvard University.

Serrano Pascual, A. (2004) *Are European activation policies converging in Europe? The European Employment Strategy for Young People*. Brussels: ETUI.

Serrano Pasqual, A. (2007) 'Reshaping welfare states: activation regimes in Europe', in Serrano Pascual, A. and Magnusson, L. (eds) *Reshaping welfare states and activation regimes in Europe*. Brussels: Peter Lang, pp. 11–34.

Silber, I.F. (2016) 'The cultural worth of economies of worth: French pragmatic sociology from a cultural sociological perspective', in Inglis, D. and Almila, A. (eds) *Sage handbook of cultural sociology*. London: Sage, pp. 159–177.

Skidelsky, R. (2009) *Keynes: The return of the master*. New York: Allen Lane.

Skocpol, T. and Pierson, P. (2002) 'Historical institutionalism in contemporary political science', in Katznelson, I. and Milner, H. (eds) *Political science: State of the discipline*. New York, NY: W.W. Norton, pp. 693–721.

Slobodian, Q. (2018) *Globalists: The end of empire and the birth of neoliberalism*. Cambridge, MA: Harvard University Press.

Slothuus, R. (2007) 'Framing deservingness to win support for welfare state retrenchment', *Scandinavian Political Studies*, 30(3), pp. 323–344.

Smith, M., J. Leschke, H. Russell, and P. Villa (2018) 'Stressed economies, distressed policies, and distraught young people: European policies and outcomes from a youth perspective', in O'Reilly, J., J. Leschke, R. Ortlieb, M. Seeleib-Kaiser, and P. Villa (eds) *Youth labor in transition*. New York, NY: Oxford University Press, pp. 104–131.

Socialdemokraterne og SF (2010) *Fair løsning: Sammen ud af krisen*. Joint party manifesto from May 2010.

Socialkommissionen (1992) *Sortering for livet: Debatoplæg om de unge*. København: Socialkommissionen.

Sode-Madsen, H. (1985) *Ungdom uden arbejde: Ungdomsforanstaltninger i Danmark 1933–1950*. København: Gad.

Standing, G. (2011) *The precariat: The new dangerous class*. London: Bloomsbury.

Standing, G. (2017) *Basic income: A guide for the open minded*. New Haven, CA: Yale University Press.

Stark, D. (2009) *The sense of dissonance*. Princeton, NJ: Princeton University Press.

Stavo-Debauge, J. (2011) 'De la critique, une critique. Sur la geste « radical » de Luc Boltanski', *espacestemps.net*.

Stoleru, L. (1974) *Vaincre la pauvreté dans les pays riches*. Paris: Flammarion.

Strand, D. (2016) *No alternatives: The end of ideology in the 1950s and the post-political world of the 1990s*. Stockholm: Stockholm University.

Streeck, W. (2013) *Buying time: The delayed crisis of democratic capitalism*. London: Verso.

Streeck, W. and K. Thelen. (eds) (2005) *Beyond continuity: Institutional change in advanced political economies*, Cary, NC: Oxford University Press.

Styrelsen for Arbejdsmarked og Rekruttering (2013) 'Orienteringsskrivelse: Nytteindsats, 17. december 2013'. Policy brief. København: Beskæftigelsesministeriet.

Styrelsen for Arbejdsmarked og Rekruttering (2014) 'Visitation: Uddannelseshjælpsmodtagere, 3. februar'. København: Beskæftigelsesministeriet.

Svallfors, S. (2003) 'Welfare regimes and welfare opinions: a comparison of eight Western countries', *Social Indicators Research*, 64(3), pp. 495–520.

Taylor-Gooby, P. (2008) 'The new welfare state settlement in Europe', *European Societies*, 10(1), pp. 3–24.

Taylor-Gooby, P. (2013) 'Why do people stigmatise the poor at a time of rapidly increasing inequality, and what can be done about it?', *The Political Quarterly*, 84(1), pp. 31–42.

Teasdale, S. (2012) 'What's in a name? Making sense of social enterprise discourses', *Public Policy and Administration*, 27(2), pp. 99–119.

Thelen, K. (2014) *Varieties of liberalization and the new politics of social solidarity*. New York, NY: Cambridge University Press.

Thévenot, L. (1984) 'Rules and implement: investment in forms', *Social Science Information*, 23(1), pp. 1–45.

Thévenot, L. (2001a) 'Organized complexity: conventions of coordination and the composition of economic arrangements', *European Journal of Social Theory*, 4(4), pp. 405–425.

Thévenot, L. (2001b) 'Pragmatic regimes governing the engagement with the world', in Knorr Cetina, K., Schatzki, T.R. and von Savigny, E. (eds) *The practice turn in contemporary theory*. Abingdon: Routledge, pp. 56–73.

Thévenot, L. (2002a) 'Conventions of coordination and the framing of uncertainty', in Fullbrook, E. (ed) *Intersubjectivity in economics*. London: Routledge, pp. 181–97.

Thévenot, L. (2002b) 'Which road to follow? The moral complexity of an "equipped" humanity', in Law, J. and Mol, A. (eds) *Complexities: Social studies of knowledge practices*. Durham, NC and London: Duke University Press, pp. 53–87.

Thévenot, L. (2006) *L'action au pluriel: Sociologie des régimes d'engagement*. Paris: Éditions la découverte.

Thévenot, L. (2007) 'The plurality of cognitive formats and engagements: moving between the familiar and the public', *European Journal of Social Theory*, 10(3), pp. 409–423.

Thévenot, L. (2009) 'Postscript to the special issue: Governing life by standards: a view from engagements', *Social Studies of Science*, 39(5), pp. 793–813.

Thévenot, L. (2011) 'Conventions for measuring and questioning policies. The case of 50 years of policy evaluations through a statistical survey', *Historical Social Research*, 36(4), pp. 192–217.

Thévenot, L. (2014) 'Voicing concern and difference: from public spaces to commonplaces', *European Journal of Cultural and Political Sociology*, 1(1), pp. 7–34.

Thévenot, L. (2015) 'Certifying the world: power infrastructures and practices in economies of conventional forms', in Aspers, P. and Dodd, N. (eds) *Re-imagining economic sociology*. Oxford: Oxford University Press, pp. 195–226.

Thompson, E. (1971) 'The moral economy of the English crowd in the eighteenth century', *Past & Present*, (50), pp. 76-136.

Torfing, J. (1999) 'Workfare with welfare: recent reforms of the Danish welfare state', *Journal of European Social Policy*, 9(5), pp. 5–28.

Torfing, J. (2004) *Det stille sporskifte: En diskursteoretisk beslutningsprocesanalyse*, *Magtudredningen*. Århus: Aarhus universitetsforlag.

Triantafillou, P. (2011) 'The OECD's thinking on the governing of unemployment', *Policy & Politics*, 39(4), pp. 567–582.

Triantafillou, P. (2009) 'The European Employment Strategy and the governing of French employment policies', *Administrative Theory & Praxis*, 31(4), pp. 479–502.

Triantafillou, P. (2012) *New forms of governing: A Foucauldian inspired analysis*. Basingstoke: Palgrave Macmillan.

Triantafillou, P. (2015) 'The political implications of performance management and evidence-based policymaking', *The American Review of Public Administration*, 45, pp. 167–181.

Triantafillou, P. (2017) *Neoliberal power and public management reforms*. Manchester: Manchester University Press.

Trickey, H. (2001) 'Comparing workfare programmes: features and implications', in Lødemel, I. and Trickey, H. (eds) *'An offer you can't refuse': Workfare in international perspective*. Bristol: Policy Press, pp. 249–294.

Tuchszirer, C. (2001) 'La nouvelle convention d'assurance-chômage: le PARE qui cache la forêt', *Mouvements*, 14(2), pp. 15–24.

Turrini, A., G. Koltay, F. Pierini, C. Goffard, and A. Kiss (2015) 'A decade of labour market reforms in the EU: insights from the LABREF database', *IZA Journal of Labor Policy*, 4(12), pp. 1–33.

Vail, M.I. (2008) 'From "welfare without work" to "buttressed liberalization": the shifting dynamics of labor market adjustment in France and Germany', *European Journal of Political Research*, 47(3), pp. 334–358.

Valverde, M. (1996) '"Despotism" and ethical liberal governance', *Economy and Society*, 25(3), pp. 357–372.

Udredningsudvalget (1992) *Rapport fra udredningsudvalget om arbejdsmarkedets strukturproblemer*, København: Finansministeriet.

van Berkel, R. and Borghi, V. (2008) 'Review article: the governance of activation', *Social Policy and Society*, 7(03), pp. 393–402.

van Berkel, R., de Graaf, W. and Sirovátka, T. (2011) 'The governance of active welfare states in Europe in a comparative perspective', in van Berkel, R., de Graaf, W. and Sirovatka, T. (eds) *The governance of active welfare states in Europe*. Basingstoke: Palgrave Macmillan, pp. 237–263.

van Berkel, R., de Graaf, W. and Sirovatkas, T. (2012) 'Governance of the activation policies in Europe', *International Journal of Sociology and Social Policy*, 32(5), pp. 260–272.

van Oorschot, W. and Roosma, F. (eds) (2017) *The social legitimacy of targeted welfare and welfare desrvingness*. Cheltenham: Edward Elgar Publishing.

van Oorschot, W., Opielka, M. and Pfau-Effinger, B. (eds) (2008) *Culture and welfare state: Values and social policy in comparative perspective*. Cheltenham: Edward Elgar Publishing.

van Parijs, P. and Vanderborght, Y. (2017) *Basic income: A radical proposal for a free society and a sane economy*. Cambridge, MA: Harvard University Press.

Villadsen, K. (2007) 'The emergence of "neo-philanthropy": a new discursive space in welfare policy', *Acta Sociologica*, 50(3), pp. 309–323.

Vlandas, T. (2013) 'The politics of in-work benefits: the case of the "active income of solidarity" in France', *French Politics*, 11, pp. 117–142.

Wacquant, L. (2009) *Punishing the poor: The neoliberal government of social insecurity*. Durham, NC: Duke University Press.

Wagner, P. (1999) 'After justification: repertoires of evaluation and the sociology of modernity', *European Journal of Social Theory*, 2(3), pp. 341–357.

Walters, W. (1997) 'The "active society": new designs for social policy', *Policy & Politics*, 25(3), pp. 221–234.

Walters, W. (2000) *Unemployment and government: Genealogies of the social*. Cambridge: Cambridge University Press.

Weber, M. (2003) *The protestant ethic and the spirit of capitalism*. Mineola, NY: Dover Publications.

Wildawsky, A.B. (1987) *Speaking truth to power: The art and craft of policy analysis*. New Brunswick, NJ: Transaction.

Wilkinson, R. and Pickett, K. (2009) *The spirit level: Why greater equality makes societies stronger*. New York, NY: Bloomsbury Press.

Wilthagen, T. and Tros, F. (2004) 'The concept of "flexicurity": a new approach to regulating employment and labour markets', *Transfer: European Review of Labour and Research*, 10(2), pp. 166–186.

Wresinski, J. (1987) *Grande pauvreté et précarité écnomique et sociale*. Paris: Conseil économique et social.

Zamora, D. (2017) *De l'égalité à la pauvreté. Une socio-histoire de l'assistance en Belgique (1895-2015)*. Bruxelles: Les Éditions de l'Université de Bruxelles.

Zimmermann, B. (2001) *La constitution du chômage en Allemagne: Entre professions et territoires*. Paris: Éditions de la Maison des sciences de l'homme.

Zimmermann, B. (2006) 'Changes in work and social protection: France, Germany and Europe', *International Social Security Review*, 59(4), pp. 29–45.

Zoberman, Y. (2011) *Une histoire du chômage: De l'antiquité à nos jours.* Paris: Perrin.

Index